P9-DXZ-256

The Social Dynamics
of Peace and Conflict

The Social Dynamics of Peace and Conflict

Culture in International Security

EDITED BY

Robert A. Rubinstein
and Mary LeCron Foster

Westview Press
BOULDER & LONDON

This Westview softcover edition is printed on acid-free paper and bound in softcovers that carry the highest rating of the National Association of State Textbook Administrators, in consultation with the Association of American Publishers and the Book Manufacturers' Institute.

All rights reserved. No part of this publication may be reproduced or transmitted in any form or by any means, electronic or mechanical, including photocopy, recording, or any information storage and retrieval system, without permission in writing from the publisher.

Copyright © 1988 by Westview Press, Inc., except Chapter 1 (© Robert A. Rubinstein) and Chapter 11 (© Alice B. Kehoe)

Published in 1988 in the United States of America by Westview Press, Inc., 5500 Central Avenue, Boulder, Colorado 80301, and in the United Kingdom by Westview Press, Inc., 13 Brunswick Centre, London WC1N 1AF, England

Library of Congress Cataloging-in-Publication Data
The Social dynamics of peace and conflict: culture in international
  security/[edited] by Robert A. Rubinstein and Mary LeCron Foster.
    p. cm.
  Includes bibliographies.
  Includes index.
  ISBN 0-8133-7614-9
  1. International relations and culture. 2. Security,
International. I. Rubinstein, Robert A. II. Foster, Mary LeCron,
1914–   .
JX1255.S62   1988
327.1′1—dc19   88-17594
                                                                          CIP

Printed and bound in the United States of America

The paper used in this publication meets the requirements of the American National Standard for Permanence of Paper for Printed Library Materials Z39.48-1984.

10   9   8   7   6   5   4   3   2   1

Contents

Preface

The main aim of this volume is to show the importance for international security studies of better understanding the social dynamics of peace and conflict. Our intention is to illustrate the crucial role that culture and symbols play in facilitating peace or fostering conflict. Our initial work on this project dates from 1985. We had earlier organized a series of symposia on peace and war in anthropological perspective for the 11th International Congress of Anthropological and Ethnological Sciences. We intended those symposia, and the book which derived from them (*Peace and War: Cross-Cultural Perspectives,* 1986), to encourage anthropologists to bring their data and theory to bear on contemporary issues of war, peace, and international security.

We thought, at the time, that the lack of anthropological presence in these areas resulted from anthropologists concerning themselves mainly with specialized questions of anthropological theory and from their presenting their research reports in journals which served mainly professional anthropologists. We thought foreign policy and international security professionals would see the value of anthropological data and embrace them, if only we and our colleagues would make our work accessible to them.

In fact, since 1983 anthropologists have been working more seriously than ever on questions of peace and war. And we were enormously encouraged by institutionalized initiatives in international security—undertaken by such organizations as the MacArthur Foundation, the Social Science Research Council, and the American Association for the Advancement of Science—intended to revitalize the field of international security analysis. We were especially pleased that the announcements for these initiatives intimated a broader role for anthropological analyses.

As we and many of our anthropological colleagues began to make efforts to participate in these initiatives, we frequently saw, or heard reports from others, that despite appearances to the contrary the representatives of the international security and foreign policy communities who dominated in these initiatives did not appreciate anthropological work. At best they characterized it as interesting but hopelessly "unscientific" and thus inadequate and unimportant for the "real world" of "hardball politics" and of rapid technological development. Especially disturbing were reports that studies of the normative and symbolic aspects of culture seemed to be particularly perplexing to these international security professionals.

We soon realized that the international security analysis community had developed an orthodoxy which accepted as valid and useful only data that derived from a select set of research methods and that they expected these data to be presented in standard formats and formal models. A supposed "scientific objectivity" was the hallmark of this analysis. Moreover, the world-view of this community could be succinctly stated (and had been in several canonical texts) in a way that anthropology's contribution could not.

We first began to redress this imbalance by organizing a symposium on "Power, Change, and Security Decisions: Anthropological Perspectives" for the 1985 annual meeting of the American Association for the Advancement of Science. That symposium was sponsored by Section H (Anthropology) of the AAAS and by the AAAS Committee on Science, Arms Control, and National Security. Several of the papers in this book (Bateson, Goldschmidt, Potter, and Worsley) were first prepared for that symposium. The American Association for the Advancement of Science gave us a small grant to cover the travel expenses of one Soviet and one British participant in that symposium. The addition of their cross-cultural perspectives enriched our discussions, and we are grateful to the AAAS for that help.

Shortly after the symposium we agreed that it would be useful to publish a volume of papers which emphasized the value of looking at the social dynamics of peace and conflict. We began to look for other papers which fit this theme. We were fortunate that at the 1986 annual meeting of the Kroeber Anthropological Society at the University of California at Berkeley a symposium was held in honor of our late colleague Professor David Mandelbaum. Several of the papers from that symposium (Anderson, Brasset, Habarad, and Sluka) seemed to us to fit especially well with the papers from the AAAS session, and these are included here.

We felt especially keenly the lack of a paper about the Fourth World. We therefore asked Alice Kehoe to write one especially for this volume. We invited Linda Pulliam's paper on the Navy community, initially presented at the 1986 meeting of the Southwestern Anthropological Association, because it provided a unique, personalized, methodological, and descriptive perspective on issues with which this book is concerned.

During the time that we worked on this book Rubinstein held a small grant from the Ploughshares Fund which supported in part his work on his paper in, and his editing of, this volume. It is a pleasure to acknowledge that support here.

We hope that the empirical analyses and theoretical materials in this volume will serve to open a continuing dialogue between anthropologists and members of the international security community. We hope, too, that this book will lead others of our colleagues to join in making the sensitive analysis of cultural materials a regular and continuing part of international security discussions. For, in our view, it is only by revitalizing the scope of those discussions that we can hope to achieve lasting peace.

Many people helped us as we shaped our ideas about the relation of anthropology to international security analysis in general and about this book in particular. We appreciate the support of all of our colleagues and friends a great deal. In particular, we are very grateful for the advice and encouragement offered by Lita Osmundsen and Sol Tax throughout this project.

Robert A. Rubinstein
Mary LeCron Foster

About the Editors and Contributors

Robert A. Rubinstein is Visiting Scholar in the Department of Anthropology at Northwestern University. Until recently he was Director of Social Indicators Research at the Chapin Hall Center for Children at the University of Chicago. He has been a member of the Organizing Board of the Commission on the Study of Peace of the International Union of Anthropological and Ethnological Sciences since its founding in 1983. He is currently Co-chair of the Commission, and was its Executive Secretary and *Newsletter* Editor from 1983 to 1988. He received his Ph.D. in anthropology from the State University of New York at Binghamton. He also holds a master's degree in public health from the University of Illinois at Chicago. He has done research in Mexico and Belize, Central America, and in the United States. His research and teaching focus on medical anthropology, health policy, research methods and social theory, and anthropology and international security. He has published widely in these areas. He is editor, with Mary LeCron Foster, of *Peace and War: Cross-Cultural Perspectives* (1986); editor, with Rik Pinxten, of *Epistemology and Process: Anthropological Views* (1984); and author, with Charles D. Laughlin and John McManus, of *Science as Cognitive Process: Toward an Empirical Philosophy of Science* (1984).

Mary LeCron Foster is Research Associate in the Department of Anthropology at the University of California at Berkeley. She has been a member of the American Association for the Advancement of Science, Committee on Science, Arms Control, and National Security, and has been a member of the Organizing Board of the Commission on the Study of Peace of the International Union of Anthropological and Ethnological Sciences since its founding in 1983. She received her Ph.D. in linguistics from the University of California at Berkeley. She has conducted fieldwork in Mexico, including long-term research in the village of Tzintzuntzan. Her interests are in the development and use of symbolism in culture and language, and as applied to the anthropology of peace. She has published widely in these areas. She is editor, with Robert A. Rubinstein, of *Peace and War: Cross-Cultural Per-*

spectives (1986); editor, with Stanley Brandes, of *Symbol as Sense: New Approaches to the Analysis of Meaning* (1980); author of *The Tarascan Language* (1969); and author, with George M. Foster, of *Sierra Popoluca Speech* (1948).

James N. Anderson is Associate Professor of Anthropology and Director of the Program for Philippine Studies, of the Institute of East Asian Studies, at the University of California at Berkeley. He received his Ph.D. from the University of California at Los Angeles. He has conducted research on economic, social, and ecological organization and change among peasant and tribal peoples in the Philippines and Malaysia for nearly thirty nears. His scholarly interests include human ecology, land tenure, indigenous agro-ecosystems, and medical anthropology. He has extensive experience in applied research relating to rural development with special concern for local organization and participation. This includes work with the Institute of Medical Research in Kuala Lumpur, Malaysia, and consulting with the Ford Foundation, UNESCO, the International Rice Research Institute, the Philippine National Economic Development Authority, and the World Bank.

Mary Catherine Bateson is Robinson Professor of Anthropology and English at the George Mason University. She received her Ph.D. from Harvard University. She has extensive research experience in the Middle East, especially in Iran. Her research and teaching interests focus on linguistic and psychological anthropology, areas in which she has published widely. She is author, with Gregory Bateson, of *Angels Fear: Towards an Epistemology of the Sacred* (1987); author of *With a Daughter's Eye: A Memoir of Margaret Mead and Gregory Bateson* (1984); and of *Structural Continuity in Poetry: A Linguistic Study of Five Pre-Islamic Arabic Odes* (1970).

Donna Brasset recently received her Ph.D. from the University of California at Berkeley. Her contribution to this book is one of many talks she has given at professional conferences in which she urges the involvement of anthropologists in global issues of war and peace. She has taught at the Santa Rosa Junior College and has been a member of the Commission on the Study of Peace of the International Union of Anthropological and Ethnological Sciences since its founding in 1983.

Walter Goldschmidt is Professor of Anthropology, Emeritus, at the University of California at Los Angeles. He received his Ph.D. from the University of California at Berkeley. A past President of the American Anthropological Association, he has been a member of the Commission on the Study of Peace of the International Union of Anthropological and Ethnological Sciences since its founding in 1983. His chief interests are in cultural ecology and the uses of anthropology in the formulation of policy. He has extensive research experience in

Africa. He is author of *The Sebei: A Study in Adaptation* (1986); of *As You Sow: Three Studies in the Social Consequences of Agribusiness* (1947, 1978); and of *Culture and Behavior of the Sebei: A Study in Continuity and Adaptation* (1976). He is editor of *Anthropology and Public Policy: A Dialogue* (1986); of *The Uses of Anthropology* (1979); of *Exploring the Ways of Mankind* (1971); and of *United States and Africa* (1963, 1970).

Jonathan Habarad is currently conducting field research among the Tonga of Gwembe Valley, Zambia, under the auspices of the University of Zambia and of the University of California at Berkeley. He received his Ph.D. from the University of California at Berkeley. Research for his paper in this book was conducted while he was assisting the late Professor David Mandelbaum in a cross-cultural study of peoples without war.

Alice B. Kehoe is Professor of Anthropology at Marquette University in Milwaukee, Wisconsin. She received her Ph.D. from Harvard University. Her primary area of research is the archaeology and ethnology of the Northwestern Plains Indians, especially Blackfoot, Plains Cree, and Saskatchewan Dakota, but she has worked also with neighboring Indian groups including the Woods Cree, Assiniboin, and Ojibwa. Kehoe has been particularly concerned with contemporary Indian political activism and its use of the rhetoric of democracy, ecological conservativism, and the promotion of peace. In addition to many articles in professional journals, she has published *North American Indians: A Comprehensive Account* (1981) and the forthcoming *The Ghost Dance Religion: Ethnohistory and Social Science.*

Jack M. Potter is Professor in the Department of Anthropology of the University of California at Berkeley. He received his Ph.D. from the University of California at Berkeley. His interests focus on peasant society and culture change. He has conducted fieldwork in Thailand, China, and the United States. He is author, with Sulamith Heins Potter, of *China's Peasants: The Anthropology of a Revolution* (forthcoming); of *Thai Peasant Social Structure* (1976); and editor, with May N. Diaz and George M. Foster, of *Peasant Society: A Reader* (1967).

Linda Pulliam received an Ed.D. from the University of Cincinnati, where she did micro-ethnographic work in classrooms and in a hospital clinic. After a hiatus from academia, she is now working on a Ph.D. in sociology at Northwestern University, specializing in the media and the performing arts.

Jeffrey A. Sluka is Lecturer in the Department of Social Anthropology and Maori Studies at Massey University, Palmerston North, New Zealand. He received his Ph.D. from the University of California at Berkeley. His interests include political anthropology, ethnicity, and social conflict. He conducted fieldwork on the Falls Road in Belfast and is author of the forthcoming book *Hearts and Minds, Water and Fish: The Social Dynamics of Popular Support for the IRA and INLA in a Northern Irish Ghetto.*

Peter Worsley is Professor of Sociology, Emeritus, at the University of Manchester. He did fieldwork among Australian Aborigines, and was awarded the Curl Bequest Prize of the Royal Anthropological Institute in 1955. He is twice past president of the British Sociological Association. He has been a Co-chair of the Organizing Board of the Commission on the Study of Peace of the International Union of Anthropological and Ethnological Sciences since its founding in 1983. He has extensive experience in international development and political and economic anthropology. He is editor, with Buenor Kofi, of *On the Brink: Nuclear Proliferation and the Third World* (1987). His authored books include: *The Trumpet Shall Sound: A Study of "Cargo" Cults in Melanesia* (1957); *Inside China* (1975); *Introducing Sociology* (1970, 1972, 1987); *Marx and Marxism* (1982); *The Third World* (1964, 1967); and *The Three Worlds: Culture and World Development* (1984).

INTRODUCTION / Revitalizing International Security Analysis: Contributions from Culture and Symbolic Process

Robert A. Rubinstein and Mary LeCron Foster

During the twentieth century anthropologists have viewed, and attempted to influence, the study of peace and war in three notably different ways. Some anthropologists have noted instances of conflict or warfare during the course of their fieldwork and have provided brief descriptions of these in the context of ethnographies that focus largely on other aspects of social life. Other, though relatively fewer, anthropologists have taken warfare as the principle topic of their work with small, well-bounded, non-western societies. These anthropologists have tried to understand war as a social phenomenon in the same way that they have tried to understand other aspects of social life. Among the aims of this work have been the development of an anthropological theory of war (usually based on "primitive war"), focusing on the issue of whether or not warfare and aggression are biologically innate parts of human behavior, or on conflict as a technical problem in the development of a more general anthropological theory of human behavior. Still fewer anthropologists have tried to show the relevance of anthropological knowledge and theory for contemporary conflicts, including conflict among nation-states, in order to contribute anthropological information to discussions about international relations and international security.

Common to all anthropological approaches is the recognition that peace and war result from complex social dynamics, as much or more than they do from other factors. Since peace and war are essentially social phenomena, a full and effective understanding of them depends upon examining the intricate connections between cultural and symbolic processes and social action. In this book we explore the nature of such connections as we try to understand better the dynamics of peace and conflict in contemporary societies.

Most social anthropological work describes in detail the social and cultural systems of particular groups. From such studies, cross-cultural theory is developed. This theory should be incorporated into political debates and social science discussions of peace and conflict. For, in our view, policies for avoiding or resolving inter-group conflicts will fail or succeed to the degree that they use theory based on the comparative analysis of detailed information about particular societies. The information needed to achieve this theoretical goal must come from studies describing social conditions which breed conflict or facilitate cooperation.

Conflict and warfare have rarely been the discipline's main focus. Yet, Sumner (1911), for example, discussed war as a topic of social inquiry early in the twentieth century. Mead (1940), Malinowski (1941), and Swanton (1943) each found enough information about war in the anthropological literature published prior to 1940 to derive from it insights about questions of war and peace.

Other anthropologists have investigated then current questions of war, peace, and international security. Bateson (this volume) describes one of the ways in which some anthropologists sought to assist in bringing a swifter end to World War II. Benedict (1946) and others developed the field of National Character Studies to inform political debate and strategic planning, based on their research about the relationship between the development of individual personality and culture.

Although, for reasons described by Bateson, National Character Studies later waned, some anthropological interest in the nature and causes of warfare continued. This interest was often tied to the pursuit of narrow anthropological questions about conflict and war, as investigated among nonliterate, nonwestern peoples.

These narrow questions led to discussions that revolved around general issues—for example, whether or not warfare is the inevitable outcome of a basic human biological imperative for aggression (Mead 1940, Swanton 1943, Ardrey 1966, Foster 1986)—or they focused on very specific issues of apparently esoteric interest only—for example, whether intervillage conflict in New Guinea or the Amazon is due to ecological factors such as protein scarcity or to factors such as kinship and biological relatedness (Rappaport 1967, Ferguson 1984, Chagnon 1988, Chagnon and Bugos 1979, and Chagnon and Hames 1979).

Anthropologists have periodically tried to bring their work to bear on current concerns and to contribute directly to public policy discussions. For example, Robert Redfield (1953) challenged the ethnocentrism of American conduct in international affairs. In 1963, the Wenner-Gren Foundation for Anthropological Research sponsored six conferences on "Anthropology and World Affairs," which examined the relevance of anthropology to then current strategic thinking, especially deterrence theory. These conferences used as a framework for discussion a collection of articles edited by Sol Tax and Ruth Adams "containing papers by strategy thinkers formulating alternative policies" (Bunzel and Parsons 1964). Later, as a result of increasing anthropological interest in cooperation and conflict in complex societies, Tax (1967) organized a conference which examined the cultural and social implications of the United States' selective service system. Concern about the United States' military involvement in Vietnam led Fried et al. (1968) to organize a symposium to discuss the anthropology of armed conflict and aggression. Anthropologists also have increasingly studied law (Nader 1965, Nader and Yngvesson 1973), the uses of power (Cohen 1974), and nationalism (Gellner 1983), all of which are themes crucial in international affairs and security policy discussions.

Anthropologists concerned about the relevance of their work to international security discussions, often find that their materials are treated as anecdotally interesting but tangential to those discussions (Foster and Rubinstein 1986:ix). They assume that their lack of policy input is due to the general image of their work as concerned with esoterica of little value to strategic planning, and that it is often presented in ways that make it available only to anthropologists. This may be partly true for some of the anthropologically narcissistic work which focuses on narrow questions treated in polemically charged theoretical discussions (for example, Harris 1974, Ferguson 1984). But, we have become convinced that it is not simply the idiom of anthropological work or the unusual nature of its concerns that block its contribution.

Our contention is that anthropological information has not been fully absorbed into international security discussions because those discussions are controlled by symbolic and social systems which define the legitimate domain of discourse in ways that systematically deny the usefulness of information and insights that derive uniquely from anthropology. As Rubinstein (this volume) shows, non-anthropological discussions in these areas rely on a technological and scientistic view of social relations that treats as valid only information that derives from "correct scientific" methods. These are taken to be methods that produce information which can be characterized as "objective" and "rational" in a logical sense. By restricting discussions to information that derives from a limited range of methods (those which are amenable to the development of formal quantitative models) international security discussions mistakenly treat social and cultural phenomena as homogeneous and stable.

Policy analysis is carried out at a macro-level in which cultural patterns are mixed together to form an aggregate whole. In the process of performing this aggregation, important symbolic, normative and motivational processes revealed by micro-level analyses are factored out of discussion. This results in policies and plans which fail to achieve desired goals because they actually ignore the human dimensions of social life.

A review of the social science literature shows that there are many alternative methodological approaches to the study of social life. These range from methods designed to imitate as closely as possible the logic of experimental analysis in the physical and biological sciences (Lieberson 1985)—and thus to yield objective, formal models of behavior—through more interpretive approaches designed to reveal the symbolic processes upon which human social interaction depends (Denzin 1970). These methodological approaches also vary in their focus on macro-level or micro-level events. In order to develop a full and effective understanding of the dynamics of social life it is important to recognize that these approaches are equally legitimate and that information from them must be integrated into a coherent account (Rubinstein et al. 1984:90).

Our view is that current international security policies often produce paradoxical results (conflict where they intended peace, despotism where they intended democracy, abuse and torture of people where they intended human rights) because they have over-emphasized one kind of method, and one level of analysis, and have mistakenly discredited the others. In this book we are concerned to show that in order to get more than a superficial understanding of the social dynamics of peace and conflict it is necessary to use a range of methods, and that these methods yield complementary information. We argue that it is wrong and dangerous to allow the idiom of "objective scientific information" to set the terms of international security policy research because this maintains a false separation between "values" and "facts," which artificially restricts the range of information considered useful in informing those policies. In addition to the particular substantive foci and method of each of the essays in this book, together the essays display the value for international security discussions of using different methods and varied levels of analysis.

Culture provides the symbolic matrix within the context of which factors contributing to social disruption or cohesion must be interpreted. From the "objective," "scientific" perspective of macro-level analysis this matrix may appear homogeneous. However, this picture of homogeneity is achieved only by ignoring the variation that exists within the cultural life of any social group. Cultures—and the symbol systems that serve them—always contain elements in tension one with the other (Foster and Brandes 1979). It is essential to recognize these tensions and the imagery that encapsulates them if we are to understand events at the macro-level. The essays in this book were selected to underscore this point, and to show that this is equally true if we wish to account for the dynamics of revolution and negotiation in Iran (Bateson this volume), for the maintenance of peaceful relations in the Philippines (Anderson this volume) or in China (Potter this volume), or for the cohesion of military units (Pulliam this volume). Failing to pay attention to the symbolic matrices in which social conflict and cohesion occur yields a lifeless and misleading picture of the social dynamics of international security affairs.

It is also our view that the methodological narrowness of international security analysis has mistakenly over-emphasized the view that human actions can be accounted for within a rational (logical) model of behavior. Another contention in this book is that such logical analysis alone always yields inadequate accounts of international affairs precisely because they fail to come to terms with moral aspects of human social life. Anthropologists have shown that fully understanding relationships of power depends upon understanding the moral and normative aspects underlying a group's behavior (Rubinstein and Tax 1985). Actions which seem irrational on the basis of logical analysis alone can be rendered understandable and even reasonable when the moral system supporting them is taken into account. The seemingly paradoxically successful resistance of small, ill-equipped peoples to pressures from more formidable adversaries becomes clearly understandable. The essays in this book also show the dynamic role of the normative aspects of culture in maintaining peace or promoting conflict. These essays show that this normative dimension is as important for understanding complex western military establishments (Brasset this volume) as it is for understanding the institutions and actions of Fourth World peoples (Kehoe this volume).

The papers in this book also show that the symbolic processes that facilitate cohesion or lead to conflict are themselves dynamically interrelated. Since the symbolic matrices that under-gird cultural systems contain within them supports for both peace and conflict it is important to understand shifts in the balance between those supports which lead to culture change. Thus, a description of these elements in a society at one time may not reflect the social reality of the society at a later time. For example, Bateson shows how an earlier balance in the tension between symbolic and normative aspects of Iranian culture could be seen to support the reign of the Shah, while at a later time it supports the Islamic revolution. Recognizing that the social relations and the symbols and normative prescriptive imperatives which they embody are in constant flux underscores the point that international security analysis errs badly when it treats cultural variables as stable. Rather, international security analysis needs to incorporate within it the continuing monitoring of the symbolic and cultural aspects of the societies of concern.

We hope that this book will illustrate the need to revitalize international security discussions by increasing the range of methodological alternatives used to produce information on which decisions can be based. We especially hope that the essays in this book will contribute to the further understanding of the importance of including information about symbolic processes and value systems together with "objective fact" in international security discussions.

One of the main ways in which anthropology can contribute to this revitalization is by providing background information and theory about the functioning of social groups, correlates among social variables, and insights into social dynamics rather than in solving immediate problems (see Bateson this volume). Because peace is as much a social as it is a technological problem, an understanding of peace and war will clearly be advanced by better social and cultural research. In this endeavor anthropology can play a unique and important role.

Despite popular perceptions of what anthropology is all about, it is *not* primarily the study of exotic or long-vanished peoples, although such study has historically been an important part of its subject matter. Instead, anthropology is about human diversity and the varieties and commonalities of human social experience. A knowledge of human diversity is essential if we are to understand ourselves and our relations to others—and we are not just our local group, or even our nation, but the entire human species. To this end, some anthropologists study peoples in remote parts of the world, while others examine social interaction closer to home. Whatever aspect of human social behavior we select as our major research focus, social theory is always a comparative enterprise. We attempt to derive generalities from a survey of cross-cultural particularities and to test them against additional social constructs.

Peoples with customs that are very different from our own often seem inscrutable. Yet, anthropologists, by living among such peoples, begin to learn the rules that guide behavior that at first seems strange—even perhaps irrational. Such analysis leads to the conclusion that the rationality behind the social behavior of any human group is much the same as that informing any other—it organizes the world in a meaningful way for its members, and is neither more nor less exotic or bizarre than our own. As one anthropologist said, "A rapidly accumulating body of evidence indicates that the bizarre and the exotic in the patterns of social behaviour are not the exclusive monopoly of pre-industrial societies" (Cohen 1974:1).

The issue is not really rationality, for culture is only rational in the remote sense of evolutionary adaptiveness. Instead, culture is driven by the dynamics of the symbolic processes as these are worked out in the activities of social actors. These actors communicate with one another through symbolic acts, and the products of such acts are meanings that social consensus has made available for exchange. This is as true of so-called "civilized" societies as of any society that we consider to be "primitive." It is this meaningful symbolic organization—the classification of experience in such a way that it can be used effectively—that has given the human species its extraordinary success in surviving, and ultimately in achieving great control over nature.

Now that we have come to a point in our social evolution at which our very survival is threatened by the magnitude of our ability to wage war, we must explore our social institutions not just in order to understand their dynamics, but also to use them to ensure the survival of the human species and its environment. This will be a long, hard task, but not necessarily an impossible one, and surely it is the most challenging one than has faced our species to date. Its success might even mean that science has come of age.

In the long history of achieving control over nature, human groups have found it expedient to achieve control over other polities. Control is power. Power is played out within every kind of social group, starting with the nuclear family. The parent is bigger and stronger, and is the source of sustenance and protection for the child. But, in order to survive, the child must come to feel that its own behavior offers some control over its destiny. Power does not necessarily mean dominance. It functions most effectively through cooperation, but without power of any kind there can be no security.

In the course of the history of warfare, conquest, often with imposition of the customs and values of western conquerors over the conquered, has steadily reduced human diversity (as, for example, in the extinction of many indigenous peoples), and ultimately has created nation-states under the aegis of which millions of today's peoples live. We say "aegis" rather than domination, because what starts as domination often ends as the "assimilation" of the conquered.

One lesson that can be derived from anthropology is that war is not a necessary outcome of a human aptitude for aggression (Foster 1986; Malinowski 1941; Mead 1940; Swanton 1943). Warfare developed as a major institution in nation-states in an attempt to achieve maximum, coercive power over other states. Warfare, as an institutionalized function of nationalism, has proved adaptive for those groups which have practiced it successfully. Through conquest, these groups have greatly increased both their power and their own security. Anthropologists have examined the role of conflict and its resolution in many societies, and have sometimes concluded that rather than being totally destructive, warfare has often had a cohesive effect on society (Gluckman 1959, Habarad this volume). Groups that are in conflict with one another within a society, commonly join together and cooperate against a common external enemy. Even between societies, such cooperation can take place and sometimes results in lasting alliances.

Discord is inevitable because human wants cannot always be equally satisfied. Societies use a variety of means to resolve conflicts, including negotiation and mediation. Human beings, like other mammals, can be aroused to commit aggressive acts, but such arousal need not lead to war, and in war, those who must fight usually feel, not so much animosity toward the enemy as a duty toward their own polity and shame before their peers if they shirk such a duty. Animosity toward an enemy can be fairly easily fomented through manipulation of symbols in order to make killing other humans—normally taboo—possible. Through such manipulation guilt feelings are rationalized away in order to make warriors able to engage effectively in battle. Anthropologists have shown that even in "primitive" tribes, where raids and intergroup fighting are frequent, feelings of fear and reluctance at undertaking battle are strong and are only subdued by a greater fear of peer contempt and loss of masculine pride if fighting is avoided (Goldschmidt this volume). Patriotism conventionally takes on sacred value, outweighing other values. This is conveyed by sayings such as "My country right or wrong," and personal values are put aside in the service of the state. In this country patriotism may obviate personal choice for or against killing by young men of draft age when war is declared (Greenhouse 1986).

War also fulfills a drive that is perhaps a human universal: that of actively seeking personal risk (Clark 1986). Men, in particular, seem to seek risk as self-validation, or as proof of personal courage. It may be that women do not have this drive, or have it to a lesser degree, or that it may be expressed differently because of the self-validating biological risk involved in child-bearing.

In many cultures in which warfare is institutionalized, masculine pride in heroism, and bravery in the face of danger, are fostered and maintained through methods of socialization and through the fear of peer contempt and ridicule (Pulliam this volume). Because this is the norm in our own culture, it may seem to us to be universal. However, anthropologists have studied societies in which the opposite is the case. In Tahiti, for example, it is reported that socialization encourages timidity, and in adulthood Tahitians are said to lack the underlying hostility that is so easily aroused in many societies (Levy 1978). This underscores the fact that aggression leading to violence is not instinctive but socially fostered. In Tahiti, as in the rest of Polynesia, warfare was frequent in the past, but was undertaken because of the ambitions of the chiefs. Since the chiefs were not only powerful but sacred, warfare in their behalf was a duty not to be avoided.

Often in the past, and still today in some parts of the world, the ruler was considered sacred, with fighting in his behalf a religious duty. Today, divinely ordained kings are more rare, but the State and locally revered God or Gods tend to coalesce in symbolic support of the nation on the battlefield. If God is assumed to be on our side, then killing in His name is justified and all evil can quite happily be attributed to the enemy. War propaganda invariably manipulates symbols to this end (see both Worsley and Brasset this volume).

Contrary to a popular belief that territoriality is a major cause of war, warfare between nation-states rarely seems to have much economic motivation. Ancient warfare was often about territory and access to territory, or was dictated by greed for booty and riches, as was the case in Spain's conquest of Latin America, where greed was rationalized as the need to save the souls of the natives through Christianity. Modern warfare between powerful nations seems mostly to be about the control of people's minds in order to force acceptance of one's own deities—or of whatever belief system substitutes for the godhead as the seat of Ultimate Truth. This is not to say that there are not also economic motivations, but these can be achieved amicably by means of international cooperation, if patience and restraint are exercised (Pinxten 1986, Silverberg 1986).

The Reagan administration is often criticized by its opponents as ruling by means of exploitation of popular symbols and the emotion that is generated by their evocation. There is no doubt that Reagan is a master of such manipulation, but it is also true that no country has ever been ruled otherwise. The symbolism may be different in each case, but without the use of emotionally invested symbols no social control would be possible, and without such control there could be no social cohesion and no government (Anderson this volume). Fortunately, as the anthropological study of symbolism demonstrates, symbols are multivocal, ambiguously supporting a variety of functions. Indeed, "The more meanings a symbol signifies, the more ambiguous and flexible it becomes, the more intense the feelings that it evokes, the greater its potency, and the more functions it achieves" (Cohen 1974:32). A variety of symbols can evoke much the same response, increasing the emotional impact of the message.

Both the tenacity and the flexibility of symbolization, as well as its capacity to fulfill emotional needs, must be understood if we are to be able to extricate the human species from the predicament in which it now finds itself. Social anthropology is making important contributions in the analysis of the symbolic process as it relates to power relationships and political dynamism.

Symbolic flexibility provides room for change, while symbolic persistence provides the continuity of culture within which change can be effected without violent destruction of the social order. Change is either fostered or hindered because of the ardor with which social symbols are embraced by society and the degree to which symbols can be adapted to changed circumstances. Symbols may also become gradually outmoded and replaced by others with more current social effectiveness (Bateson this volume). Because of their multivalence, symbols can be manipulated as easily by destructive as by constructive forces. By coming to understand potentially socially destructive aspects of symbols at work in our own society we can significantly reduce their potency.

In recent years, nuclear weapons have been made to seem more benign by giving them names such as "Peacekeeper," or by planning to "house them in silos," evoking the sanctity of peaceful domesticity and agricultural productiveness. Often weapons or weapon systems are given names so abstracted from their reality as to distance the danger, such names as "Strategic Defense Initiative," or at even further distance from reality, the acronym of "SDI" (Cohn 1987). Interestingly, the opponents of "SDI" thought to ridicule it as a fanciful notion by dubbing it "Star Wars," but this instead served a promotional purpose by elevating it in the popular fancy to the potent but distant level of science fiction, comfortably familiar but reassuringly nonthreatening to many from the Star Wars and Star Trek films.

Many forms of symbolic behavior serve to distance us from reality in this way. It is even probable that our society is more impelled by fantasy than any other in the history of the world. First of all, literacy is distancing in that through reading about events we can feel almost as if we have experienced them without having actually lived them. Radio and television have enhanced the feeling of immediacy but kept us at a safe distance from personal risk. Advertising, as well as media exposure to the glamour of the life of others, creates wants that are difficult or impossible to fulfill, making us constantly dissatisfied with whatever we have achieved.

Not only does constant media bombardment distance us from events, it also conflates events that are actually happening, viewed on the evening news, with events that are imaginary, portrayed in entertainment programs. One kind of event that we are exposed to in this way is war. At a safe distance, we can have the thrill of risk without experiencing bodily danger. War becomes both familiar and unthreatening and seems, at the same time, inevitable. If it is inevitable, we can put it out of our minds, as we necessarily must exclude from consciousness the possibility of unanticipated but ultimately expectable acts of nature such as earthquakes, storms and floods, or even our own deaths (Becker 1973, 1975). Since war is not inevitable but man-made, this distancing and abdication of responsibility for war is a very dangerous thing. Yet, it is precisely this kind of objectification and distancing that political realism asserts is important and possible (Rubinstein this volume). It is only if we take personal and group responsibility for it that it can be avoided.

In western culture, science has steadily replaced the supernatural as the object of belief. If we are not scientists, or only scientists in a specialized discipline, we put ourselves in the hands of scientists with other specialized knowledge in the expectation of miracles. In modern society, scientists and technologists have replaced the shamans of less "civilized" peoples, whose practices have been studied by many anthropologists. Our most fervent modern western belief is in technology and in the benefits that it can confer, with little thought for its potential for social destruction.

Mathematics has been put in the service of technology, and quantification is the new mystique (Cohen 1982). Unfortunately, the study of symbolism does not lend itself readily to quantification because some aspects of symbolic experience do not yield to purely formal models of causality, constructed from the causal relationships of logic: "Symbolic behavior is dramatic behaviour and its analysis cannot be effected through the computer" (Cohen 1974:52). Like the communication media, quantification is a distancing mechanism. If we can quantify, we begin to feel that we have solved our problems.

The ritual symbolism of arms control needs to be carefully examined. The term itself is reassuring: if we control arms they cannot destroy us. However, this conceals the reality of arms control ritual as it is being played out today, which encourages each side to attempt to manipulate the arms race to its own advantage within the fiction of control. Much of the problem is created by our mystical reliance on the "objectivity" of numbers. If numbers are balanced between contending forces it is believed that our security will be increased. Yet, just by stating the problem in terms of numerical balance, instead of promoting a steady decrease in deadly weapons arms control has promoted a competitive effort for weapons advantage. The symbolism of this process and its meaning to the protagonists needs to be studied. It is exactly the kind of symbolic process that easily goes unexamined because the very fact that such a mutual effort exists seems reassuring. In the meantime, the process itself is promoting rather than hampering arms stockpiling and the development of new weapon systems.

We are strongly affected by the manipulation of symbols that takes place around us. If we understand the process and the kind of affect that certain kinds of symbolic manipulation produce, it is likely that their affect will be lessened, or at least by becoming conscious of their workings we will be freed from their mesmerizing influence and can choose the symbolic systems that have the greatest chance of fostering global security. Since governments and politicians are skilled in manipulating symbols in order to achieve the kind of social consensus that will allow them to pursue their own ends, if we are aware of the way that this is done, and the subtlety with which this power is wielded, we will be able to make informed choices between those symbolic constructs that promise some measure of long term security and those that may ultimately foster global destruction.

References Cited

Ardrey, R. 1966. *The Territorial Imperative.* New York: Atheneum.

Becker, E. 1975. *Escape from Evil.* New York: Free Press.

———. 1973. *The Denial of Death.* New York: Free Press.

Benedict, R. 1946. *The Chrysanthemum and the Sword: Patterns of Japanese Culture.* Boston: Houghton Mifflin.

Bunzel, R. and A. Parsons. 1964. Anthropology and World Affairs as seen by U.S.A. Associates: 1. Report on Regional Conferences. *Current Anthropology* 5:430, 437–442.

Chagnon, N. 1988. Life Histories, Blood Revenge, and Warfare in a Tribal Population. *Science* 239:985–992.

———, and P. Bugos. 1979. Kin Selection and Conflict: An Analysis of a Yanomamo ax Fight. In *Evolutionary Biology and Human Social Behavior: An Anthropological Perspective.* N. Chagnon and W. Irons, eds., North Scituate, MA: Duxbury Press, Pp. 213–238.

Chagnon, N. and R. Hames. 1979. Protein Deficiency and Tribal Warfare in Amazonia: New Data. *Science* 203:910–913.

Clark, M.M. 1986. The Cultural Patterning of Risk-Seeking Behavior: Implications for Armed Conflict. In *Peace and War: Cross-Cultural Perspectives.* M.L. Foster and R.A. Rubinstein, eds., New Brunswick, NJ: Transaction Books, Pp. 79–90.

Cohen, A. 1974. *Two Dimensional Man.* Berkeley: University of California Press.

Cohen, P.C. 1984. *A Calculating People: The Spread of Numeracy in Early America.* Chicago: University of Chicago Press.

Cohn, C. 1987. Slick'ems, Glick'ems, Christmas Trees, and Cookie Cutters: Nuclear Language and How We Learn to Pat the Bomb. *Bulletin of the Atomic Scientists* 43(5):17–24.

Curry, M. 1986. Beyond Nuclear Winter: On the Limitations of Science in Political Debate. *Antipode* 18:244–267.

Denzin, N. 1970. *The Research Act: A Theoretical Introduction to Sociological Methods.* Chicago: Aldine.

Ferguson, R.B., editor. 1984. *Warfare, Culture, and Environment.* New York: Academic Press.

Foster, M.L. 1986. Is War Necessary? In *Peace and War: Cross-Cultural Perspectives.* M.L. Foster and R.A. Rubinstein, eds., New Brunswick, NJ: Transaction Books, Pp. 71–78.

———, and S. Brandes, editors. 1979. *Symbol as Sense.* New York: Academic Press.

Foster, M.L. and R.A. Rubinstein, editors. 1986. *Peace and War: Cross-Cultural Perspectives.* New Brunswick, NJ: Transaction Books.

Fried, M., M. Harris, and R. Murphy, editors. 1967. *War: The Anthropology of Armed Conflict.* Garden City, NY: Natural History Press.

Gellner, E. 1983. *Nations and Nationalism.* Ithaca: Cornell University Press.

Gluckman, M. 1959. *Custom and Conflict in Africa.* Glencoe, IL: The Free Press.

Greenhouse, C. 1986. Fighting for Peace. In *Peace and War: Cross-Cultural Perspectives.* M.L. Foster and R.A. Rubinstein, eds., New Brunswick, NJ: Transaction Books, Pp. 49–60.

Harris, M. 1974. *Cows, Pigs, Wars, and Witches: The Riddles of Culture.* New York: Vintage Books.

Levy, R. 1978. Tahitian Gentleness and Redundant Controls. In *Learning Non-Aggression.* A. Montagu, ed., Oxford: Oxford University Press.

Lieberson, S. 1985. *Making it Count: The Improvement of Social Research and Theory.* Berkeley: University of California Press.

Malinowski, B. 1948. *Magic, Science and Religion and other Essays.* Boston: Beacon Press.

———. 1941. An Anthropological Analysis of War. *American Journal of Sociology* 46:521–550.

Mead, M. 1940. War Is Only an Invention—Not a Biological Necessity. *Asia* XL:402–405.

Nader, L. 1965. Choices of Legal Procedure: Shia Moslem and Mexican Zapotec. *American Anthropologist* 67:394–399.

———, and B. Yngvesson. 1973. On Studying the Ethnography of Law and its Consequences. In *Handbook of Social and Cultural Anthropology.* J.J. Honigman, ed., Chicago: Rand McNally, Pp. 883–922.

Pinxten, R. 1986. The Developmental Dynamics of Peace. In *Peace and War: Cross-Cultural Perspectives.* M.L. Foster and R.A. Rubinstein, eds., New Brunswick, NJ: Transaction Books, Pp. 269–280.

Rappaport, R. 1967. *Pigs for the Ancestors.* New Haven: Yale University Press.

Redfield, R. 1953. Does America Need a Hearing Aid?. *The Saturday Review* 36(26 September):11–45.

Rubinstein, R.A., C.D. Laughlin, and J. McManus. 1984. *Science as Cognitive Process: Toward an Empirical Philosophy of Science.* Philadelphia: University of Pennsylvania Press.

Rubinstein, R.A. and S. Tax. 1985. Power, Powerlessness and the Failure of "Political Realism." In *Native Power: The Quest for Autonomy and Nationhood of Indigenous Peoples.* J. Brøsted, J. Dahl, A. Gray, H. Gulløv, G. Hendriksen, J. Jørgensen and I. Kleivan, eds., Bergen: Universitetforlaget AS, Pp. 301–308.

Silverberg, J. 1986. The Anthropology of Global Integration: Some Grounds for Optimism about World Peace. In *Peace and War: Cross-Cultural Perspectives.* M.L. Foster and R.A. Rubinstein, eds., New Brunswick, NJ: Transaction Books, Pp. 281–291.

Swanton, J. 1943. *Are Wars Inevitable?* Washington, DC: Smithsonian Institution.

Tax, S., editor. 1967. *The Draft: A Handbook of Facts and Alternatives.* Chicago: University of Chicago Press.

Part 1
Confronting Peace and War

1 / Anthropology and International Security

Robert A. Rubinstein

International security analysis is conducted by a community of practitioners which has a well-developed world-view. Robert Rubinstein describes the major features of this world-view, often called "Political Realism." International security professionals use the principles of "political realism" to set the terms of discussions about questions of peace and conflict. Rubinstein shows that this results in their dismissing as not useful, theoretical and empirical information which is not consistent with these principles. Much of this information, he argues, is precisely the kind which anthropologists often consider crucial for understanding societies—facets of symbolism and social process. Rubinstein argues that as a result international security professionals base their discussions on an inadequate conception of the complexity of human culture and society. The result, he shows, is that while international security discussions of the technological aspects of peace and conflict are very sophisticated, discussions of the social dynamics of peace and conflict are impoverished and misleading. Using information about societies in situations of prolonged environmental deprivation to critique discussions of "nuclear winter," Rubinstein shows that the inadequate conception of human culture and society held by the international security community obscures rather than clarifies critical points of discussion. He argues that international security discussions should be revitalized by insuring that multiple levels of analysis—including considerations of symbolic and cultural processes—are treated as equally necessary and legitimate.—The Editors

Copyright © Robert A. Rubinstein, 1988

17

Maintaining international security and avoiding nuclear war requires both technological and social understanding.[1] Accurate information about the social and cultural dynamics of groups involved in the conduct of international affairs is a necessary complement to the formal and technological analyses now routinely conducted in the field of international security (Schwartz and Derber 1986).[2] This is because wise strategic decision-making requires, at a minimum, taking account of a wide variety of information and using it in flexible ways (Rubinstein 1986:350). In general, however, social and cultural information is not regarded by the strategic studies community as particularly useful, except, perhaps, for *post hoc* regional analyses (Booth 1979).

Some anthropologists are concerned that a preoccupation with technical models of, and technological factors in, world affairs is dangerous (see, Foster and Rubinstein 1986). They argue that policies based on a view that sees all international security problems from a perspective of inter-state power conflicts leads to the mistaken belief that these problems can be solved by reference to material power and models of technical rationality (Beeman 1986). This belief in the existence of "technical fixes" (Pacey 1983:7) for all international security problems inevitably leads to recommendations that are out of touch with social and cultural realities.

The potential value of social and cultural information for international security studies is now often noted. Yet, the international security literature remains heavily dominated by technical analyses and technological concerns (Hamburg 1986). International security professionals have found that it is very difficult to integrate substantive social science knowledge into their models and policy recommendations.

There are many different accounts of why social science knowledge has not been more fully integrated into international security analysis. Some focus on the economics of the military industrial complex (Melman 1983, 1986). They argue that the economic and political self-interests of those in positions of power make impossible the fuller use of social and cultural information which threatens the status quo. Others focus on the epistemological differences between the quantitative approaches of the international security community and the qualitative methodologies needed to gain social and cultural information (Knudsen 1987). These people argue that the vastly different rules of evidence and inference of the approaches make them incompatible. Others argue that the professionalization of the international security field produced an orthodoxy that socially enforces a narrow definition of what kind of knowledge is useful in international security work (Korany 1986:548). Each account captures an important aspect of the difficulties that meet attempts to bring cultural considerations to bear on strategic studies.

Anthropologists who wish to contribute to international security discussions also are handicapped because the relevant anthropological literature appears to those in the international security community to be a collection of local-level, often exotic studies. In contrast, the disciplines that form the core of traditional strategic thinking embrace general and generalizable principles of analysis and method (like game theory or econometric modeling, see Ball and Richelson 1986). Anthropological studies are thought to be tangential to problems of international security, in part because the anthropological literature contains no clear statement about the substantive and methodological principles of anthropology that unify this work and relate it to international security concerns. This paper describes some of the common themes in the anthropological literature related to peace and war and indicates some of the ways that the resulting anthropological data provide important information for international security studies.

International Security and
the Paradigm of "Political Realism"

When anthropologists seek to contribute to discussions of peace and international security they enter a community of practitioners who share a common paradigm. As Kuhn (1962, 1970) points out, a paradigm limits how a community defines the domain in which it is interested. At the group level, paradigms function by providing (1) theoretical statements about a class of phenomena, (2) shared belief in particular models that legitimate the use of particular analogies and metaphors, (3) common values about what is important, and (4) concrete problem solutions that are firmly accepted by the community and that constitute a critical aspect of the training of young researchers (Rubinstein et al. 1984:63). The paradigm that characterizes the world view of the international security community has been called "political realism."[3]

The paradigm of "political realism" proceeds from a number of theoretical premises about (1) what the proper unit of analysis is for understanding world affairs, (2) what kinds of information ought to be taken into account by decision makers (3) how "rational" decision makers act, and (4) the nature of power.

The state as unit of analysis. "Political realists" assert that in international affairs the State is the most important unit of analysis (Kim 1983, Beeman 1986, Korany 1986). Thus, in this view, international security is to be understood on the basis of the actions and interests of Nations. Discounted (if not completely ignored) are questions of inter-group relations at levels other than the state, issues of meaning and symbolism, and local-level views of the significance of conflict situations.

Useful knowledge as objective fact. Underlying "political realism" is the view that useful knowledge must be based on "objective," "scientific" facts. Most frequently, quantitative indices of interstate relations are taken as the hallmark of useful knowledge. That it is the "political realist" paradigm itself that determines what counts as fact and what as fantasy is rarely discussed, and is most often expressed in the rejection out-of-hand of descriptions of world affairs that do not conform to "realist" expectations (Kim 1983:9).

Yet, scientific facts are never "just facts." Indeed, they depend upon value judgments that can be consciously presented and explored, or, for whatever reasons, hidden. As Myrdal (1969:51–52) observed:

> biases in social science cannot be erased simply by "keeping to the facts" and refining the methods of dealing with statistical data. Indeed data and the handling of data are often more susceptible to tendencies towards bias than is "pure thought." . . . Biases are thus not confined to the practical and political conclusions drawn from research. They are more deeply seated than that. They are the unfortunate results of concealed valuations that insinuate themselves into research at all stages, from its planning to its final presentation. As a result of their concealment, they are not properly sorted out and can thus be kept undefined and vague.

The state as rational actor. A corollary of the first two aspects of the "political realist" paradigm is the belief that once States have the objective facts they (through their leaders) will act rationally. Actions are judged more or less rational to the degree that they conform to the behavior that is predicted by formal models (of econometric analysis or game theory) that are based on objective facts. Such "technical rationality" excludes a wide range of substantive cultural and social information (Simon 1983), and is perhaps more appropriately described as logical rather than rational.

Power as material. To understand world affairs and ensure international security, the "political realist" view calculates the relative power of states acting "rationally" on the basis of "objective" knowledge. Only physical and material resources are included in the calculations of power. Kim (1983:9) notes that,

> the concept of "power" in mainstream realism is excessively narrow and limited. This realism respects only material and physical power and is contemptuous of "normative power," . . . It denies the existence of the world normative system.

One result of this is that powerful actions based on normative or nonmaterial strength are difficult to understand from the "realist" perspective. Yet normative imperatives form an important basis for many activities important for international security. Indigenous peoples have successfully challenged the actions of materially more powerful groups, and stopped the self-interested actions of those more powerful groups. For example, the Dené (Kehoe this volume) successfully oppose uranium mining and other nuclear related actions, and the Cherokee successfully resist economic and cultural extinction (Rubinstein and Tax 1985). The Dené, Cherokee, and other indigenous peoples' resistance is based on normative, not material, resources. Normative cultural aspects play important roles in the affairs of many countries, like Iran (Bateson this volume; see also Beeman 1986) and China (Potter this volume).

Some Current Implications for Strategic Studies

Although the "political realist" view has for a long time been criticized as over-narrow (see the articles collected in Mendlovitz 1975, Falk and Kim 1980, and Falk et al. 1982) it has dominated discussions of international affairs for the past four decades. The principles underlying it were given clear statement by scholars like Morgenthau and Thompson (1956), Aron (1966) Morgenthau (1973). Despite mounting evidence that such a preoccupation with technical analysis and technological concerns is inadequate for achieving international security, "political realism" remains the predominant paradigm.

In fact, the "political realist" view is the most widely taught approach to international affairs. In a review of the literature in this field, Olson and Onuf (1985) report that Morgenthau and Thompson's (1956) work is "the most influential textbook of the early post-war period," and Rosenau et al. (1977) report in their study of university training that it ranked as the top textbook. Korany (1986:549) notes that the influence of "political realism" has become widespread:

> the power paradigm has been presented to the Third world as the most valid, since *Politics Among Nations* has been translated into such languages as Arabic, Chinese, Turkish and Swahili.

The cross-cultural experiences central to anthropological work lead to the recognition that different groups conceptualize security and power differently, and that such concepts are always socially situated. Frequently these conceptions employ symbols and metaphors other than those acknowledged by "political realists" as those that guide actions.

Once one acknowledges the legitimacy of these alternative conceptions it is difficult to accept the "realist" analysis as satisfactory. Indeed, cultural and social considerations are as important as technical and technological concerns in reaching a satisfactory understanding of world events.

Before discussing some selected themes that unify anthropological work, it is useful to mention two examples of how "realist" models of strategic thinking ignore social and cultural information. These examples illustrate many that could be selected from the international security literature.[4]

The United States' positions at disarmament negotiations are guided in part by estimates of how many and what kinds of weapons systems need to be retained in order to ensure the country's security. These "bottom line" positions result in part from estimates of how much damage our weapons would inflict on the Soviet Union in the event of a nuclear war. One measurement of this damage is the length of time it is estimated it would take the Soviet economy to recover to its pre-attack level. Published information suggests that after a nuclear war the Soviet economy would recover in between four and fifteen years (United States House of Representatives 1977:212). Kennedy and Lewis (1986:195) report that,

Typical results suggest full recovery to prewar GNP within about five years if a U.S. attack destroys, say, less than half of Soviet capital and relatively little labor; seven to ten years with population-only civil defense; and perhaps fifteen years in any event. The U.S. force committed to the attack in such models often runs to several thousand warheads.

Kennedy and Lewis critique these models from a technical perspective, showing that the speed of recovery that this modeling predicts depends upon the use of statistical assumptions about capital and labor that may not be warranted. They demonstrate that these models may in fact overestimate the speed of a recovery.

From an anthropological perspective, models of post nuclear war economic recovery (even Kennedy and Lewis's critique) are unrealistic. This is because they include in their calculations only considerations of the survival of labor and capital (the quantitative fact that they are still here after an attack *not* the quality of that existence) and the acceptance of technical, *a priori* assumptions about the operation of any economy. To an anthropologist, such models are unacceptable because they do not recognize the internal dynamics of human societies in general (see below) or include any specifically Soviet elements.

For example, United States' strategic calculations include assumptions about the resources that the Soviets would commit to a nuclear exchange. These influence estimates of how much capital and labor would be left after the exchange on which the Soviet's could rebuild their economy. These assumptions are based, in turn, on the further assumption that each side would seek to limit the damage resulting from a nuclear war by preserving the chance for a cease-fire. This is called "escalation control." In theory, escalation control will be achieved by using only the minimally necessary amount of arms to bring the Soviets to negotiations. Thus, particular patterns of nuclear attack on the Soviet Union are seen by United States' strategic planners as being more or less severe than others. This depends on Soviet strategists giving the same meanings to patterns of attack as do United States' strategists. From the Soviet perspective, however, due to geographic considerations an all out United States attack would be indistinguishable from a small-scale attack (Ball 1986:20–23).

Technical models are also used to guide actions in non-nuclear areas of international affairs. One vivid example is the recent history of the United States' policy and actions toward Iran. The United States' thoroughly "realist" approach to dealing with Iran is reflected in its handling of the 1979–1981 Iranian-American hostage crisis (Beeman 1986) and more recently in the administration's attempt to cultivate "moderates" in Iran (leading to "Iran-Contragate"). In both instances, the United States analysts consistently failed to treat as legitimate normative rather than material considerations, especially those actions that stemmed from social dynamics in Iran "below" the state level (Bateson this volume). United States policy failed because it did not include a specifically Iranian element in its analyses of these situations. This left foreign policy officials frustrated by the Iranians seeming "irrationality" and "untrustworthiness."

With these considerations in mind I turn to some themes that unify the anthropological literature and make it particularly important for work in international security.

Consequences of Environmental Deprivation and Stress

Anthropological analyses of situations of environmental deprivation and stress can add an important human dimension to discussions of the consequences of the effect of nuclear war. One such discussion focuses on whether a nuclear exchange—meaning nuclear war—would cause a "nuclear winter." The technical question is: will enough smoke enter the earth's atmosphere after nuclear war so that enough sunlight would be absorbed by the smoke to cause the earth's surface to cool significantly. Considerable technical literature analyzes variations in the atmospheric system resulting from various sorts of nuclear exchanges. It is not always agreed that sufficient smoke would be injected into the atmosphere to cause a wide-scale problem. Yet, the assumption among people working on this as a technical problem is that if a sufficient amount of smoke is produced it will precipitate significant changes in the earth's atmospheric and geological systems.

This technical work has not been equally concerned with projecting the effect of a nuclear winter on human social systems. Although common-sense tells us that if there is a nuclear war which causes nuclear winter life as we know it will be significantly changed, and perhaps disappear, even very recent work has focused on the narrow technical questions of whether the atmospheric systems will be greatly affected. Much of the nuclear winter debate results from researchers refining their models of the environmental impact of nuclear war and asserting that its consequence for people will be much less than imagined (hence we should plan more for post-nuclear war life).

For instance, in May 1987 the Federal Emergency Management Agency (FEMA) released a report asserting that life after nuclear war will be better than strategists had earlier concluded (Treichel 1987). The report used "refined" targeting assumptions to show that only 130 million people would be in the high risk category in the event of a nuclear war (this category is the group that has a "sure probability of being injured or killed"). This contrasts with earlier FEMA estimates that 156 million people would be in this category.

In a similar vein, Thompson and Schneider (1986) review the scientific literature about nuclear winter and conclude that it is unlikely to happen. They say that they

> show on scientific grounds that the global apocalyptic conclusions of the initial nuclear winter hypothesis can now be relegated to a vanishingly low level of probability. Thus the argument that nuclear winter provides the sole basis for drastic strategic arms reductions has been greatly weakened. But, at the same time, there is little that is thoroughly understood about the environmental effects of a nuclear war (Thompson and Schneider 1986:983).

Missing from nearly all of these discussions is a principled understanding of the effects of prolonged environmental deprivation and stress on the dynamics of human societies.

Anthropological studies of situations of prolonged environmental deprivation and stress can help predict the dimensions of changes in social relationships that would result from nuclear disaster. There is a growing body of studies of societies that have experienced extreme environmental stress and of societies in which there has been massive destruction due to war or natural disasters (including studies of Hiroshima and Nagasaki after they were atom-bombed).

Nuclear war would bring about very real changes in the way that people treat one another. The result would be ways of interacting that might be called "not human." Recognizing this can clarify the effects of nuclear winter, perhaps especially in terms of the common social goal of preserving particular cultural patterns, or "defending *our* way of life."

Models predicting change in human social systems also make it clear that, for human beings, it won't matter whether a nuclear winter actually occurs because the stress on human systems in the event of nuclear war will be so severe that it will trigger social changes even before nuclear winter comes to pass (Greene et al. 1982). Consideration of the effect of nuclear war on human systems, in conjunction with consideration of its effect on physical or environmental systems forces a change in the definition of the international security problem: The question ceases to be, will there be a nuclear winter?, and becomes, what are the implications of the changes that will occur in the environmental and human systems as a result of nuclear war? The implications for human life are grave.

For example, anthropologists recognize that human society is based on reciprocity—the exchange and manipulation of goods, services, affections, symbols. Food sharing—how food is distributed and with whom we eat—serves as a primary example of this. We know from studies of societies undergoing prolonged stress that their patterns of food sharing change in particular sorts of ways. To oversimplify a bit, these changes can be characterized as a pulling in of the bounds of social relations so that societies become increasingly atomized or individualistic. The ethnographic record is replete with reports of general increases in competition and decreases in cooperation, increased incidence of infanticide, of older and ill members of society being allowed to fend for themselves and to starve, decreases in parental displays of affection for their children, and secrecy rather than sharing in the consumption of food. In other words the kinds of caring, positive affective relationships that we have come to consider as characteristic of humanity disappear (Laughlin 1974, Rubinstein 1975, Laughlin and Brady 1978, Dirks 1980, 1985).

Turnbull (1967, 1972, 1968), for instance, describes the effects of prolonged environmental stress on the Ik of northeastern Uganda. For historical reasons, the Ik have during the last thirty or forty years been living in an environment that has become increasingly depleted.

Ik society has adjusted to the insufficiency of the environment by dramatic shifts in the patterns of social relations among its members. Parents report separating from their children at younger ages than their own parents left them as children. In fact Turnbull says,

> the family itself has, *as a socioeconomic unit,* become dysfunctional. It simply does not exist in any form recognizable to us as such. Even the conjugal pair, whether formally married or not, does not form a cooperative unit except for a few specific purposes (Turnbull 1978:59).

This fragmented social life is reflected in the architecture of Ik settlements. Historical construction patterns that fostered social interaction by providing common and central meeting places has been replaced by architecture that includes no common spaces and orients entrances to homes so as to emphasize privacy and, perhaps, secrecy.

In the face of this fragmentation and the disappearance of the family support structure children form age-gangs. These gangs differ from traditional age-grades in that they have no cooperative purpose other than to fend off predators, including adults.[5]

> A new meaning of *marangik* "goodness" emerged in this predatory context: any adult who found a child with food and could take the food and eat it was a "good" adult. . . . But since adults normally pursued their food quest alone, only a solitary child was in danger. [I] never heard of any adult rash enough to take food from a child with a gang nearby. The gangs roamed the ravines and when food was seen; [sic] the first child to reach it consumed it instantly. The others did not expect it to be shared . . . (Turnbull 1978:63).

Turnbull also describes how the general economic system among the Ik is characterized by a retraction of bounds of reciprocity, resulting in the expendability of people unable to fend for themselves. The Ik are not a unique case. Laughlin (1974, 1978) describes similar social shifts among the So, also of northeastern Uganda.

The dramatic scaling back of reciprocity relations in response to environmental deprivation is also not unique to pastoralists in east Africa. Bishop (1978) describes similar changes in the adaptive strategies of the Northern Ojibwa in Canada during the 1800s. Bishop (1978:221–224) observes changes in the traditional social organization of the Ojibwa (for example, post-marital residence patterns became less regular). Further, reciprocity relationships became more competitive (in Sahlins' 1965 terms, more negative).

Parallel shifts in patterns of social organization, cooperation and reciprocity have been described in urban societies as well (Lomnitz 1986). Rubinstein (1975) describes the impact of stressful ecological circumstances on reciprocity among the poor in Mexico City. In the face of prolonged resource deprivation, exchange among the residents of the Panaderos *vecindad* is characterized by a shrinking of the social sphere within which generalized and balanced reciprocity occur and an increase in the kinds of people with whom negative reciprocity occurs, including even other family members (Rubinstein 1975:259–261).

Anthropologists distinguish situations of deprivation from those of disaster (Laughlin and Brady 1978:18, Torry 1979:518). While environmental deprivation involves ongoing ecological degradation, disasters are unique events,

> that culminate in physical damage to a community, or communities, so severe that most or all major public and private facilities no longer provide essential social and economic services without extensive replacement or repair. This definition applies whether or not people are killed (Torry 1979:518).

Although many technical aspects differ, Torry's (1979) recent review of the ethnographic literature shows that the social and cultural effects of disasters parallel those of prolonged environmental deprivation. These changes are mostly in the direction of the more frequent occurrence of negative reciprocity (increased intergroup conflict) and less spontaneous cooperation among members of society ("dispersal of residences" as an economic strategy, "retrenchment of social activity"). In general "imperfections in the decision apparatus of government itself diminished effective community response to peril" (Torry 1979:523).

Dirks (1985:19) describes social responses to environmental deprivation in the context of the possibility of nuclear winter and projects that the resulting social changes would lead to considerable atomism of social relations, approximating what we today see as the least cooperative extremes of human social life. "The generosity, the trust, the affective warmth, the closeness that is generally valued in our culture will undergo serious erosion . . . [there will be] little latitude for relationships and actions that are not closely calculated in terms of their instrumental value." In short, not only would nuclear war "compound the ruin of the earth and its habitats, but [it would] degrade . . . the very qualities and relationships which we have come to realize as the fulfillment of our human potential."

This anthropological picture is frightening, especially in relation to the non-western, tribal, and preliterate peoples about whom the anthropologists' ethnographies most often speak. Some might object that because we are much more technologically sophisticated than they, we will be able to compensate for these ecological perturbations by either importing food supplies from other areas of the world, or by achieving a technological solution to the problem.

The response to this objection depends on understanding another very important anthropological principle: that the various facets of cultural and social life—political, legal, economic, religious, educational, symbolic, to name but a few—are critically interdependent. I have used food sharing as an example, but, the effects of ecological stress would extend into other parts of social and cultural systems, and cause social perturbations. Thus, a long-term food deficit cannot reasonably be treated in isolation because other social institutions will undergo similar changes. Perhaps most crucial will be the effect on the symbolic systems that undergird and support social and cultural life. Indeed, the record of the social effects of the atom-bombing of Hiroshima and Nagasaki show that severe nuclear disaster will lead to the "total breakdown of human life" (see, Committee for the Compiliation of Materials on Damage Caused by the Atomic Bombs in Hiroshima and Nagasaki 1981:339).

Culture in International Security

A recurrent theme in the anthropological literature is that all social behavior has a symbolic dimension. Although warfare and the construction of peaceful social relationships have much to do with considerations of economics and material force, they also have symbolic aspects that must be taken into account in order to resolve conflicts, avoid war or maintain an established peace.

One premise of anthropological work is that it is necessary to understand the social dynamics of the societies involved in world affairs. In the same way, it is important to recognize that international security work is conducted by a community, the social and cultural dynamics of which affect the decisions taken by its members. These dynamics produce a world view that is embodied in symbols and that evokes both cognitive and affective responses in community members. All such symbols direct attention to a limited part of the world, and thus models based on them can easily be overly narrow. In fact, symbols can even "normalize the unthinkable" (Peattie 1984). A self-conscious awareness of symbols and the content they convey can help to decrease that danger (Foster this volume).

In a general sense, the disciplines on which international security and strategic studies is based embrace a world view which discounts the importance of symbolic aspects of human social life when considering political relations. There is a specific sense in which the activities of this community have been institutionalized. Social mechanisms set up to perform particular functions lose their capacity for achieving their goals if they undergo a process of institutionalization (Melko 1974, Britan and Cohen 1980, Rubinstein 1984, Justice 1986), in which the social mechanisms set up for some purpose begin to receive more attention than the goal they were set up to achieve. Evidence that the international security community has been institutionalized is found in the elaborate system of symbols that it has created (Foster 1987) and in the complex ritual processes for manipulating these symbols that it has developed to ensure common problem definitions and responses (Pulliam this volume, Rubinstein 1988).

Anthropologists learn about a group's system of implicit meanings by looking at what the group does and listening to and observing the ways the group expresses itself in relation to its environment. When we do this we seek to understand the group's symbolic environment and to learn how symbols are manipulated. The importance of some symbols is that they evoke powerful responses from group members because they encompass both shared cognitive meanings and shared affective values (Lakoff and Johnson 1980).

Anthropological studies of the strategic community confirm that the community maintains its own world view—at times in the face of large amounts of evidence that it is inadequate—in part through the manipulation (not necessarily conscious) of symbols. Cohn (1987; see also Brasset this volume) for instance, describes how learning to use the acronyms and imagery of the strategic community led to a subtle shift in her own perceptions of the danger of nuclear war.[6] As she described the experience:

Nearly everyone I observed—lecturers, students, hawks, doves, men, and women—took pleasure in using the words; some of us spoke with a self-consciously ironic edge but the pleasure was there nonetheless. Part of the appeal was the thrill of being able to manipulate an arcane language, the power of entering the secret kingdom. But perhaps more important, learning the language gives a sense of control, a feeling of mastery over technology that is finally not controllable but powerful beyond human comprehension. The longer I stayed, the more conversations I participated in, the less I was frightened of nuclear war. . . . My energy was focused on the challenge of decoding acronyms, learning new terms, developing competence in the language—not on the weapons and wars behind the

words. By the time I was through, I had learned far more than an
alternate, if abstract, set of words. The content of what I could talk
about was monumentally different (Cohn 1987:21).

The international security community uses linguistic symbols to
maintain an inadequate conception of the complexity of human culture
and society. Nuclear strategic planning has incorporated the notion of
escalation control; this presupposes that the political and other social
processes necessary for the exercise of restraint exist. Thinking about
escalation control depends, in the language of international security
analysis, on there being a surviving command, control, communications
and intelligence system (Ball 1986:19)—or, as it is called, a surviving
"C³I." By assuming that assuring a surviving C³I is a technological
problem which can be solved, the international security community is
able to imagine scenarios about post-nuclear attack society such as the
estimates of the time needed for economic recovery discussed earlier.

From an anthropological perspective *these projections are logical but
not very realistic.* Yet, because they are taken to be based on "hard,"
quantifiable data there develops around these projections a false sense
of the adequacy of the problem definitions. The fact that such projections are based on partial information is obscured. Indeed, "No
formal recovery model . . . incorporates the coordination function, and
all models instead simply assume that it can be accomplished" (Kennedy and Lewis 1986:205). It is only possible to take so lightly information about such symbolically based social processes if one generally discounts the importance of cultural analysis.

Using linguistic symbols in support of the "realist" world view is
not simply the result of continuing to use now out-of-date strategic
concepts. Rather, these symbols are part of a powerful belief system
underlying the conduct of international security analysis. At present
international security analyses do not include information on the local-
level, social and cultural dynamics of groups other than the state.
Inconsistencies in the ways that people act from one point in time to
another are too often dismissed as puzzling but unimportant. Attempts
are often made to "factor out" these inconsistencies from the decision-
making process. Treating these inconsistencies in this way may mask
their importance but experience demonstrates that their importance is
not diminished.

Strategic decision-making usually requires generating and considering
multiple options. Wise strategic decision-making requires an informed
choice of the data considered and flexibility in the use of interpretive
strategies. Only then can we expect the decision-making process to

lead to appropriate policy decisions and ways of implementing those decisions.

What is needed is a kind of revitalization of international security analysis. This, in fact, is what anthropology's role can usefully be: to help create a potential for re-expanding this world view and building a continuing flexibility into the resulting analyses. All culturally significant tasks require continuing tension and adjustment between varied ways of generating novel alternatives and of integrating those alternatives in useful ways. Perhaps anthropology can provide a way of rebuilding flexibility into what is probably the most culturally significant task for us today: achieving a stable world peace.

Notes

1. Preparation of this paper was supported in part by a grant from the Ploughshares Fund, which I gratefully acknowledge. Earlier versions of this paper were read at the 1987 annual meetings of the American Association for the Advancement of Science, Chicago, Illinois, and of the American Anthropological Association, Chicago, Illinois. For their comments on earlier drafts of this paper, I thank Sol Tax, Janet D. Perloff, Mary Anna Thornton, and Jeffrey J. Ward.

2. Academic writing in the international security area includes work conducted under a variety of disciplinary names including: "national security studies," "international affairs," and "strategic studies." Although there are some differences in approach all share commitment to the "realist" approach to international affairs outlined by Morgenthau and Thompson (1956). Therefore, in this paper I use these terms interchangeably.

3. I place quotes around "political realism" because from an anthropological perspective this view is not realistic (Rubinstein and Tax 1985:302). That this is so will become clear later in this paper.

4. Similar examples can be drawn from Soviet strategic literature. The United States is used in this example simply because this information is more accessible.

5. Age grades are part of a form of social organization in which groups of people of similar age fulfill distinct and different roles in their society according to the age that is attained. Typically, members of an age grade maintain close ties throughout their lives.

6. William Broad (1985) presents a similar, though journalistic, account of how world view shifts in response to the use of nuclear language.

References Cited

Aron, R. 1966. *Peace and War: A Theory of International Relations.* New York: Praeger.

Ball, D. 1986. Toward a Critique of Strategic Nuclear Targeting. In, *Strategic Nuclear Targeting.* D. Ball and J. Richelson, eds. Ithaca, NY: Cornell University Press, Pp. 15–32.

Beeman, W.O. 1986. Conflict and Belief in American Foreign Policy. In *Peace and War: Cross-Cultural Perspectives.* M.L. Foster and R.A. Rubinstein, eds., New Brunswick, NJ: Transaction Books, Pp. 333–342.

Bishop, C. 1978. Cultural and Biological Adaptations to Deprivation: The Northern Ojibwa Case. In *Extinction and Survival in Human Populations.* C.D. Laughlin and I. Brady, eds., New York: Columbia University Press. Pp. 208–230.

Booth, K. 1979. *Strategy and Ethnocentrism.* New York: Holmes and Meier.

Britan, G. and R. Cohen, editors. 1980. *Hierarchy and Society: Anthropological Perspectives on Bureaucracy.* Philadelphia: Institute for the Study of Human Issues.

Broad, William. 1985. *Star Warriors: A Penetrating Look Into the Lives of the Young Scientists Behind our Space Age Weaponry.* New York: Simon and Schuster.

Cohn, C. 1987. Slick'ems, Glick'ems, Christmas Trees, and Cookie Cutters: Nuclear Language and How We Learn to Pat the Bomb. *Bulletin of the Atomic Scientists* 43(5):17–24.

Committee for the Compilation of Materials on Damage Caused by the Atomic Bombs in Hiroshima and Nagasaki. 1981. *Hiroshima and Nagasaki: The Physical, Medical, and Social Effects of the Atomic Bombings.* New York: Basic Books.

Dirks, R. 1985. Long-Term Effects of Famine on Human Societies, In *Nuclear Winter: The Anthropology of Human Survival: Proceedings of a Session at the 84th Annual Meeting of the American Anthropological Association, December 6, 1985, Washington, D.C.* M.P. Bumstead, ed., Los Alamos, NM: Los Alamos National Laboratory Document LA-UR-86-370, Pp. 11–19.

————. 1980. Social Responses During Severe Food Shortages and Famine, *Current Anthropology* 21:21–32.

Falk, R. and S. Kim, editors. 1980. *The War System: An Interdisciplinary Approach.* Boulder: Westview Press.

Falk, R., S. Kim, and S. Mendlovitz, editors. 1982. *Toward a Just World Order, Volume 1.* Boulder: Westview Press.

Foster, M.L. 1987. Suggestions from Anthropology for Increasing International Understanding. Paper presented at the 153rd Annual Meeting of the American Association for the Advancement of Science, 18 February 1987.

————, and Rubinstein, R.A., editors. 1986. *Peace and War: Cross-Cultural Perspectives.* New Brunswick, NJ: Transaction Books.

Greene, O., B. Rubin, N. Turok, P. Webber, and G. Wilkinson. 1982. *London After the Bomb: What a Nuclear Attack Really Means.* Oxford: Oxford University Press.

Hamburg, D.A. 1986. New Risks of Prejudice, Ethnocentrism, and Violence. *Science* 231:533.

Justice, J. 1986. *Policies, Plans, and People: Culture and Health Development in Nepal.* Berkeley: University of California Press.

Kennedy, M. and L. Lewis. 1986. On Keeping Them Down; or, Why Do Recovery Models Recover So Fast? In *Strategic Nuclear Targeting.* D. Ball and J. Richelson, eds, Ithaca, NY: Cornell University Press, Pp. 194–208.

Kim, S.S. 1983. *The Quest for a Just World Order.* Boulder: Westview Press.

Knudsen, B.B. 1987. The Paramount Importance of Cultural Sources: American Foreign Policy and Comparative Foreign Policy Research Reconsidered. Paper presented at the *European Consortium for Political Research Joint Session of Workshops,* Amsterdam, April 10–15.

Korany, B. 1986. Strategic Studies and the Third World: A Critical Evaluation. *International Social Science Journal* 110:546–562.

Kuhn, T.S. 1962. *The Structure of Scientific Revolutions.* Chicago: University of Chicago Press.

———. 1970. Logic of Discovery or Psychology of Research? In *Criticism and the Growth of Knowledge.* I. Lakatos and A. Musgrave, eds., Cambridge: Cambridge University Press, Pp. 1–23.

Lakoff, G. and M. Johnson. 1980. *Metaphors We Live By.* Chicago: University of Chicago Press.

Laughlin, C.D. 1974. Deprivation and Reciprocity, *Man* 9:380–396.

Laughlin, C.D. and I. Brady, editors. 1978. *Extinction and Survival in Human Populations.* New York: Columbia University Press.

Lomnitz, L. 1986. The Uses of Fear: "Porro" Gangs in Mexico. In *Peace and War: Cross-Cultural Perspectives.* M.L. Foster and R.A. Rubinstein, eds., New Brunswick, NJ: Transaction Books, Pp. 15–24.

Melko, M. 1974. The Termination of Peace as a Consequence of Institutionalization. In *War: Its Causes and Correlates.* M. Nettleship, R.D. Given, and A. Nettleship, eds., The Hague: Mouton, Pp. 549–558.

Melman, S. 1983. *Profits Without Production.* New York: Knopf.

———. 1986. The War-Making Institutions. In *Peace and War: Cross-Cultural Perspectives.* M.L. Foster and R.A. Rubinstein, eds., New Brunswick, NJ: Transaction Books, Pp. 193–208.

Mendlovitz, S., editor. 1975. *On the Creation of a Just World Order.* New York: The Free Press.

Morgenthau, H. 1973. *Politics Among Nations: The Struggle for Power and Peace, 5th edition.* New York: Knopf.

———, and K. Thompson. 1956. *Principles and Problems of International Politics.* New York: Knopf.

Myrdal, G. 1969. *Objectivity in Social Research.* Middletown, CN: Wesleyan University Press.

Olson, W. and O. Onuf. 1985. The Growth of a Discipline. In *International Relations: British and American Perspectives.* S. Smith, ed., London: Basil Blackwell.

Pacey, A. 1983. *The Culture of Technology.* Cambridge, MA: MIT Press.

Peattie, L. 1984. Normalizing the Unthinkable. *Bulletin of the Atomic Scientists* 40(3):32–36.

Rosenau, J., G. Gartin, E.P. McClain, D. Stinziano, R. Stoddard, and D. Swanson. 1977. Of Syllabi, Texts, Students, and Scholarship in International Relations. *World Politics* 29:263–341.

Rubinstein, R.A. 1975. Reciprocity and Resource Deprivation Among the Urban Poor in Mexico City. *Urban Anthropology* 4:251–264.

———. 1984. Epidemiology and Anthropology: Notes on Science and Scientism. *Communication and Cognition* 17:163–185.

———. 1986. The Collapse of Strategy: Understanding Ideological Bias in Policy Decisions. In *Peace and War: Cross-Cultural Perspectives*. M.L. Foster and R.A. Rubinstein, eds., New Brunswick, NJ: Transaction Books, Pp. 343–351.

———. 1988. Ritual Process and Images of the Other in Arms Control Negotiations, *Human Peace* 6(2):3–7.

———, C.D. Laughlin, and J. McManus. 1984. *Science as Cognitive Process: Toward an Empirical Philosophy of Science*. Philadelphia: University of Pennsylvania Press.

Rubinstein, R.A. and S. Tax. 1985. Power, Powerlessness and the Failure of "Political Realism." In *Native Power: The Quest for Autonomy and Nationhood of Indigenous Peoples*. J. Brøsted, J. Dahl, A. Gray, H. Gulløv, G. Hendriksen, J. Jørgensen and I. Kleivan, eds., Bergen: Universitetforlaget AS, Pp. 301–308.

Sahlins, M. 1965. On the Sociology of Primitive Exchange. In *The Relevance of Models for Social Anthropology*. M. Banton, ed., London: Tavistock, Pp. 139–236.

Schwartz, W. and C. Derber. 1986. Arms Control: Misplaced Focus. *Bulletin of the Atomic Scientists* 42:39–44.

Simon, H. 1983. *Reason in Human Affairs*. Stanford: Stanford University Press.

Thompson, S.L. and S.H. Schneider. 1986. Nuclear Winter Reappraised. *Foreign Affairs* 64:981–1005.

Torry, W.I. 1979. Anthropological Studies in Hazardous Environments: Past Trends and New Horizons. *Current Anthropology* 20:517–529.

Treichel, R. 1987. *Nuclear Attack Planning Base—1990*. Washington, DC: Federal Emergency Management Agency.

Turnbull, C. 1967. The Ik: Alias the Teuso. *Uganda Journal* 31:63–71.

———. 1972. *The Mountain People*. New York: Simon and Schuster.

———. 1978. Rethinking the Ik: A Functional Non-Social System. In *Extinction and Survival in Human Populations*. C.D. Laughlin and I. Brady, eds., New York: Columbia University Press, Pp. 49–75.

United States House of Representatives. 1977. *Department of Defense Appropriations for 1978*. Washington, DC: United States Government Printing Office.

2 / Compromise and the Rhetoric of Good and Evil

Mary Catherine Bateson

In the following paper, Mary Catherine Bateson explores one way in which anthropological research can contribute to international security. She argues that our understanding of international events will be confounded if we assume that these events result from the operation of homogeneous cultural processes within nations. Using an analysis of Iranian popular culture, as expressed in films, she shows that cultures contain within them alternative ways of valuing actions. The methods of content analysis and in-depth interviewing yield data which are very different from the aggregated quantitative data used in "political realist" models of international affairs. Instead, her approach identifies normative themes in Iranian culture which affect international affairs. Iranian popular culture contains two distinct values for approaching situations of choice—a pragmatic style (which emphasizes compromise and calculation) and an ideal style (which stresses absolute integrity and precludes compromise). Bateson describes how these two styles of acting are always present in Iranian culture, and uses the concept of "editing" to explain why one style appears ascendant at a particular time, later to be replaced by the other style. She argues that by taking into account the coexistence of these two styles in Iranian culture members of the United State's foreign policy community would find events in the Islamic Republic far less perplexing. As in the case of nuclear winter, discussed by Rubinstein, taking account of the complexity of cultural processes forces the analyst to reframe the international security question. Thus, as Bateson points out, the goal of policy task shifts from deciding whether Iran is "rational" or "irrational," in some abstract sense, to attempting to understand the implications of shifts in Iranian world view.—The Editors

The attempt to use cultural analysis to improve policy making in the area of international relations has run into repeated frustration, and yet seems intuitively to be promising and valuable.[1] Events occur in the international arena which reflect national decision-making processes and ways of interpreting available data; these become intelligible if they are interpreted in cultural terms. Yet clearly, cultural analysis based on the study of individuals, like historical analysis based on previous foreign policy decisions, is not adequate for prediction, particularly since the stakes in international relations are often too high to make probabilistic forms of prediction useful. We would like our anthropologists to tell us that the people of such and such a nation share a given characteristic and therefore will behave in a given way, expressed in singular and centrally determined policies of immense moment. Unfortunately, culture is not determinative or predictive in any such simple sense. If it were, the world would be a very much duller place.

The problem of prediction may even include the possibility of diametrically opposed styles, a problem anthropologists have become increasingly aware of. My own recent work on the history of cultural anthropology, in the context of a familial memoir (Bateson 1984), has involved a reconsideration of how anthropologists account for the presence of apparently contradictory possibilities within a culture. Margaret Mead, Ruth Benedict, and Gregory Bateson were among the first anthropologists to attempt to use generalizations about culture to anticipate the policies of nation states. A few years earlier, they had been among the first to attempt to extend psychological categories appropriate to the description of individuals to whole societies. We will only be able to mobilize an effective use of anthropology in this area if certain problems in the earlier work are confronted, problems more clearly present in that work as it was popularly understood than in its original statements.

In her writing and teaching in the 1920s, Ruth Benedict developed the powerful but flawed concept of a cultural configuration as "personality writ large." This concept is most fully elaborated in *Patterns of Culture* (1934), but was already expressed in "Psychological Types in the Cultures of the Southwest," (1930), which was read by Mead in 1928 before going to Samoa and reflected in *Coming of Age in Samoa* (1928) and *Social Organization of Manua* (1930). This approach, which sought for psychological homogeneity, was, however, rapidly left behind by further theoretical advances. By 1932, Mead and Bateson were already noting that a culture might be organized around contrasting psychological themes rather than around homogeneity, beginning in their consideration of sex roles in two Sepik River cultures, the Iatmul and the Tshambuli (now Chambri). This insight was reflected in war-time work such as Benedict's on the Japanese, in which she expressed the presence of contradictory cultural themes in the evocative title, *The Chrysanthemum and the Sword* (1946), and other wartime and postwar efforts to apply anthropological modes of analysis to such complex entities as modern nation states. The early work has been extensively criticized, most recently by Freeman (1983) who unfortunately replicates the original error by assuming that an accurate account of Samoan culture will describe psychological homogeneity. Freeman differs from Mead in depicting an equally monochrome Samoa, simply emphasizing his own perception of conflict as pervasive and failing to see that an adequate account of Samoan culture must account both for the harmonious ethos perceived by Mead and for the conflictual ethos emphasized by himself—and for the mechanisms of selection and alternation (described in a more modern mode by Bradd Shore, 1977). A contemporary approach would recognize that cultural systems work with alternatives, many of them discontinuous, often embracing contrasts or complementarities along culturally defined axes.

Thus, theories of psychological homogeneity do not work to account for foreign policy, much less to predict it. The central question remains whether we can express the sense in which policy decisions are framed by cultural rules in a useful way. Even if it is not possible to predict a given outcome or to attach a statistical probability to it, it may be useful to be able to define the set of alternatives from which a selection is being made, and indeed to define the sequence of operations of selection through which a policy is generated.

In this context, the analogy frequently made between language and other cultural forms is useful. Grammar constrains speech, but does not allow the prediction of any single utterance, and indeed the number of possible grammatical utterances that may be generated by a speaker is infinite. Happily, this is a very exclusive infinitude. Linguists look at possible sentences in terms of whether they are "well formed," or "grammatical," acknowledging that many actual utterances are not even well formed, are, for instance, interrupted, or produced by speakers who are drunk or aphasic or deliberately violating grammatical rules—linguists shaping hypothetical examples, for instance. Similarly for actions, an individual at a given moment of time often has a great many alternatives open to him which an observing member of the same culture would find plausible, would regard as "making sense" in relation to a diversity of possible goals, and information available to the actor. Some actions may be so likely as to seem almost determined, others may be much less likely but still culturally plausible, and a few occur which simply do not make sense in cultural terms. An example would be the filing of an an income tax return: there is no doubt a predictable distribution of filing dates, around the first weeks of April, as well as a series of intelligible reasons for failure to file, ranging from ideological protest to incompetence, and once in a while one may run into a case that simply does not "make sense" in terms of available information.

Yet in this case we are not dealing with convention (say the mailing of a mother's day card) but with legislation, an aspect of the cultural system that attempts to be determinative. Cultural rules are not like natural laws; knowledge of the rules will not allow prediction for any single case. Indeed, because some culturally inappropriate instances are always liable to arise, cultural forms of prediction are least likely to be useful where single instances are of high importance. Not surprisingly, cultural analysis seems at first glance to be more useful to advertisers, say, than to secretaries of state.

Cultural forms of prediction are most likely to be useful in relation to behavior that involves large numbers of actors. This is obviously true for multiple actions which allow for statistical prediction, but significantly, it also includes behavior that produces a single outcome but only after undergoing extensive review by many members of a society considering whether it seems to them appropriate, wise, or intelligible—what we might call "editing." Under most circumstances, the actions of governments on matters of international relations and security are very heavily edited.

An example will clarify this: the sentences which I am likely to generate as I sit by my word processor are in general well formed, recognizably English sentences, even when the ideas I put forward have a certain *soupçon* of originality, but I review them before printing them, and they will be further reviewed before they appear in a publication. Any one who has tried to include an odd or informal turn of phrase, for instance, in an op ed piece for the *New York Times* knows that what e.e. cummings could get away with, they cannot. The foreign policy establishment of a nation is a bit like the copy editing office of a newspaper—sentences don't get through that are not seen as plausible, that do not make sense, except under very special circumstances, for instance, an insane despot, an incompetent or quixotic chief of state, or a private action that gets converted into policy.

A heavily bureaucratic nation, or one in which decision-making is clearly collective, is much easier to deal with than one in which decisions reflect individual creativity. Similarly, movies are much more useful for cultural analysis than novels: a movie is a collective project, involving a great many different minds who reshape the materials given to them so that they make sense, and furthermore it is a commercial product, it must have plausibility at the box office, even if that plausibility is based on its shocking character—it cannot seem simply arbitrary or irrelevant. A Khrushchev or a Sadat may make decisions that disconcert and scandalize their bureaucracies—clearly, if members of their societies are surprised, we cannot assume that their actions were predictable in any simple sense. Truman, recognizing the new state of Israel, is said to have surprised and scandalized the State Department, but the decision worked at the box office. A novel may reflect an idiosyncratic vision, may fail or be ignored for many years and then recognized as great art. No system of anthropological analysis would have predicted *Finnegan's Wake,* and such a work can only be used evidentially with the greatest of care—but formula books, such as Gothic novels, are far more immediately useful to the anthropologist—you have only to see them displayed in a supermarket to know that they fit with some existing concern in the society.

Actions taken by governments, then, are in general heavily edited. Not only are they formulated by one or more individuals, they usually have to pass through a filter of plausibility for a considerable number of others involved in decision-making, implementation, or other kinds of concurrence, a filter which in no way precludes disagreement with the wisdom of a given policy, just as the copy editing at the *New York Times* does not signify agreement with content. Just as the *New York Times* is hospitable to contradictory opinions, the culturally plausible foreign policy decisions of a nation-state may contrast sharply.

The purpose of this paper is to examine a situation in which the foreign policy community was taken by surprise by events in a nation-state of some significance to the United States, namely Iran, and in which assumptions about Iranian political styles proved inaccurate. I will examine these events in relation to a research project conducted in Tehran in the years 1973–1976 which suggested that Iranians pose alternatives in terms of two sharply contrasting cultural styles. On the one hand a style that emphasized opportunistic maneuvering under circumstances of moral ambiguity and allowed for practicality, dissimulation, and negotiation, and on the other hand an absolute style, dealing with binary opposites, in which good and evil are contrasted and compromise devalued. We found both styles present in the popular culture and in the accounts given by individuals of the way in which alternatives present themselves in personal life, although they are as dissonant as the harmonious and violent pictures of Samoa presented by Mead and Freeman.

Iranian public policy and public rhetoric, both domestically and internationally, went through an apparent radical change at the time of the revolution into a style that appeared totally different and therefore unpredictable, but we would argue that the two styles—and more significantly the tendency to think of them as alternatives facing individuals and societies—were and still are both implicit in Iranian culture. The change was more like shifting gears in a car, in which the system has built into it multiple modes of operation, than like the replacement of something old by something new; the post-revolutionary style was always implicit. Thus, a second purpose of this paper is to demonstrate the way in which a given technique for studying popular culture is able to define a given *axis* on which alternatives may be formulated, although it cannot predict which pole will be chosen or when. A given initial decision will generally involve subsequent sequences of choices. The particular shift that occurred in Iran, from a rhetoric of opportunism accessible to compromise to a binary rhetoric of good and evil, is of immense importance because of the way it structures subsequent decisions and alternatives. Then, too, partial analogues can be found in other contexts, including United States policy, which goes through cycles of being more or less pragmatic or moralistic in its rhetoric.

Our original work (Bateson et al. 1977), which included interviewing and the analysis of popular stories and films, was done by a group consisting of Iranians and Americans trained in a variety of social science disciplines, including J.W. Clinton, J.B.M. Kassarjian, H. Safavi, and M. Soraya (and several others for shorter periods), as well as myself. I must take responsibility for the 1985 formulation in this paper. The research should be regarded as preliminary, oriented toward the identification of themes and the development of hypotheses, since historical events have precluded the kind of follow-up that would have been desirable.

This work was done prior to the Iranian revolution, and was not primarily oriented towards public issues. We were concerned to clarify the values that motivate individual Iranians in their private lives and inform their judgments and evaluations of others, whether or not these were reflected on the larger political scene. In the event, we found that we got a set of composite images, each of which evoked a certain ambivalence. On the one hand, there was the image, often devalued, of someone who is opportunistic and calculating, but disapproval was mixed in this image with appreciation of cleverness, and it was suggested that only such a person could be successful. On the other hand, we found several variant forms of an ideal character type whose absolute integrity precludes maneuvering and compromise, summed up in the title of one of our papers, *safa-yi batin* (inner purity). Attitudes toward such a person were ambivalent, since he was seen as unlikely to be successful, and yet informants expressed the sense that at some deep level they longed for and were capable of that kind of integrity, conformed to it in certain relationships, and were nostalgic for a society in which it would be the norm. Thus, we collected many statements of conflict even within private life—narratives of individuals torn between two sets of values—and repeated statements that public values were in contradiction to the more idealized vision that was seen as viable only in a private context. Interestingly enough, whether or not our informants were prepared to say that they repudiated the values represented by the Shah's government *per se* (not a risk we encouraged them to take), we observed a wide-spread agreement that it is of the nature of social life to distort virtue. We were struck by the fact that the basic contrast depicted was not between good and bad but between two ways of approaching situations of choice.

Two different readings of these results are possible. One reading suggests that the true Iranian self-image is that of integrity and the situation of living under a corrupt despotism left many feeling they could not be true to themselves, a temporary distortion during the Pahlavi dynasty. This reading would predict the revolution rather nicely but dismisses the pre-revolutionary situation as an aberration, as un-representative. Pro-revolutionary Iranians would of course concur. It is satisfying to find that a study of popular culture identifies the value themes that would predict a social upheaval, but I would argue that the governmental structures and policies during the monarchy involved large numbers of individuals who had considerable scope for what I have called editing, so that an adequate account of Iranian national culture must account for both the Pahlavi dynasty and the Islamic Republic as representative variants—an example of the need to account for sharp contrast within a tradition. This is not a view that would be popular with any group of Iranians on first hearing it, and yet it allows the pointing out of a number of other continuities. In effect, it requires that partisans recognize that both they and their adversaries are acting within a culturally defined range of possibilities, a potential contrast built into the tradition. This alternative reading, then, is one that recognizes ambivalence as built into the culture, sometimes visible in a public-private contrast, but always present as a dual potentiality. The question to ask in attempting to forecast policy is when and how the pragmatic emphasis will be ascendant and when and how the idealized emphasis will be ascendant, and how these two stylistic preferences will be interwoven in the relationship between rhetoric and implementation.

An example may clarify this. In our work on Iranian popular culture, we observed a number of films in which there is a turning point of decision, when the protagonist rejects a dishonorable course, often one which he has followed in the past or which members of the audience say most people would choose, and takes an honorable course that will be costly to him, perhaps costing him his life. We wrote then,

> Overriding commitment, pushing an individual out of the sphere of calculation, beyond the need to balance one course of action against another, so that what he does is a complete and direct expression of who he is, is profoundly admired. Such an individual cannot be moved by threats or co-opted or bribed, all of which are strongly supported in most people most of the time by the habit of living in ambiguity (Bateson et al. 1977:271).

Against this background, the admiration for Ayatollah Khomeini's intransigence and unwillingness to negotiate or compromise four years later becomes intelligible. More complex is the process whereby individuals who had always felt a certain admiration and nostalgia for the stance of unambivalent commitment—combined with a degree of pity for the failure or martydom it may imply—shifted gears at a personal level and became identified with the revolution, accepting the risks involved.

Calculation involves recognizing and weighing a multiplicity of alternative courses, each having advantages and disadvantages. Once a decision has been made to conceive of a situation in terms of a binary choice, to focus on only two alternatives, valuing one and devaluing the other, the stakes are set so high that the outcome is predetermined. One thinks of High Noon: "Oh to be torn twixt love and duty . . . " or of the old Presbyterian hymn, "Once to every man and nation, comes the moment to decide, in the strife of truth and falsehood, for the good or evil side." There are still many members of this society who would limit alternatives to "Live free or die." The choice of the "good" is already committed once the alternatives have been formulated in this way, and the maintenance and consideration of multiple alternatives depends on avoiding the rhetoric of binary choice.

It is not, however, sufficient to say that under certain circumstances Iranians (or Americans) formulate decisions in heavily value laden binary terms, unless one can define when this framework comes into play and how the binary axis is defined. Even binary decisions may contrast on different axes. Some of the most familiar are right versus wrong, fair versus unfair, good versus evil, honorable versus dishonorable. The rhetoric used by representatives of the Iranian government during the hostage crisis, and since, implies that Iran, in the form of the Islamic Republic, is pitted against evil, the Great Satan. The rhetoric of the United States during that same period asserted that Iran, in tolerating and endorsing the hostage taking, was acting wrongly—against the rules of the game. Where they spoke of good versus evil, we spoke, with equal certitude, of right versus wrong—there is more than one variety of self righteousness.

The posing of binary alternatives is such a radical simplification that it would seem extremely important to know when it comes into play. Will the actor conceptualize a given situation as presenting many alternatives, with a decision to be made pragmatically, or will he conceptualize it as binary? Indeed, as noted above, the binary phrasing may predetermine the subsequent decision: once you label a decision point as offering good or evil, honor or dishonor, have you not committed yourself to choose the good, to seek honor?

To sum up, a study of cultural patterns of decision-making must visualize multiple stages of culturally formulated decision before the formulation of action, in some cases starting from sharply contrasting and discontinuous alternatives that exemplify dissonant themes coexisting in the culture. However, even though multiple decisions follow the basic decision to define a given situation as appropriate for subsequent opportunistic decisions or as appropriate for binary decision—posing an absolute choice—these subsequent decisions are inevitably constrained by the initially established premise: either there is a *RIGHT* (good, true) answer, or there is a *BEST* (most advantageous, most appropriate) answer. The community operating on a rhetoric that asserts that its policies are right, rejecting evil, may be able to mobilize very strong feeling, but it will have limited flexibility and be subject to the dangers that Iranians see for individuals with integrity, the danger of martyrdom. (Incidentally, the actual dangers may be even greater for societies in which many people believe that rightness leads to success, as they sometimes do in our own, in which the hero may triumph precisely because his heart is pure—unless they believe, as we on the whole do, that he is simultaneously clever. Perhaps only heroes who are both clever and virtuous are likely to prosper.)

Thus, it seems clear that although alternative modes of posing issues for decision exist for both the United States and the Islamic Republic (and may create apparent inconsistencies and unpredictabilities in both cultures), the contexts in which they are evoked differ. However, the tendency to formulate alternatives in absolute terms must represent a dangerous loss of flexibility wherever it arises. Whether the rhetoric concerns the United States as the "Great Satan" or the Soviet Union as the "evil empire," it sets up a context that may tend to preclude effective negotiation and needed compromise.

One of the advantages of recognizing that the tendency to define a decision-making context as opportunistic or binary is part of Iranian culture is that we should recognize that the opportunistic mode is present within the Islamic Republic instead of failing to see it as many observers failed to see the idealism present within the Shah's Iran. Just as there was a reservoir of self-sacrificing idealism present in the Shah's Iran, so there is a reservoir of cynicism in the Ayatollah's Iran. Iranians expect, on the whole, to find that power corrupts and that wealth or success are associated with moral ambiguity—this expectation is referred to as *badbini*—and it is one of the ever-present problems for the state. In order to survive, there must be a certain capacity to compromise, and yet Khomeini's intractable integrity must precisely not be compromised, and so the government is both trapped in the war with Iraq and dependent on it to establish its adamant conviction.

In summary, decision-making in Iran, both public and private, is characterized by the prior adoption of a mode that constrains subsequent decisions, a mode that is either opportunistic or binary/moralistic. Each mode is characterized by a degree of ambivalence. Individuals may shift from one mode to the other, often having been quite clear about the two kinds of alternatives. The state too may shift from one mode to the other, as it ostensibly did at the time of the revolution, and yet both modes continue to be implicitly present. An informed foreign policy would note the opportunistic willingness of the Khomeini government to exclude certain issues from its moralistic fervor, and thus to deal with the Israelis when convenient. Similarly, we should cultivate in our own polity the appreciation of compromise and pragmatism as premises that must be adopted well before a given policy is up for debate. As anthropologists, we may contribute most to thinking about such matters as international relations by analyzing styles of decision-making rather than styles of outcome, attempting to characterize the tensions within a procedure rather than seeking homogeneity.

Notes

1. This paper was originally presented at the Symposium, "Power, Change, and Security Decisions: Anthropological Perspectives," at American Association for the Advancement of Science, Annual meeting, Los Angeles, California, 31 May 1985.

References Cited

Bateson, G. 1936. *Naven: A Survey of the Problems Suggested by a Composite Picture of the Culture of a New Guinea Tribe Drawn from Three Points of View.* Cambridge, England: Cambridge University Press.
Bateson, M.C. 1984. *With a Daughter's Eye: A Memoir of Margaret Mead and Gregory Bateson.* New York: Morrow.

_____, J.W. Clinton, J.B.M. Kassarjian, H. Safavi, and M. Soraya. 1977. Safa-yi Batin: A Study of a Set of Iranian Ideal Character Types. In *Psychological Dimensions of Near Eastern Studies.* L.C. Brown and N. Itzkowitz, eds., Princeton: Darwin Press, Pp. 257–73.

Benedict, R. 1930. Psychological Types in the Cultures of the Southwest, *Proceedings of the 23rd Congress of Americanists.* Pp. 572–81.

_____. 1934. *Patterns of Culture.* Boston: Houghton Mifflin.

_____. 1946. *The Chrysanthemum and the Sword: Patterns of Japanese Culture.* Boston: Houghton Mifflin.

Chomsky, N. 1957. *Syntactic Structures.* The Hague: Mouton.

Freeman, D. 1983. *Margaret Mead and Samoa: The Making and Unmaking of an Anthropological Myth.* Cambridge: Harvard University Press.

Mead, M. 1928. *Coming of Age in Samoa: A Psychological Study of Primitive Youth for Western Civilization.* New York: Morrow.

_____. 1930. *Social Organization of Manua.* Honolulu: Bernice P. Bishop Museum Bulletin 76.

_____. 1935. *Sex and Temperament in Three Primitive Societies.* New York: Morrow.

_____, and Rhoda Metraux, editors. 1953. *The Study of Culture at a Distance.* Chicago: University of Chicago Press.

Shore, B. 1982. *Sala'ilua: A Samoan Mystery.* New York: Columbia University Press.

3 / Inducement to Military Participation in Tribal Societies

Walter Goldschmidt

War does not result from homogeneous cultural processes. Why then do men fight? Walter Goldschmidt explores this question by using data from preliterate societies to show that human aggressiveness does not necessarily lead to warfare. Instead, in societies that reward soldier-heroes the social pressures for aggression are powerful enough to overcome personal reluctance to fight. As Bateson's paper showed that careful analysis of values and symbols in a single society can reveal the basis for socio-political change, in this article, Goldschmidt shows that the institutionalization and internalization of cultural premises, rather than innate aggression, make war an acceptable social option. In other terms than Bateson's, Goldschmidt again shows that peace and conflict result from the differential management of competing normative themes in cultures. His paper therefore continues the argument for including in international security analysis detailed information about particular cultural institutions and the symbols that support them.—The Editors

Why do men fight?[1] Why do men leave the comfort and security of ordinary life to engage in an activity that has been described as long stretches of tedium interspersed with moments of terror? This is a different question from "Why warfare?"—an issue many anthropol-

This chapter was previously published in a slightly different form and is reprinted by permission of Bergin & Garvey Publishers, Inc., from Paul R. Turner and David Pitt, eds., *Cold War and Nuclear Madness: An Anthropological Analysis* (South Hadley, Mass.: Bergin & Garvey, 1988).

ogists have addressed with indifferent success. Here we are asking: why individuals willingly undertake such unpleasant, life-threatening activity. This issue is important and the ethnographic literature has something to say to us about it.

My procedure has been to examine the literature on a sample of 27 tribal communities and preliterate systems drawn to represent the universe of all such communities in which military activity is salient (see Appendix). I will only give frequencies of reported behavior and not any correlational analysis, for the ethnography of warfare leaves much to be desired and, while one can generally accept at face value specific described forms, one can never be certain that the blanks in the literature represent the absence of such traits or merely the failure of ethnographers or their informants to mention the matter.

Diversity of War in Tribal Societies

The literature shows that the character of military operations varies widely among tribal societies. In those societies where there is something approaching a nation-state warfare is a matter of national policy serving expansionist ambitions, territorial protection, and possibly also the preservation of internal structure (Baganda, Fon, Kazak, Wolof, and probably Shilluk and Creek). In three of the societies, military operations, though important, were designed primarily for defense (Hopi, Papago, and Thonga). Among the Mapuche, Chuckchee, Ainu, and probably others, defensive operations were mainly against the encroachment of so-called civilized societies. Patterns of raiding and counter-raiding appear to have been characteristic of the remaining societies examined. Land was clearly at issue in some (Ainu, Haida, Maori, and Mae Enga), loot or booty (often livestock) more frequently (Abipone, Apache, Cheyenne, Chuckchee, Klamath, Mapuche, Pawnee, Rwala, and Nyakyusa).

A few societies are found that are more like the popular stereotype where raiding and counter-raiding seem to be ends in themselves, where taking trophies and acquiring honor is the sole apparent purpose. These attitudes dominated the behavior of the Igorot, the Jivaro, and the Mundurucu, and to a lesser extent the Andamanese and Aranda, among whom warfare is less important. Even in these instances, economic consequences are potentially present. For instance, in the detailed description of military activities among the Tsembaga (Rappaport 1967), who are not in our sample but who share this pattern, territorial transfers do result from wars, and there is some evidence that the military action of the Jivaro has territorial consequences.

One of the most consistent elements in the ethnography of warfare that I found was the perception that the purpose of warfare was vengeance or retaliation. Aside from the three state-organized peoples (Baganda, Fon and Wolof), only the Ainu, Mundurucu and Pawnee were not described as having such motivation. Two defense-oriented people, Hopi and Papago, expressed this as retaliation, the others as vengeance for murder, wife stealing or the taking of property.

While I am not analyzing these data to determine the cause of warfare, they do make it clear that the popular anthropological notion that primitive war is merely a "game" and without economic consequences is wrong. Land or territorial considerations were frequently found to be salient elements (Ainu, Andamanese, Baganda, Haida, Kazak, Maori, Mae Enga, Mapuche, Rwala, Shilluk, and Wolof), acquisition of goods of some kind in 19 instances, and in only three instances was such booty specifically denied (Igorot, Papago, Hopi). Tribal warfare is usually serious economic business.

Fear and Counterfear

Lest you think my perception of war is culture-bound, I will first show that men in tribal societies themselves often, public statements to the contrary notwithstanding, display fear of their own military pursuits. Consider the Yanomamo, who have come to represent the quintessential nature of tribal warfare in the modern literature, having been given the sobriquet "the fierce people." They boast and posture on the eve of their departure to avenge a death; they brag:

> I'm so fierce that when I shoot the enemy my arrow will strike with such force that blood will splash all over the material possessions in the household (Chagnon 1977:129)!

But let us watch what actually happens. For instance, the leader of one expedition, though ill and in great pain, insisted on going, "*suspecting others would turn back* if he did not lead it" (Chagnon 1977:130, emphasis added). He was right:

> The raiders had not been gone five hours when the first one came back, a boastful young man, complaining that he had a sore foot and could not keep up with the others. The next day a few more men returned, complaining that they had malaria and pains in the stomach. They enjoyed participating in the pomp of the *Wayu Itou* [the preparatory war ritual], for this impressed the women, but they were, at heart, cowards. . . . On the last evening [before the actual attack, while sleeping

in the bush], the raiding party's fierce ones have difficulties with the younger men; most of them are afraid, cold, and worried about every sort of hazard, and all of them complain of sore feet and belly aches (1977:130).

Later, when Chagnon took a group of warriors part way to their battle area in his power boat, he noted that the leader

. . . was not enthusiastic about going on the raid, despite the fact that he lectured the younger members of the raiding party about their overt reluctance and cowardice. He was older, however, and had to display the ferocity that adult men are supposed to show. In short, although Hukoshikuwa probably had very little desire as an individual to participate in the raiding, he was obliged to do so by the pressures of the entire system (1977:35–6).

So much for ferocity!

Similar attitudes are found among the Abipone, described by Dobrizhoffer a century and a half ago. Though he emphasizes their military exploits and ferocity, he also says:

Should a report be spread . . . that the enemy are coming in a few days, it is enough. Numbers, dreading the loss of life more than fame, will desert their Cacique, and hasten with their families to some well-known retreats. Lest, however, they should be branded with the name of deserters and cowards, they say they are going out to hunt (Dobrizhoffer 1822:105).

And elsewhere, he notes that they do not "hazard an attack unless confident of victory" (1822:363).

The Creek of the southern United States, who share these public values of military prowess, have institutionalized their reluctance, for

if their dreams portend any ill, they always obey the supposed divine intimation and return home, without incurring the least censure. They reckon that their willingness to serve their country should not be subservient to their own knowledge or wishes, but always regulated by the divine impulse. I have known a whole company who set out for war, to return in small parties, and sometimes by single persons, and be applauded by the united voice of the people; because they acted in obedience to their *Nana Ishtohoollo,* or 'guardian angels,' who impressed them in their visions of night, with the friendly caution (James Adair, quoted in Swanton 1909:408–9).

The description of warfare among the Mae Enga is the most detailed, intimate and unromanticized in the ethnographic literature (Meggitt 1977). They too tend to express self confidence, but are quite aware of fear. A youth who is afraid in combat might be excused and encouraged by his elders to raise his spirits and confidence, or will be reminded that, in any case, his death is foreordained by the sun and thus inescapable. Such a youth may also be shamed. But an older man who tries to evade his military duties—among the Mae Enga warfare is over land—will be ridiculed and told to remain among the women, who are viewed as polluting. To escape calumny, such a man will depart with his family for a period of time, but even so will suffer loss of reputation and political influence.

Ritual Catharsis

There are, the saying goes, no atheists in foxholes. The Creek use of religious belief in the support of fear, as just noted, is reflected elsewhere in the religious practices associated with war. Consider the war dance, the rituals that are designed to psych the men up for their endeavor (see Table 1), which were reported in 18 of our 27 instances. In four of these, some kind of drugs (alcohol, tobacco, or "medicines") were an important element in their rituals. Such rituals were not reported for the Fon, Kazak, and Wolof—tribes in which military pursuit is more-or-less in the hands of a professional soldiery.

The Apache, for instance, have religious dances for four nights preceding a raiding party. It is a dramatization of the war itself; they dance through the night with "fierce dancing," as they call it. The men are dressed as for war and appear at the ceremony to show their intention. Men who do not appear are called by name in the songs "You, So-and-so, many times you have talked bravely. Now brave people . . . are calling you." If a man doesn't come out and make good his boasts, he is not considered a man. "The dance is a profound religious experience for the man who takes part in it," according to Opler (1941:336–7), but it is religion in the service of emotional reinforcement.

In addition to such efforts to get psyched up for battle, there are other practices that help to allay fear. In eight instances a shaman, priest, or medicine man is actively involved in the preparation for warfare, often responsible for magically determining or predicting the outcome of the conflict, and sometimes accompanying the warriors. In twelve instances amulets, fetishes, or other special devices are carried by the soldiers as magical protection and support. Clearly, tribal soldiers enter into combat with apprehension and concern; tribal warriors are both serious and fearful.

Table 1. Ritual Reinforcements for War

Preparatory rites	18	Abipone, Andamanese, Apache, Aranda, Baganda,[1] Cheyenne, Creek, Haida, Hopi, Igorot, Jivaro, Klamath, Maori, Mapuche, Papago, Pawnee, Shilluk, Thonga
Use of drugs	4	Abipone (alcohol), Creek ("black medicine"), Jivaro (beer, tobacco), Thonga ("war medicine")
Shaman's services[2]	8	Abipone, Apache, Creek, Haida, Klamath, Mundurucu, Papago, Wolof
Amulets or Talismans[3]	12	Apache, Aranda, Baganda, Cheyenne, Chuckchee, Creek, Hopi, Jivaro, Klamath, Maori, Pawnee, Thonga

1. Baganda ritual consists of an oath of allegiance and therefore may serve more to assure the Kabaka that the men will not defect.

2. Sometimes shamans accompany the battle, at others predict the outcome. Among the Wolof, it is the Griote who serves, and this may be a social rather than a magico-religious reinforcement.

3. Occasionally special dress "to give the men courage."

Warfare as Masculine Career: Preparation

Men's careers in these societies involved them in military pursuits and in most of them social standing—acceptance, prestige, material goods and influence—depended largely upon their performance as warriors. Military performance was something that was taken for granted, much as in our society men expect to work to earn a living. Even where warfare was generally viewed as "necessary evil," as among the Papago (Underhill 1946:165) and Hopi, with their self-image as peaceable, this attitude appears to have prevailed. Only among political societies where the military operations are in the hands of professionalized soldiers was this not the case, though even there military accomplishments were a source of status to the soldier group.

Table 2. Elements in Training of Warriors

Training in skills	6	Abipone, Apache, Chuckchee, Maori, Mae Enga, Papago
Apprenticeship	7	Apache, Cheyenne, Creek, Fon, Mae Enga, Nyakyusa, Pawnee
Games and contests	7	Ainu, Cheyenne, Chuckchee, Hopi, Mae Enga, Mapuche, Rwala
Pain endurance tests	12	Apache, Abipone, Andamanese, Aranda, Cheyenne, Fon, Hopi, Mapuche, Pawnee, Rwala, Thonga, Wolof
Other endurance tests	9	Apache, Chuckchee, Fon, Haida, Klamath, Maori, Pawnee, Rwala, Thonga
Legends and stories	7	Ainu, Apache, Cheyenne, Chuckchee, Maori, Pawnee, Wolof

Only a few ethnographers describe in detail the training of soldiers, but many give certain specifics. In our sample, six mentioned training in skills, seven apprenticeship in warfare, and seven games and contests designed to establish military qualities (Table 2). Youths were made to endure pain in 11 societies and endurance of other hardships in seven.[2] Legends and stories designed to reinforce militaristic attitudes were mentioned in seven instances. Most societies consciously inculcate military virtues in some ways, and I am confident that if our data were more complete, they would all do so in many ways.

Where ethnographers have investigated the matter directly, we find elaborate schooling for the warriors. Among the Apache the emphasis on being brave and tough is strong and pervasive, though to be brave meant not to be afraid, but yet to be cautious. "The man who blindly ran into trouble without fear was a fool, not a brave man" (Baldwin 1965:97). According to Opler (1941:65), "the child and adult often listen together to accounts of the rigors of the hunt, of the hardships and glories of war, and of the cruelties of the enemy. 'As soon as I was old enough to know,' said one informant, 'I was told who were our enemies'." The elaborate training of Apache youths included practical education to make them strong and increase their endurance and skills and religious rites to ensure their safety. Older people tell the youth that the enemy is as frightened as he is and that "if he puts on a brave front and charges, the enemy may run" (Opler 1941:72). Boys are warned that girls will not marry a cowardly or lazy person. Youths are particularly trained in endurance and in running. One test involves running a course with a mouth full of water which may not be swallowed (if the boy swallows the water on the way, the trainer sees that he doesn't do it a second time). They match youths of the same age and have them engage in running contests and fighting. They were even expected to take on known superior fighters. They also engage in mock fights with slings to learn both attack and defense. Later they fight in teams with bows and arrows, and though the arrows are small, they can inflict severe damage. Later still, they are trained in handling horses, and in long cross-country journeys without food or sleep.

> The boys who achieve a position of superiority during this training period rise to pre-eminence in their age group . . . the foundations of status recognition are laid in the training period . . . (Opler 1974:74).

When a boy wants to volunteer, his relatives tell him of the hardships and dangers, and only if he feels prepared is he allowed to go. He remains a novice during his first four military expeditions, and during this time he is thought to be particularly vulnerable—comparable to a girl during her puberty ritual—and receives special instruction from a relative or a shaman. Only after this lengthy training is an Apache recognized as a warrior and as a full member of the tribe.

Jivaro indoctrination starts early. According to Stirling, when a boy is about the age of six, he is instructed each morning on the necessity of being a warrior and incited to avenge the feuds in which his family is involved. Such admonishment "is repeated every morning regularly for more than five years, until the parent sees that the son has been thoroughly inoculated with the warlike spirit and the idea of blood revenge" (Stirling 1928:51). From the age of seven, boys are regularly taken on war expeditions with their fathers and, though they do not actually engage in combat, they get accustomed to the methods of warfare, and learn to defend themselves and not to be afraid. At the age of 15 or 16 the Jivaro youth undergoes an initiation during which he must observe numerous taboos and in which he is given a narcotic drink and tobacco to smoke in order to transfer the power of the tobacco to him. "This power will automatically show itself in all the work and occupations incumbent on him as a male member of society.

He will be a brave and successful warrior and be able to kill many enemies. . . . " (Karsten 1935:242).

Among the Mae Enga (Meggitt 1977:61–4), the training is less formalized and intrusive but equally pervasive. At the age of eight, boys move into their fathers' homes and spend much time in the company of men—avoiding women, who are viewed as polluting and enervating. Boys are expected to do useful work, but fathers watch with approval any evidence of a son's aggressiveness in childhood scuffles. Boys also play at warfare over imaginary houses and gardens and go on to "negotiate settlements." Later they receive specific and detailed instructions in the handling of weapons and tactics, and get practice in the handling of scaled-down weapons that have been made for them. Soon thereafter a boy will get his first sentry duty, and will be beaten if he is reluctant. No fuss is made over early wounds so that the youth will learn "what pain is all about." When a boy is about fifteen he joins the bachelors' association and receives a full complement of weapons. After another two or three years he participates in the warfare, but not on the front line of fight. He is urged to participate in the battles of neighboring friendly groups so that he can become enured to the dangers of battle.

Such descriptions make it clear that it takes a major effort to make aggressive warriors out of tribal children. When Carol and Melvin Ember examined the social and psychological correlates to warfare in tribal societies, the only significant relationship with intensity of warfare they found was the socialization and training of boys for aggressiveness (Ember and Ember 1984:6). They rightly note that this indoctrination is probably a consequence rather than a cause of war, for they also found a strong tendency for such aggression-training to disappear among peoples who have been "pacified" by colonial powers.

Warfare and the Masculine Career: Rewards

In virtually every society examined, the successful warrior is rewarded with booty, slaves, women (either as concubines or wives) or the opportunity to adopt captives (see Table 3). In only four (Andamanese, Igorot, Jivaro, and Mae Enga) of the 27 societies examined was no material reward for the soldier mentioned, though in four (Aranda, Creek, Hopi, and Mundurucu) these rewards are slight or rare.

But it is the non-material rewards that really induce men to fight. In almost every society examined, the returned warrior receives accolades of some kind—honor or prestige (5 cases), special titles or membership in special societies (10 cases), political influence or positions of leadership (18 cases). Only for three societies (Ainu, An-

Table 3. Rewards to Warriors

Booty	14	Abipone, Apache, Baganda, Cheyenne, Chuckchee, Fon, Klamath, Maori, Nyakyusa, Pawnee, Rwala, Shilluk, Thonga, Wolof (probably also Creek, Haida and Hopi)
Slaves	11	Abipone, Ainu, Apache, Chuckchee, Fon, Haida, Kazak, Klamath, Maori, Mapuche, Shilluk (the adoption of captives also among Mundurucu and Pawnee)
Women[1]	9	Ainu, Aranda, Baganda, Creek, Maori, Rwala, Shilluk, Thonga, Wolof
Trophies[2]	13	Abipone, Apache, Cheyenne, Creek, Haida, Hopi, Jivaro, Klamath, Mapuche, Mundurucu, Papago, Pawnee, Thonga
Honors or prestige	15	Abipone, Andamanese, Apache, Baganda, Cheyenne, Creek, Hopi, Igorot, Jivaro, Maori, Mundurucu, Pawnee, Rwala, Shilluk, Tonga
Titles or membership	10	Abipone, Baganda, Chuckchee, Creek, Hopi, Maori, Mundurucu, Pawnee, Thonga, Wolof
Political influence or leadership	18	Abipone, Apache, Cheyenne, Chuckhee, Creek, Fon, Hopi, Kazak, Klamath, Jivaro, Mae Enga, Mapuche, Mundurucu, Papago, Pawnee, Rwala, Wolof

1. As wives or concubines.

2. Usually heads or scalps.

damanese, and Haida) is there no mention of any such rewards, but for the Haida the ethnographic data suggest that the house-group, rather than the individual, is rewarded. The same ambiguity applies to the Igorot, for the successful head-hunter gets a special tattoo—but so does his whole group. In three of the societies listed, death in battle was recognized as a special virtue and presumably involved some post-mortem status for the slain. Giving special status to the warrior is also the most effective means of socializing the new generation into military activity. Young boys see the rewards, the prestige, the strutting, and have for themselves role models which they naturally emulate.

Warfare and Women

The role of women in the conduct of war in tribal societies varies widely. Battalions of Amazons existed among the Fon, who had a professional military group; indeed, women constituted approximately a third of the army of the king. They engaged in warfare quite like the men, emulating and even exceeding their masculine counterparts. Some Klamath women

> are said to fight like the men, shouting and jumping about to add to the the terrifying effect of the surprise. Armed with short spears they help to catch the women and children and to slay the aged as they run to hide (Spier 1930:31).

Women also engaged in fighting among the Ainu. Ainu battle was hand-to-hand combat between individuals, and the women fought the women. Mundurucu women accompanied the military expeditions but did not engage in combat, only serving the soldiers from a safe distance. Elsewhere, women goaded men to battle (Rwala women bared their breasts and urged their men to war), while among the Andamanese, women tried to settle quarrels and bring fighting to a conclusion. Repeatedly, women were expected to engage in ceremonial activities or to maintain extreme decorum while their men were away fighting; among the Jivaro they danced each night, among the Haida they stayed home and acted out the war, while the wives of Baganda soldiers were expected to remain chaste during their husbands' absence. Women, too, can be socialized to the demands of war.

Conclusion

War is a cultural phenomenon. As with all matters cultural, the society shapes natural human capacities and potentialities to its accepted purposes, reinforcing some and suppressing others. It does this by systematically rewarding and punishing, by indoctrinating youth, creating role-models to be emulated, and honoring those who perform well with special influence. In short, it guides behavior and sentiment to the kinds of performance that define the human career.

Even among those societies where warfare is important, war is dealt with variantly. More accurately, there are both surprising consistencies and remarkable variations in how war is perceived. Among the continuities are the centrality of ideas of vengeance and retaliation, the willingness to exploit strangers, and the need for religious reinforcement to accomplish the essentially secular ends. Furthermore, beyond the mundane rewards of loot and women, there is the consistent ennobling of the warrior himself—even among societies such as the Papago and Hopi, who view war as a necessary evil.

Yet for all these consistencies, one cannot read about warfare in diverse societies without realizing that military operations are differently perceived. There are some, like the Apache and Abipone, for whom it is a major source of economic well-being through preying on neighbors; others, like the Plains Indians, East African cattle herders and the Mae Enga, who are caught in patterns of raiding for goods or land; still others like the Jivaro and Mundurucu, where fighting seems to be an end in itself, an elaborate and deadly game. In some societies, not all men undergo a military career. Maori and Apache men may honorably opt out, whereas elsewhere there is no escape without opprobrium. In state-organized societies, most ordinary citizens must be conscripted. There are some societies in which, in contrast, women can join.

I saw this variance at first hand among the Sebei (Goldschmidt 1976). On the plains, where the cattle had to be protected from marauding neighbors, militarism was honored, but on the mountain, the farming Sebei viewed fighting as foolish and looked down on the plainsmen for even living in a war-infested area.

To say that war is a cultural phenomenon may seem to my fellow anthropologists the belaboring of the obvious. Yet there are those who argue that mankind, particularly *man*kind, fights wars because he is naturally aggressive. What these data clearly show is that this aggressive potentiality—which manifestly is present—must be carefully nurtured and shaped. This is accomplished by making military action central to the pursuit of the careers of individual citizens. That, in my opinion, is what culture is all about.

Indeed, this examination of tribal behavior suggests that human aggressiveness is *not* the salient personality element leading to warfare. It is, rather, something else, something more difficult to define. It is pride, self-concern, the desire for recognition and influence in the community and the counterpart of these, the sense that the action of others is threatening to these aims. I call this the concern with the "symbolic self." The symbolic self is defined—as are all symbols—by the community. It is in the service of this symbolic self that men engage in the actions that the society considers essential or for which it gives rewards in material satisfaction and public influence. It is in the service of this symbolic self in militaristic societies that men seek the bloody trophies of war.

That is why men fight.

Appendix: Societies Selected for Examination

Societies selected for detailed examination were, with a few exceptions, drawn from the Standard Ethnographic Sample (Murdock and White 1969), so as to assure world-wide distribution, but chosen for high scores on militaristic involvement as established by Ross (1983) and eliminating modern nations or communities that are contained within such nations, since war is not a local matter under these conditions.

Table A1. Societies Examined

PEOPLE	LOCATION	BASIC ECONOMY	SOURCES
Abipone	Chaco, Paraguay	mounted foragers	Dobrizhoffer 1822
Ainu	Sakhalin & Hokaido, Japan	foragers, fishing	Batchelor 1927 Watanabe 1973 Murdock 1934
Andamanese	Andaman Islands	foragers	Postman 1899 Radcliffe-Brown 1933
Apache (Chiricahua)	SE Arizona	foragers	Opler 1937, 1941 Baldwin 1965
Aranda	Central Australia	foragers	Spencer & Gillen 1927
Baganda	Uganda	horticulture	Roscoe 1965 (1911)

PEOPLE	LOCATION	BASIC ECONOMY	SOURCES
Cheyenne	Northern Plains of USA	mounted foragers	Grinnell 1962 Llewellyn & Hoebel 1941
Chuckchee	Northeast Siberia	reindeer pastoralists	Bogaras 1904-09
Creek	Southern USA	horticulturists	Swanton 1928
Fon	Dahomey	horticulturists	Herskovits 1967 (1938)
Haida	British Columbia	maritime foragers	Murdock 1934 Stearns 1981 Swanton 1909 van der Brink 1974
Hopi	Northeast Arizona	horticulture	Hough 1915 Murdock 1934 Simmons 1942 Stephens 1936 Thompson 1950 Thompson & Joseph 1944 Titiev 1944
Igorot (Bontoc)	Northern Luzon, PI	terraced agriculture	Jenks 1905
Jivaro	Eastern Ecuador and Peru	horticulture	Harner 1962 Karsten 1935 Stirling 1938
Kazak	Kazakstan, USSR	mounted pastoralists	Hudson 1938 Murdock 1934
Klamath	SW Oregon	foragers	Gatschet 1890 Spier 1930

PEOPLE	LOCATION	BASIC ECONOMY	SOURCES
Maori	New Zealand	horticulture	Buck 1949 Best 1924 Penniman 1938
Mae Enga	New Guinea highlands	horticulture	Meggitt 1977
Mapuche	South Central Chile	horticulture & pastoralists	Berdichewsky 1975 Faron 1961, 1968 Titiev 1951
Mundurucu	Para, Brazil	horticulture	Murphy 1956
Nyakyusa	So. Tanzania	horticulture & pastoralists	G. Wilson 1938 M. Wilson 1950, 1951
Papago	SW Arizona NW Sonora	horticulture	Thompson 1951 Underhill 1939, 1946
Pawnee	Central Plains USA	horticulture	Grinnell 1889 Hyde 1957 Weltfish 1965
Rwala Bedowin	Asia Minor	mounted pastoralists	Musil 1928 Raswan 1942
Shilluk	South Sudan	pastoralists & horticulture	Westerman 1912 Seligman & Seligman 1932 Dempsey 1955
Thonga	Eastern South Africa	horticulture & pastoralists	Junod 1927
Wolof	Senegal & Gambia	horticulture	Gamble 1957 Charles 1977

Notes

1. I thank Carol and Melvin Ember, Douglass White and Valerie Wheeler for advice in planning this paper, and Laurie Kroshus and Michele Zack for the literature search they made.

2. While ten of the societies had initiation rites for youth and such initiation inflicted physical pain and hardship, in many the initiation rituals were often totally disassociated from any military involvement. Thus, the elaborate initiations among the Aranda that have been so fully described and widely discussed, have no specific relationship to the engagement in warfare.

References Cited

Baldwin, G.C. 1965. *The Warrior Apaches.* Tucson, Arizona: Dale Stuart King.

Bachelor, J. 1927. *Ainu Life and Lore.* Tokyo: Kyobunkwan.

———. 1892. *The Ainu of Japan.* London: Religious Tract Society.

Berdichewsky, B. 1975. *The Araucanian Indian in Chile.* Copenhagen: International Work Group for Indigenous Affairs.

Best, E. 1924. *The Maori As He Was.* Wellington: Dominion Museum.

Bogoras, W. 1904–09. *The Chuckchee.* Memoir of the American Museum of Natural History, v. 11. New York: American Museum of Natural History.

Brink, J. H. van den. 1974. *The Haida Indians.* Leiden: Brill.

Buck, P.H. 1949. *The Coming of the Maori.* Wellington: Maori Purposes Fund Board, distributed by Whitcombe and Tombs.

Chagnon, N.A. 1977. *Yanomamo: The Fierce People, 2nd edition.* New York: Holt, Rinehart and Winston.

Charles, E.A. 1977. *Precolonial Senegal: The Jolof Kingdom 1800 to 1890.* Boston: African Studies Center, Boston University.

Dempsey, J. 1955. *Mission on the Nile.* London: Burns & Oates.

Dobrizhoffer, M. 1822. *An Account of the Abipones, An Equestrian People of Paraguay.* 3v. London: J. Murray.

Eggan, F. 1937. The Cheyenne and Arapaho Kinship System. In *Social Anthropology of North American Tribes.* F. Eggan, ed., Chicago: University of Chicago Press, Pp. 33–95.

Ember, C.R. and M. Ember. 1984. Warfare and Aggression: Cross-Cultural Results. Paper presented at 83rd annual meeting of the American Anthropological Association, Denver, Colorado, 16 November 1984.

Faron, L. C. 1961. *Mapuche Social Structure.* Urbana: University of Illinois Press.

———. 1968. *The Mapuche Indians of Chile.* San Francisco: Holt, Rinehart and Winston.

Gamble, D.P. 1957. *The Wolof of Senegambia.* London: International African Institute.

Gatschet, A.S. 1890. *The Klamath Indians of Southwestern Oregon.* U.S. Geographical and Geological Survey of the Rocky Mountain Region, Department of the Interior. Washington: United States Government Printing Office.

Goldschmidt, W. 1976. *The Culture and Behavior of the Sebei.* Berkeley: University of California Press.

Grinnell, G.B. 1889. *Pawnee Hero Stories and Folk Tales.* New York: Forest and Stream Publishing Co.

————. 1915. *The Fighting Cheyennes.* New York: Scribner's.

————. 1923. *The Cheyenne Indians.* 2v. New Haven: Yale University Press.

Harner, M.J. 1962. Jivaro Souls. *American Anthropologist* 64(2):258–272.

Herskovits, M.J. 1967. *Dahomey, An Ancient West African Kingdom, Second Edition.* Evanston: Northwestern University Press (first published 1938).

Hoebel, E. A. 1960. *The Cheyenne.* New York: Holt.

Hough, W. 1915. *The Hopi Indians.* Cedar Rapids, IA: Torch Press.

Hudson, A. E. 1938. *Kazak Social Structure.* New Haven: Yale University Press.

Hyde, G.E. 1951. *The Pawnee Indians.* Denver: University of Denver Press.

Jenks, A.E. 1905. *The Bontoc Igorot.* Ethnological Survey Publication, Vol. 1. Manila P.I.: Bureau of Public Printing.

Junod, H. A. 1927. *The Life of a South African Tribe.* London: Macmillan.

Karsten, R. 1935. The Head-Hunters of Western Amazonas. *Societas Scientiarum Fennica: Commentiones Humanarum Litterarum* 71. Helsingfors, Centraltryckeriet.

Llewellyn, K.N., and E.A. Hoebel. 1941. *The Cheyenne Way.* Norman: University of Oklahoma Press.

Meggitt, M. 1977. *Blood Is Their Argument: Warfare among the Mae Enga of the New Guniea Highlands.* Palo Alto, CA: Mayfield.

Murdock, G.P. 1934. *Our Primitive Contemporaries.* New York: Macmillan.

————, and Douglas R. White 1969. Standard Cross-Cultural Sample. *Ethnology* 8:329–369.

Murphy, R.F. 1956. Matrilocality and Patrilineality in Mundurucu Society. *America Anthropologist* 58:414–434.

————. 1957. Intergroup Hostility and Social Cohesion. *American Anthropologist* 59:1018–1035.

————. 1960. *Headhunter's Heritage.* Berkeley: University of California Press.

Musil, A. 1928. *The Manners and Customs of Rwala Bedouins.* New York: published under the patronage of the Czech Academy of Sciences and Arts and of Charles M. Crane.

Opler, M.E. 1937. An Outline of Chiricahua Apache Social Organization. In *Social Anthropology of North American Tribes.* F. Eggan, ed., Chicago: University of Chicago Press, Pp. 173–239.

————. 1941. *An Apache Life-Way.* Chicago: University of Chicago Press.

Penniman, T.K., editor. 1938. *The Old-Time Maori, by Makereti, Sometime Chieftainess of the Arama Tribe, known in New Zealand as Maggie Papakura.* London: V. Gollancz.

Postman, M. V. 1899. *A History of our Relations with the Andamanese.* Calcutta, India: Office of the Superintendent of Government Printing.

Radcliffe-Brown, A.R. 1933. *The Andaman Islanders.* Cambridge: Cambridge University Press.

Rappaport, Roy A. 1967. Ritual Regulation of Environmental Relations among a New Guinea People. *Ethnology* 6:17–30.

Raswan, C.R. 1947. *Black Tents of Arabia.* New York: Creative Age Press.

Ross, H.M. 1983. Political Decision Making and Conflict: Additional Cross-Cultural Codes and Scales. *Ethnology* 22:169–192.

Seligman, C.G., and B.Z. Seligman. 1932. *Pagan Tribes of the Nilotic Sudan.* London: G. Routledge and Sons.

Simmons, L. 1942. *Sun Chief, the Autobiography of a Hopi Indian.* New Haven: Yale University Press.

Spier, L. 1930. *Klamath Ethnography.* Berkeley: University of California Press.

Stearns, M.L. 1981. *Haida Culture in Custody.* Seattle: University of Washington Press.

Stephen, A.M. 1936. *Hopi Journal.* E.C. Parsons, ed., New York: Columbia University Contributions to Anthropology, v. 38, pt. 1.

Stirling, M.W. 1938. Historical and Ethnographical Material on the Jivaro Indians. *Bulletin Bureau of American Ethnology* 117:1–148.

Suguira, S. and H. Befer. 1962. Kinship Organization of the Saru Ainu. *Ethnology* 1:287–298.

Swanton, J.R. 1909. Contributions to the Ethnology of Haida. *Memoirs of the American Museum of Natural History* 8:1–300.

_____. 1928. *Social Organization and Social Uses of the Indians of the Creek Confederacy.* Annual Report of the Bureau of American Ethnology, 1922–23. Washington: U.S. Government Printing Office, Pp. 25–472.

Thompson, L. 1950. *Culture in Crisis.* New York: Russell and Russell.

_____. 1951. *Personality and Government.* Mexico: Grafica Panamericana.

_____, and Alice Joseph. 1944. *The Hopi Way.* Chicago: University of Chicago Press.

Titiev, M. 1944. *Old Oraibi, A Study of the Hopi Indians of Third Mesa.* Papers of the Peabody Museum, Number 22. Cambridge: Harvard University.

_____. 1951. *Araucanian Culture in Transition.* Ann Arbor: University of Michigan Press.

Underhill, R.M. 1939. *Social Organization of the Papago Indians.* New York: Columbia University Press.

_____. 1940. *The Papago Indians of Arizona and Their Relatives the Pima.* U.S. Bureau of Indian Affairs, Sherman Pamphlets no. 3.

_____. 1946. *The Papago Indian Religion.* New York: Columbia University Press.

Watanabe, H. 1973. *The Ainu Ecosystem: Environment and Group Structure.* Seattle: University of Washington Press.

Weltfish, G. 1965. *Lost Universe, with a Closing Chapter on "The Universe Regained."* New York: Basic Books.

Westerman, D. 1912. *The Shilluk People.* Philadelphia: The Board of Foreign Missions of the United Presbyterian Church of North America.

Wilson, G. 1938. *The Land Rights of Individuals Among The Nyakyusa.* Livingston, Northern Rhodesia: The Rhodes-Livingston Institute.

Wilson, M. 1950. Nyakyusa Kinship. In *African Systems of Kinship and Marriage*. A.R. Radcliffe-Brown and D. Forde, eds., London: Oxford University Press, Pp. 111–139.

_____. 1951. *Good Company, A Study of Nyakyusa Age-Villages*. London: Oxford University Press.

Part 2
Dynamics of Conflict

4 / Images of the Other

Peter Worsley

In Peter Worsley's description of the institutionalized images of the Soviet Union and the United States, held by each of the other, we see again the importance of symbols and values in forming the dynamic basis on which peace and conflict rest. Drawing on his experiences as a foreign anthropologist in both countries, and upon newspaper articles and other literature, Worsley shows how images institutionalized as stereotypic beliefs contribute substantially to foreign policy decisions. He shows that when this happens our images of the other can become dangerously out of touch with the reality of their life. He calls attention to a set of political, economic, and ethnic images that are now out-of-date, if ever they were accurate. He uses these and other concepts to illustrate the process of "cultural lag," the failure of culturally-based images and values to keep pace with the reality of a changing world. Worsley, like Bateson, shows that our images contain conflicting elements, and suggests that most people operate with a mix of these. Anticipating Sluka's discussion later in this volume, Worsley calls attention to the importance for understanding the dynamics of situations of conflict and aggression to the role played by the manipulation in propaganda of symbols and stereotypes. In common with other contributors to this volume, Worsley suggests that anthropology has a critical role to play in international security affairs by contributing accurate information about the social and cultural life of those with whom we must interact in a changing world.—The Editors*

Societies are systems, whose component parts fit together and influence one another.[1] Some societies are more integrated than others, sometimes because they have strong central institutions, sometimes because they have highly coherent cultures. Americans think of the Soviet Union, for instance, as an exceptionally systematic, indeed totalitarian society—one which would break up into its component parts if it were not for the apparatus of State and Party. This model, I believe, is dangerously over-simplified.

Soviet views of the United States, by contrast, emphasize the division of the society into classes. America is certainly a class society, as a recent diagram of social stratification in the United States shows (Rose 1983). People in California have long resisted the idea that New York is the center of gravity of the United States—America, they insist, is not just the Big Apple. But the American class system is pear-shaped. Most people live in the bulge of the pear, and a sizable proportion of them below the official poverty-line. But what no diagram can show (except logarithmically) is the stalk to the pear, far higher than Jack's legendary bean-stalk, for the stalk of the pear, if projected on the same scale to show the incomes of the astonishingly rich, would be sixty stories high. And by the end of the century, some have asserted, there could be a million millionaires (Davis 1983).

We normally think of science in terms of discovery and problem-solving—of finding answers to questions. But it is equally important to ask the right questions in the first place, including questions about things we take for granted as *un*problematic—so obvious that they don't call for an answer. Thus, Finer (1962) discussing military take-overs in Third World countries, raised the awkward question as to why the military—who, after all, control the decisive apparatus of force—do not use that power to take over in *every* society.

Given the distribution of wealth we have just seen, a foreigner such as myself from Western Europe, or my Soviet colleague, Dr. Tishkov, or some future visitor from Mars, might well ask why it is that the poor accept their lot in the United States; indeed, why there is not chronic social unrest on a large scale. That question, indeed, was classically asked nearly eighty years ago by the German economist, Werner Sombart (1906), who asked why is there no socialism in the United States. Of course, there was a socialist movement of some importance, but unlike those in Europe, it never became a serious alternative to capitalism.

There have been many explanations of this "American exception-alism:" the availability of an "open frontier;" the divisions within a new working class composed of immigrants from many countries; the belief, shared by conservatives and populists alike, that Americans, in the end, share the same basic values—that people should be rewarded in accordance with their contribution to society, and that all should have the chance of rising from log cabin to the Presidency.

Those values are still alive today but they are not very convincing to those who live in the South Bronx or Watts rather than in log cabins. Those underprivileged areas did witness massive disturbances in 1967. But such violent public unrest is abnormal. There has been no need, therefore, for physical repression. Social peace has persisted despite marked social inequalities and recession.

A second type of explanation focuses on mechanisms of redistribution through which the poor are saved from total destitution through welfare programs, and on the phenomenon of social mobility. The reality is that most of this mobility is very short-ranged indeed, and the American belief that the Welfare State is a peculiarly Western European phenomenon is belied by statistics which show that the proportion of Gross National Product (GNP) devoted to publicly-funded programs of this kind, from medical care to food stamps, is remarkably similar in every industrialized Western country, the United States included, even given the "rollback" of the last few years.

A third type of explanation is non-economic: that people acquire their ideas about the world from the mass media, which never question the basic institutions or values of United States society and give minimal space and time to possible alternative ways of life. All these kinds of explanation, a fourth one holds, are beside the point. For, Blacks in ghettos do not compare themselves with stockbrokers on Wall Street or Sunbelt millionaires, even less aspire to join them. Rather they compare their lot with that of people close to them: women with men; married men to single men without family responsibilities; auto workers with steel workers; those at one plant with those in the same branch of industry.

Most people, social scientists included, operate with a personal mix of all of these—and other—explanations. But most of the time, unless we are professional social scientists, we don't think about Society as a whole, with a capital 'S'; we simply get on with the business of living, and that takes time and is problematic enough. That is why C. Wright Mills once said that most people had what he called a "middle level" consciousness. We don't think about bigger questions or higher levels of society unless we have to—when we're forced to because we find ourselves with serious personal problems. But when those problems are not purely idiosyncratic, but are faced, too, by millions of other people, because they are the result of national and even international events and decisions, and therefore persist, "personal troubles" become transformed into "public issues" (Mills 1959:8).

To someone from a small island off the coast of continental Europe, it is understandable that in the United States and the Soviet Union, or in China, which are virtual continents rather than countries, what goes on outside their borders may seem remote and unimportant. But I found it disturbing the last time I was in California to find that the headline on the front page of the famous *Los Angeles Times* concerned a mud-slide on a nearby major freeway. In the United States, it is actually difficult to get anything like adequate knowledge about what is going on, not only in the outside world but at times even about what is going on in this enormous country, unless one subscribes to national newspapers and periodicals. Few do so. Hence, as far as other countries are concerned, people rely on capsule newscasts for their information.

The gaps are filled with a limited repertoire of stereotypes. Some of these are very ancient indeed. The division of Europe into Western and Eastern segments, for instance, recent historiography suggests (Anderson 1974a, 1974b, Wallerstein 1974) goes back far beyond the rise of modern communism. An outstanding history written in California, for instance (Stavrianos 1981), argues that the Third World began, not in Africa, Asia or Latin America, but in Europe, when Eastern Europe, which up to the fifteenth century had had a positive balance of trade with the Western part, began to slip behind, and eventually became a backward agrarian zone, while the West modernized its agriculture and then went on to develop mercantile and later industrial capitalism. The possibility of catching up was further blocked because autocratic political institutions in Tsarist Russia, plus a powerful Church, blocked the possibility of any cultural transformation similar to the Protestant Reformation and the Renaissance in Western Europe. Instead, Russia embarked upon an expansion eastward that was to turn it into a vast Empire, reaching the Pacific across Siberia far faster than the Thirteen Colonies were to expand into the West. This only reinforced Tsarist rule so that it was not until as late as 1917 that that polity was overthrown and the modernization of Russia began.

When we speak of the "United States," we do not mean to insult the United States of Mexico or the United States of Brazil by appropriating the term for this country alone. Equally, what we loosely call "Russia"—the Soviet Union, to give it its proper name—was from the beginning, and still is, a federation, made up of 15 Republics, 20 Autonomous Republics, 8 Autonomous Regions, and 10 Autonomous Areas. Unlike the United States, where a dominant, homogenized culture, based on the WASP culture of the Founding Fathers, emerged, the Soviet state is made up of many different nationalities, from the Russians (130 million) and the Ukrainians (41 million), through the 9 million Uzbeks, the million Estonians, down to the smallest peoples such as the 29,000 Nenets of the Siberian tundra. In principle, they have, or had, the right to secede, and Finland was actually allowed to do so in 1917, even though it was likely to become what in fact it did become—a firmly anti-Bolshevik state. Armed intervention by fourteen foreign powers soon changed that policy, since the Bolshevik leadership feared that Japan, Britain, France and other countries would back separatist movements from the Ukraine to the oil-rich Caucasus, Central Asia and Siberia. Under the far worse occupation by the Nazis, from 1941–1944, some minority nationalities such as the Chechen-Ingush and the Volga Germans, suspected by the paranoid Stalin of potential disloyalty, were deported in hundreds of thousands, just as the Nisei Japanese were interned in this country.

But Stalin has been dead for over thirty years, and the cohesion of the Soviet Union is no longer based on the mass terror that sent millions to their graves in the 1930s, however severe the control exercised over dissidents. For the Soviet Union was transformed by the experience of World War II, in which all suffered alike at the hands of the Nazis who recruited minority nationalities into the Waffen SS but did not give them their own states. As a result, a new consciousness, of *Soviet* identity, emerged: what one might call a first-order national identity as against the second-order identities of Russians, White Russians, Uzbeks, Tadjiks, Armenians, Georgians, and other nationalities: a new identity born of common suffering, common sacrifice, and pride in victory.

The situation of the United States during World War II was very different. That great chronicler of America, Studs Terkel, recently published a book based on hundreds of interviews with Americans who lived through that war (Terkel 1985). The central message of his book is very clear: that the vast majority of Americans had a very good war. But, I spent my school days preparing for my Cambridge entrance examinations in air-raid shelters on the school football-pitches, and 60,000 British civilians died in air-raids on our cities. But this is an utterly insignificant number compared to the twenty million who died in the Soviet Union, most of them civilians.

To us in Britain, the United States Forces lived at a standard that aroused both the envy and the admiration of the rationed British. America symbolized, too, jazz, Hollywood, modernity. So, as the film *Yanks* vividly and nostalgically recaptures, Americans were popular. Tens of thousands married British women, and tens of thousands died, in part to defend us.

We have not forgotten that, because we knew them as individuals. (What the film did not capture was the other side of the ambivalent relationship expressed in the wartime joke about the differences between the Americans and the British: Americans, it ran, were over-sexed, over-paid, over here, and over us; the Brits were under-sexed, under-paid and under Eisenhower.)

But we did not get to know the Russians as individuals, and it has therefore been much easier to forget the decisive contribution they made, when, in Churchill's words, they "tore the guts out of the German fighting-machine." Forty Soviet citizens died for every one American. Hence, despite official ideological commitment to "proletarian internationalism," that war is officially known in the Soviet Union not as the Anti-Fascist War, but as the Great Patriotic War. The result is an obsession with avoiding any repetition of those appalling losses, an obsession which has led the Soviet leadership into a nuclear arms-race with the United States that on any basis of statistical probability must lead to the eventual use of those weapons, whether by accident or design. To anthropologists, the idea of defending oneself with nuclear weapons is perhaps the supreme instance of the phenomenon of cultural lag, for "defense," "survival," and "victory" are concepts that had meaning forty years ago, but no longer do.

The history of World War II is not familiar to young people today. Historians and anthropologists, who make a special study of how the past gets reinterpreted in the light of present-day preoccupations, have shown that what we often take to be authentic "tradition" is, in fact, quite modern invention. Thus, Scottish clan tartans, the Druidic ceremonies solemnly enacted every year in Wales, or the annual celebrations of the Viking invasions of the Shetland Islands were all invented in the nineteenth century by Romantic and nationalist intellectuals (Hobsbawm and Ranger 1983).

In tribal societies, anthropologists have shown, myths of this kind flourish not just because people simply find intellectual satisfaction in them, but because myths of how the ancestors came out of the ground at the beginning of the world—as in the Australian Aborigines' "Dreamtime"—legitimize the rights of their living descendants over the land where these miraculous events took place.

Traditions are still being invented today, with similar social rationale. The long period of the Cold War necessitated the symbolic transformation of an ally into an enemy. That process was ritually completed in 1984, when Britain and France celebrated the D-Day landings in Normandy. Present at the ceremonies was a representative of a country which is now an ally but was then the enemy—Germany. Absent was the ally of 1941–1945 which had many times more divisions in the field than the armies of the Western Powers put together.

I began by saying that societies are systems. Modern anthropology, from the functionalist cultural anthropology of the 1930s to the structuralism of Lévi-Strauss, has also insisted that the ideas and values which make up the culture of any society and which sustain its institutions and self-images also constitute systems—that the myths about ancestral Beings and their doings are not just so many separate Just-So stories, but all contain common themes, which, taken together, display logical and mythological coherence (Lévi-Strauss 1966). But other anthropologists have argued that the degree of coherence is often greatly exaggerated and that all societies, even tribal ones, change and are changed from the outside, though changes take place at different rates in different institutions of society. Some parts change faster than others and in different ways. Hence complete overall consistency is less likely than contradictions, whether between institutions or values, and especially so in rapidly-changing modern societies. Ideas can change overnight—as a result of the magical experience of reading a book or hearing a charismatic speaker. But, they can also lag behind events because, being things of the mind, whilst we can be made to conform in our outward behavior, ideas are more difficult to police.

Such unevenness in the rate of change between different social institutions, different cultural domains, and popular perceptions of these social and cultural changes, have been designated by some anthropologists "cultural lag."

The theory of cultural lag, however, assumes unevenness to be an immanent phenomenon, and underestimates the extent to which social change does not simply happen but is made to happen as a consequence of both positive decisions—as when the Cold War was launched as an act of policy—and negative decisions—such as the priority given to what Galbraith has called "private affluence," whose consequence is necessarily "public squalor," including inadequate education about national and international matters. Both, however, are the outcome of societal decisions: positive decisions to promulgate a hostile image of the Soviet Union, and negative decisions limiting the allocation of social resources to education in the world's richest industrialized country. The "lag" in American consciousness of social change in the Soviet Union, then, is a consequence of the deliberate institutionalization of ignorance which began with the launching of the Cold War in 1945. The end-product, today, is that nearly half (44%) of the Americans in a *New York Times Magazine* survey in 1985 did not know that the Soviet Union and the United States fought together on the same side in World War II, while nearly a third (28%) thought they had actually fought each other. Yet, at the same time, more than 200 books and 2,500 articles per year are written by Americans about the Soviet Union. This apparent paradox is readily explained: these books and articles are read only by specialists, not by the general public (Shipler 1985).

Americans are ignorant not only about the Soviet Union, however. They do not know much about the United States, either. In 1943, fewer than one in four could name two achievements of Abraham Lincoln, Thomas Jefferson, Andrew Jackson or Theodore Roosevelt; less than 15% could identify Samuel Gompers as a leader of organized labor, or Susan B. Anthony as an advocate of women's rights; less than 6% could name the thirteen original colonies. By 1976, after an explosion of tertiary education, only 44% knew that the term "cold war" referred to United States-Soviet relations; only 62% knew that the Supreme Court had the power to declare acts of Congress unconstitutional. Two-thirds of 17-year-olds in the 1980s could not place the Civil War in the period between 1850–1900; a third did not know that the Declaration of Independence was signed between 1750 and 1800; a third could not find Britain, West Germany or France on a map of Europe; about half could not identify Winston Churchill or Josef Stalin (Ravitch 1985).

These examples of specific factual knowledge are less disturbing than the wider ideological conditioning of the United States population. Today, the dominant American images of the Soviet Union are seriously out-of-date. The first, a political image, is the image of that country as a totalitarian system only held together by the exercise of mass terror. As Mr. Khrushchev told the world, that image was not too far from the truth during the Stalin period, when millions of Soviet citizens perished. A second, economic, image, established as early as the famine of the 1920s, is that of the Soviet Union as a desperately poor country in which the cities are only islands in a sea of peasants, and where people spend all their time queuing for even the basic necessities of life. A third, ethnic, image is of a country which would fly apart into its constituent national components were the Soviet gridiron removed.

Let us take these stereotypes in reverse order. There is a widely-held view, in some United States circles, for instance, that the Soviet Union possesses a time-bomb which threatens the survival not of the West, but of the Soviet Union itself: the ethnic/national time-bomb of the Baltic, Caucasian and Central Asian minority nationalities. Today, the argument runs, the Soviet Union has crossed a watershed, for those nationalities now outnumber the Russians proper. Hence, before long, they will begin to flex their political muscles and use their new power to throw off Russian control.

I would not want to underestimate such potential nationalistic tendencies. But what this model omits (apart from the unlikelihood that fissiparity would be tolerated) is that all but a few of the highest administrative positions in these republics (and, of course, the central State and Party institutions in Moscow) are now staffed by members of the national minorities; secondly, that when Tadjiks and Uzbeks, Armenians and Georgians, look across their borders to Turkey, Iran and Afghanistan, they find little to envy either in the wretched poverty of people who are often of the same ethnic stock as themselves. And Armenians know, too, that while they have their own Republic, their ethnic kin in Turkey were massacred in their millions.

As for the peasantry, the archetypal *muzhik* is no longer the typical Soviet citizen, but is today well out-numbered by the urban population. Shortages of consumer goods certainly exist, because they get lower priority than defense and heavy industry. But despite this, between 1965 and 1980, the monthly wage rose from 96.5 rubles to 168.5; by 1980, 85% of all families had television sets as against 25% fifteen years earlier, and 84% now have refrigerators. Where they were mainly eating bread and potatoes two decades ago, they now eat a lot more meat and vegetables (Steele 1982). The number of doctors has doubled, and housing is no longer calculated in terms of families per room, but of rooms per family. A recent United States report similarly notes that automobile production has quadrupled since the late sixties; that over 80% of urban housing now includes bathrooms, with central heating in nine out of ten residences; while nearly thirty million telephones are now in use where there were less than 4 1/2 million in 1960 (Schmemann 1985).

Life has improved materially, and is a matter for both satisfaction and pride. In the Soviet economy, however, defense has priority. It can produce equipment of the highest quality and precision, comparable with anything the West can produce, as the sputnik proved nearly a quarter of a century ago. It can do so because it is allocated capital, scientific resources and the best managers. The second level, heavy industry, is also as efficient, often better, than its Western counterpart. But industry supplying consumer goods is notoriously inadequate both in terms of quality and quantitatively; hence the notorious queues. Lowest priority in terms of inputs is given to agriculture, the Soviet Union's chronic problem (Medvedev 1981). The stresses and strains are reflected in alcoholism and in deteriorating health services and health conditions (Worsley 1984:334–335).

The United States, likewise, which had the lowest standards of infant and neo-natal mortality in the 1950s, had fallen behind France, Belgium, Germany, and England by 1972, while drug addiction and unemployment have brought misery to millions. These declines are in part due to differences in political priorities: to what, for the United States, John Kenneth Galbraith described as a preference for private affluence which inevitably meant public squalor (Galbraith 1969). But they are also exacerbated by something common to both countries: the priority given to military expenditure (Melman 1974). The United States now runs a negative balance of payments with Japan in respect of manufactured goods, a gap only bridged by the export of foodstuffs (jet planes apart), including, ironically, rice and soya. The machine-tools used in United States industry are twice as old as those used in Japan. The reason is—and the reason for the similar "miraculous" pre-eminence of that other ruined wartime economy, in Western Germany—that Japan and West Germany spend only 7% of their research and development (R&D) budget on defense whereas Britain and the United States spend 30%. In my country, the Ministry of Defense is the largest employer of nuclear scientists and engineers.

Many Cold War myths are mirror-images. Those who resent United States power—and few Americans realize how much their world-domination is resented, even in countries whose governments are friendly—often argue that the United States now has its own ethnic time-bomb, in the shape of millions of new Hispanic immigrants. Given time, the argument runs, they will combine with the similarly-under-privileged Blacks in a militant Rainbow Coalition. This is about as likely, I believe, as an American working-class revolution.

Yet life for tens of millions in both countries is certainly unenviable, as a recent brilliant study by a Cambridge (Britain) anthropologist—on an admittedly extremely marginal part of the Soviet Union, Buryat Mongolia—shows (Humphrey 1983). But it also shows that people do not simply conform to official plans and that even the most bureaucratic system can be and is manipulated by folk who cooperate with officials who need their support only when they get benefits in return: favorable target-figures for production and favorable prices for the products of the collective farm as a whole, as well as personal favors for individuals: scholarships, the right to live in the village, to visit the city, and so on.

Studies of institutions in the West, even of those institutions Erving Goffman called "total" institutions—such as hospitals, prisons, ships, etc.—show that the powerless often exercise considerable power over those formally in authority over them (Goffman 1961). It is a more illuminating model of how society works, I believe, than uncritical Manichaean assumptions about the Other as total Evil and one's own society as totally Good. That mutual paranoia is grimly embodied in two maps, one from the Soviet Ministry of Defense, showing the Soviet Union ringed by United States bases; the other issued from Washington, under the name of Caspar Weinberger, showing Soviet expansion outside her borders (Chaliand 1983).

Co-existence with the Soviet Union is a very unsatisfactory and fragile condition: little more than armed balance of terror. It seems unlikely, for some time, to be replaced by what is needed and is technologically possible—actual joint cooperation to wipe out world poverty—because we mistrust one another. One prerequisite for building confidence is much more knowledge and much more exchange. I hope, therefore, that before too long we will have studies by Soviet scholars, sponsored by, for example, the University of California, similar to the studies by British anthropologists sponsored by the Institute of Ethnography in Moscow (Dragadze 1984), not only of ethnic minorities, but of life in the great cities of the United States and of the great shrines of national culture, from Arlington Cemetery to Disneyland.

Notes

1. This paper was originally prepared for the symposium "Power, Change, and Security Decisions" held at the 1985 annual meeting of the American Association for the Advancement of Science, Los Angeles, California.

References Cited

Anderson, P. 1974a. *Passages from Antiquity to Feudalism.* London: New Left Books.

———. 1974b. *Lineages of the Absolutist State.* London: New Left Books.

Chaliand, G. 1983. *Atlas Politico-Stratégique.* Paris: Flammarion.

Dragadze, T. 1984. *Kinship and Marriage in the Soviet Union.* London: Routledge and Kegan Paul.

Finer, S.E. 1962. *The Man on Horseback: The Role of the Military in Politics.* London: Pall Mall Press.

Galbraith, J.K. 1969. *The Affluent Society.* London: Deutsch.

Goffman, E. 1961. *Asylums: Essays on the Social Situation of Mental Patients and other Inmates.* New York: Anchor Doubleday.

Hobsbawm, E.J. and T. Ranger. 1983. *The Invention of Tradition.* London: Cambridge University Press.

Humphrey, C. 1983. *Karl Marx Collective: Economy, Society and Religion in a Siberian Collective Farm.* London: Cambridge University Press.

Lévi-Strauss, C. 1966. *The Savage Mind.* London: Weidenfeld and Nicolson.

Medvedev, R. 1981. Why the Russians Can't Grow Grain. *New York Times,* 1 November:1, 17.

Melman, S. 1974. *The Permanent War Economy: American Capitalism in Decline.* New York: Simon and Schuster.

Mills, C.W. 1959. *The Sociological Imagination.* New York: Oxford University Press.

Ravitch, D. 1985. Decline and Fall of History Teaching. *New York Times Magazine,* 17 November:50–56, 101–117.

Rose, S.J. 1983. *The American Profile Poster: Who Owns What, Who Makes How Much, Who Works Where, and Who Lives with Whom,* Poster designed by D. Livingston and K. Shagas. New York: Pantheon Books.

Schmemann, S. 1985. Gorbachev Tries to Shift Economy into Top Gear. *New York Times,* 12 December.

Shipler, D. 1985. The View from America. *New York Times Magazine* 10 November:32–48, 72–82.

Sombart, W. 1906. *Warum gibt es in den Vereinigten Staaten keine Sozialismus?* Tubingen: J.C.B. Mohr.

Stavrianos, L.S. 1981. *Global Rift: The Third World Comes of Age.* New York: Morrow.

Steele, J. 1982. The New Russia the Old Guard Inherits. *Guardian* London, 12 November.

Terkel, S. 1985. *The Good War: An Oral History of World War Two.* New York: Ballantine.

Wallerstein, I. 1974. *The Modern World System.* New York: Academic Press.

Worsley, Peter 1984. *The Three Worlds: Culture and World Development.* Chicago: University of Chicago Press.

5 / Values and the Exercise of Power: Military Elites

Donna Brasset

As we have seen in previous articles, values and symbols give social life its dynamism. It is therefore important to understand the roles they play in relation to international security analyses. Just as we are concerned to better understand these cultural dynamics among other people, Donna Brasset's description of the role of values in the strategic thinking of senior officers in the United States' military makes clear that we also need to be conscious of our own values and manipulation of symbols. Basing her conclusions on a year-long study in which she interviewed senior military officers, Brasset describes the symbolism that supports the institutionalization of the military in the United States. As Worsley reports a cultural lag between our general "images of the other" and the realities of their lives, Brasset identifies a lag in the culture of the military officers between their strategic concepts and the technological context of their profession. Thus, in the course of her interviews she found that military decisions were often justified by reference to normative aspects of society, through a belief in the moral "rightness" of the officer's strategic position. She argues that such justifications reflect a dangerous ethnocentrism in the training and experience of military officers. This includes a mistaken tendency to treat all conflict situations as though they are fundamentally a part of the struggle between the communist East and the democratic West. She suggests that anthropologists can contribute importantly to international security studies by illuminating the roots of discontent among people, whose desire for change has little to do with the Soviet and American ideological and economic agendas. In common with other chapters in this book, Brasset suggests that one way to approach this is by

explicating the language, symbols, and values of the military.—
The Editors

In 1963, the Cuban missile crisis impressed a number of anthropologists with the need to conduct research having to do with the problem of war among nation-states.[1] At a conference organized to that end, Ruth Bunzel and Anne Parsons (1964:437) commented in a paper that, "The military establishment with its ramifying structure, its mythology, symbols, ideology, and systems of action, like any other sub-culture, is an appropriate object of anthropological study."

Influenced by Bunzel's call for research on the subculture of the military establishment, I decided on a project that would explore the attitudes and values of United States military elites. The purpose was to show how social and cultural factors impinge on military perceptions of world events, and which therefore influence strategic and foreign policy decisions. I spent nearly a year in Washington, D.C. interviewing active and retired senior officers at the highest levels in each of the major service branches. I also talked to others in the Washington "defense community"—to CIA directors, to civilian appointees, and strategic analysts in the Department of Defense. I have been to their homes, to their offices in the Pentagon, the National Defense University, liberal and conservative think tanks in the area, and the offices of some who are in the employ of major and minor defense contractors.

Most of the officers I spoke to were friendly, articulate, hard-working, dedicated, and deeply loyal to their services and academies—in short, they shared the qualities of the "honorable men" that C. Wright Mills (1956) spoke of in *The Power Elite*. During many hours of conversation, I developed an understanding of, and an appreciation for, their world, as they see and experience it: of their combat experience in Vietnam, Korea and in World War II, of the complicated and demanding responsibilities that go with their roles, and of the richness and complexity of military culture.

Despite such appreciation however, my preliminary conclusion about their beliefs and perceptions of world problems has emerged as a kind of military permutation of the "Peter Principle" (Peter 1969:7)—that is, that military socialization and selection processes tend to raise into command individuals with talents best suited to a time when (1) the military was more insulated than it is at the present from the political and economic sectors of American society, when (2) the destructive potential of its weapons was much less, and when (3) the intellectual demands on its leaders were far less pressing.[2] I believe this is because advances in weapons technology in the past forty years have outpaced the ability of the military to make the necessary, adaptive institutional adjustments.

Pragmatic and Absolutist Military Thinking

The military sociologist, Morris Janowitz (1960), discusses the "pragmatic" versus the "absolutist" schools of military thought, which have divided individuals in the military and defense communities for decades, if not longer. The pragmatists, whose views probably dominated military and political thinking during the Vietnam war, tend to see warfare as one of many instruments of international relations. Though they are committed to the long-range political goal of active competition with the Soviet Union, their tendency has been to support the idea of the co-existence of political democracies with communist and socialist nations.

Pragmatists endorse the policy of "graduated deterrence"—that is, the "measured" or "flexible" use of force to achieve specific political goals. In reference to nuclear war, pragmatists tend to take the position that traditional concepts of military victory are not applicable; they retain strategic nuclear retaliation as one of their options, however, and this is accompanied by the belief in an inevitable recovery from the devastation of a nuclear "exchange" with the Soviet Union.

"Absolutists" on the other hand, having derived their views from the traditions of the "frontier punitive expeditions" against the Native Americans, are those who subscribe to more conventional ideas of achieving total military victory in all-out war. Although they understand the implications of nuclear destruction, absolutists tend to see nuclear war as limited and unlikely to escalate into large-scale war. Their view of Soviet intentions is based on the idea of Soviet world domination through military force. Communist nations and "free" nations cannot survive indefinitely in the same world, and the absolutist long-range goal is both to work towards maintaining the status-quo in the non-communist world, and to "liberate" communist-dominated political systems wherever they may emerge on the globe.

Absolutists also tend to see international relations in terms of a pattern which has remained essentially unchanged since 1945, to lump all communist and socialist-like nations together, and to believe that a similar political and military stand must be taken against all of them regardless of difference in history or geography. In addition to having different strategic conceptions than pragmatists, absolutists are more likely to hold to a strong belief in orthodox religion, because, as Janowitz (1960:264) put it, " . . . belief in the necessity of violence requires strong prescriptions for sanctioning its use."

None of the officers whom I met fit these categories exactly, but my impression is that the military failure in Vietnam—associated as it was with both the strategy of "graduated deterrence" and more civilian "interference" in military matters than many officers cared for, has led in recent years to a strengthening in power of more officers with perceptions approximating Janowitz's "absolutists."[3] On the subject of the use of nuclear weapons, the majority of active-duty generals and flag-rank officers whom I interviewed, expressed views very similar to that of one of my "informants," a 3-star Army general:

> I am not uncomfortable with our nuclear war-fighting strategy. That doesn't mean I am enthusiastic about it. But I won't turn my back on the use of nuclear weapons if [it] meets the proper moral criteria. I don't believe the use of nuclear weapons is immoral if it fits Judeo-Christian values. I believe it is moral to fight with nuclear weapons in someone's defense, for example, in the defense of others who can't protect them-selves; to fight soldiers, not civilians, and to fight in proportion to the kinds of weapons used against us. . . . Nuclear war is just a conflict extension of any kind of war. True, civilians would also be killed in a nuclear war, but collateral damage goes with it, as it does in any war . . . I don't waste a lot of time worrying about nuclear war because I have faith in the Lord. I have a strong faith that if we're on the right side, He'll be on our side . . . [because] a life *worth living* is what we are fighting for (original emphasis).

As anthropologists, we are predisposed to understand that individuals in all economic and status groups seek solace in the supernatural to assuage their fears, to justify their decisions and actions, or as moti-vation to survive in a world experienced as oppressive or dangerous (see Nash 1982). The problem as I see it, is that the kinds of religious beliefs which were a perfectly usual, and perhaps functional, way of viewing the universe in the seventeenth century, are especially dys-functional in the nuclear era if it should happen that vital military and political decisions are ever guided by them, or if such beliefs facilitate decisions dangerous to the survival of great masses of people.

Ethnocentrism in the Military View of the World

For reasons having to do with military socialization in general (see Pulliam this volume), and socialization into American society in par-ticular, the role of the American military in international politics is also accompanied by an especially ethnocentric view of the world on the part of its members—despite Janowitz's prediction in 1960 that the military was to become more internationally oriented, and less ethnocentric. A substantial majority of all those whom I interviewed expressed a belief in the superiority of American social and religious institutions, an impassioned anti-Soviet ideology, and a predilection to perceive the world's other peoples as "frustrated, or potential Americans" (Baritz 1985:31).

Each of these themes has its own history, but the anti-Soviet ideology, and the military build-up that has emerged from it, are significantly linked to the perceptions held by American political and economic leaders involved in shaping the post World War II world. In the wake of Hitler's hegemonic goals, in a climate of rising suspicions about Soviet expansionism, and as a result of an interest in pursuing foreign trade as a solution to America's economic problems, President Harry Truman and his advisors envisioned the entire globe as a potential economic, political, ideological and military contest between the United States and the Soviet Union. American foreign policy became substantially militarized as a result (Yarmolinsky 1971, Barnet 1972, Ambrose 1972). According to Truman (1956:2), the idea was for the United States to " . . . take the lead in running the world the way the world ought to be run."

In the Cold War political environment of 1947 the National Security Act was formulated, providing the bureaucratic framework for direct military participation in the formulation of foreign policy. With the passage of "NSC–68" in 1950, the military had been authorized to acquire in peacetime unprecedented amounts of national and international resources of all kinds to deal with every conceivable kind of threat to perceived American interests anywhere in the world.[4] An enormous expansion of military responsibilities ensued: the ability to acquire and manage a vast range of industrial and manpower resources, developing the capability to fight any kind of war in any area of the globe in any conditions at any time, and to plan for one-and-one-half to two such wars at a given time; acquiring knowledge of the most sophisticated weapons systems; cultivating extensive international military networks, assuming a greatly expanded role in the political arena, and accepting (albeit reluctantly) "collateral damages" of modern warfare in terms of "megadeaths."

Despite such greatly expanded responsibilities, and because all institutions and cultures are slow to change, military officers continue to spend their lives in an institution that presses for great conformity of thought, requires unquestioning loyalty to the state, profoundly distrusts dissenting opinions, encourages ideological and religious legitimation of its policies, and idealizes concepts of battlefield victory which have been part of military history and culture since there have been standing armies in the world (Pulliam this volume). Intellectual judgment can be compromised as a result. A number of senior officers whom I interviewed, for example, asserted variations on the following comment made by one informant:

> If it came down to a choice between ourselves as a nation, versus the survival of a species, I would have to say, we as a nation would have to look out for ourselves first and the species second.

In my judgment, military officers say such things out of a type of loyalty to the state that has become outmoded in the nuclear era— their best and most honorable intentions to the contrary, notwithstanding.

My data also show that many senior officers, along with younger officers contending for higher ranks, have rejected some of the more substantive lessons of the Vietnam war in favor of those of a strictly tactical nature. Among the active-duty officers I spoke with, the short and long term consequences of ethnocentrism are not on their list of lessons learned from the Vietnam experience, but there are retired commanders who admit that greater attention to the French experience in Vietnam, better understanding of the relations between the Chinese and Vietnamese, or the attitude of a great bulk of Vietnamese towards Ho Chi Minh, would have called for a different appraisal of the plans to intervene. One vice-admiral explained that he and his group went about making war plans for Vietnam " . . . without any of us having read anything about the French experience there." The presumption was that superior American technology and "know-how" was all that was sufficient to win the war. Few knew much about the history and culture of the Vietnamese people, nor were they interested. As one retired army general put it "We never took into account the cultural difference" (Kinnard 1977:92).

All human societies tend to sustain traditions which bolster ethnocentric attitudes and values. Historian Loren Baritz (1985:37) discussed the recurring theme in American culture, originating with the Puritans, that Americans have a mission "to convert others to the truth as they understand it." This was a persistent theme in the speeches and memoranda of the military and political leaders during the Vietnam war. As Baritz (1985:27) put it, the United States was consistently depicted as "Chosen to lead the world in public morality and to instruct it in political virtue." Beyond "containing" the communists, the goal of our presence in Vietnam was to make the Vietnamese people more like ourselves, with social and cultural institutions reflecting American concepts of morality and "progress."

This attitude is ubiquitous in the military (and in many civilian sectors as well) and continues to be projected onto other people and other nations; but a few retired colonels, passed over for promotion to higher ranks, expressed sentiments similar to those of several in a survey of retired army generals in 1974: "We erroneously tried to impose the American system on a people who didn't want it, couldn't handle it and may lose because they tried it" (Kinnard 1977:92).

The great preponderance of active duty officers to whom I spoke do not hold these views, however. Adherents of an operational, "can do" philosophy, their tendency has been to confine the lessons of Vietnam to tactical problems, and to work on ways to redress what they perceive to be the real reasons for the military failure in Vietnam: too much interference from the political sector; biased media coverage, and a concomitant failure of the general population to support the war. Their sights have become directed towards achieving greater control of a wide range of decision-making factors pertaining to military matters—towards more influence over the media by restricting journalistic coverage of military maneuvers; towards redoubling efforts to use TV, radio, newspaper and other communicative means to bring the population around to military values and interests, towards curbing political interference with military matters once war has broken out; and, in the event of war, towards the "absolutist" aspiration of achieving military victory in a short, but all-out war.[5]

Two Structural Notes

There are two points I would like to make before specifying some of the contributions anthropologists can make to the subject of war and peace. First, there are responsible senior officers who are very concerned that the United States not become involved in ventures which it cannot effectively control—to become "bogged down" in another Vietnam, or have the military placed in the kind of vulnerable position the Marines found themselves in at the time of the terrorist attack on the Marine compound in Lebanon in 1983. A number of those I talked with felt that the political appointees in the Department of Defense are "hawkier" than the military when it comes to plans of an interventionist nature. A similar stance for restraint was taken by many military leaders after the Korean war as well; but their worry about being "bogged down" in another "Korea" did not prevent military personnel from being sent to Vietnam as advisors a mere six years later, or from remaining there in full force for 10 years after that. Clearly, aspects of the interventionist lessons of Korea and Vietnam, learned by some in the military leadership, have little utility if they are not also learned by civilian leadership (see Sarkesian 1986).

I see the military—in I.F. Stone's phrase (personal communication)— as "our brothers entrapped:" entrapped by a constricted pool of ideas emanating from our militarized foreign policies, by cultural values and socialization patterns that legitimize an ethnocentric world view, by conceptions of battlefield victory which originated in conditions very different from those of the nuclear era, and, perhaps most important, by the intrinsic characteristics of the nation-state.

Conclusion

There are diverse areas where anthropological insights can enrich and humanize the constructs of those who comprise the defense and foreign policy communities—the military and political sectors, the scientists, strategic analysts and scholars of international relations who have laid down the ground rules for thinking about war.

First, and perhaps most obvious, I think we need to redouble our efforts to instruct future generations of politicians and the general citizenry about the dangers of ethnocentrism in general, and ethnocentrism among super-powers in the nuclear age, in particular. Excessive interest in the well-being of one's own group or class or nation, coupled with failure to understand the roots of discontent among others, has been a factor in the world's greatest military travesties (Booth 1979). We also need to renew our efforts at dispelling the fears that people tend to have of people and social systems unlike their own. It was Ruth Benedict's (1946:15) view that to demand uniformity as a condition of respecting another individual or another nation is neurotic. "The tough-minded," she said, "are content with differences . . . Their goal is a world made safe for differences."

Second, anthropologists need to bring their expertise in regional studies to the attention of the plethora of those policy-makers who see the world in bi-polar terms. The world is abundant with examples of ethnic, religious, political and economic groups whose desires for social change transcend Soviet and American ideological or economic agendas. Moreover, not all of the law and order forces of the world can prevent the conflict and strife that emerges from internal and international, social and economic inequalities, or from the desire of people simply to retain their identities with some semblance of dignity. Our literature is rich with such examples, and we can bring them to bear on the discourse among policy makers on the causes of conflict and aggression among the world's countless peoples and cultures. William Beeman (1986), a consultant to the State Department during the Iranian hostage crisis a few years ago, has been urging anthropologists for a number of years to write about their understandings of other cultures in the prominent journals and periodicals read by members of the foreign policy community.

Finally, there are numerous interesting topics—normally the domain of political scientists, which could be substantially enriched by anthropological insights. Foster (1986:77) suggested that "The interplay between technology and ideology involved in the generation of war is a natural target for anthropological inquiry." Mandelbaum (1984:14), in suggesting that anthropologists can contribute to research on the basis of the United States and Soviet fears which propel the arms race, says:

> The fears aroused by the realities of target missiles are viewed by each side from different cultural perspectives and placed within differing social expectations. Anthropological studies of these differences will scarcely change the circumstances of nations in confrontation. But when circumstances and public opinion are altered during a major turning, such studies may be of considerable use, especially if they have already been widely discussed.

The insights of anthropologists may contribute to such a major turning of public opinion—or they may not. But I agree with Gerald Berreman (1980:12) who, commenting on a similar topic, said "I do not think we have much chance, but I think it is worth a try for we have nothing to lose."

Notes

1. A version of this paper was presented at the 1986 annual meetings of the Kroeber Anthropological Society, at the University of California, Berkeley, 8 March 1986.

2. The reference is to Peter's theory that " . . . an individual within a hierarchy tends to rise to his or her level of incompetence." Upon promotion to that level, the individual "usually remains (there), frustrating co-workers, eroding the efficiency of the organization, or at the highest level, leading the country into one disaster after another."

3. According to Janowitz, "absolutists" have always been in the majority of the military; but they were eclipsed during the Vietnam war by "pragmatists" in both civilian and military sectors. General Maxwell Taylor is depicted by Janowitz as belonging to the pragmatic "school."

4. The reference is to the National Security Council paper—entitled "NSC–68"—drawn up by State Department and Defense Department officials during the Truman administration. NSC–68 called for extensive changes in United

States foreign policy, including a dramatic build-up of American and Western European military arsenals. For details, see "NSC–68: A Report to the National Security Council by the Executive Secretary on United States Objectives and Programs for National Security," in the *U.S. Naval War College Review* (14 April 1950).

5. I have many statements to this effect in my interview notes, and other sources (for example, Pentagon newsletters, papers and speeches of military officers, and the like).

References Cited

Ambrose, S. 1972. The Military and American Society: An Overview. In *The Military and American Society: Essays and Readings*. S. Ambrose and J.A. Barber, Jr., eds., New York: Free Press.

Baritz, L. 1985. *Backfire*. New York: William Morrow.

Barnet, R. 1972. *The Roots of War*. New York: Atheneum.

Beeman, W.O. 1986. Conflict and Belief in American Foreign Policy. In *Peace and War: Cross Cultural Perspectives*. M.L. Foster and R.A. Rubinstein, eds., New Brunswick, NJ: Transaction Books, Pp. 333–342.

Benedict, R. 1946. *The Chrysanthemum and the Sword: Patterns of Japanese Culture*. Boston: Houghton Mifflin.

Berreman, G. 1980. Are Human Rights Merely A Politicized Luxury in the World Today? *Anthropology and Humanism Quarterly* 5(1):2–13.

Booth, K. 1979. *Strategy and Ethnocentrism*. New York: Holmes and Meier.

Bunzel, R. and A. Parsons 1963. Anthropology and World Affairs as Seen by U.S.A. Associates: Report on Regional Conferences. *Current Anthropology* 5:430, 437–442.

Foster, M.L. 1986. Is War Necessary? In *Peace and War: Cross Cultural Perspectives*. M.L. Foster and R.A. Rubinstein, eds., New Brunswick, NJ: Transaction Books, Pp. 71–78.

Janowitz, M. 1960. *The Professional Soldier*. New York: The Free Press.

Mandelbaum, D. 1984. Anthropology for the Nuclear Age. *Bulletin of the Atomic Scientists* 40(6):11–15.

Mills, C.W. 1956. *The Power Elite*. New York: Oxford University Press.

Peter, L.J. 1969. *The Peter Principle*. New York: William Morrow.

Sarkesian, S. 1986. The Nature of War and the American Military Profession. In *Peace and War: Cross Cultural Perspectives*. M.L. Foster and R.A. Rubinstein, eds., New Brunswick, NJ: Transaction Books, Pp. 209–222.

Truman, H.S. 1956. *Harry Truman: Memoirs, Vol. 2.: Years of Trial and Hope*. New York: Doubleday.

Yarmolinsky, A. 1971. *The Military Establishment*. New York: Harper and Row.

6 / Achieving Social Competence in the Navy Community

Linda Pulliam

The following article by Linda Pulliam complements earlier articles by providing an insider's view of the symbols and values of military life, and by giving an account of how these are shaped by social processes. Her methodological approach marks a point on a continuum which proceeds from comparisons of secondary data (Gold-schmidt), through closer inspection of primary sources, like newspaper accounts and literature (Worsley), and in-depth interviewing of people (Bateson and Brasset) to participant observation, perhaps the major anthropological research method. Although there are many technical differences among these various methodological approaches—like whether or not one believes it is possible to discover "objective facts" which are distinct from a society's values—each produces information that is important for better understanding societies. One argument of this book is that it is important to integrate all of these approaches into a coherent account, and to reconcile the information produced by each. Each method needs to be valued for the level of information that it provides. Brasset describes the role of values in military strategic thinking. In this paper, Pulliam describes the social processes through which these values are fostered and maintained by the military community. Her account helps us understand the tensions among ways of acting in the military community—just as Bateson described similar tensions in Iran. Pulliam's discussion of the relations among naval personnel of various ranks anticipates Anderson's discussion of the avoidance of class-based conflict in the Philippines. Like Bateson, Brasset, and Potter, Pulliam suggests that one of the important roles that anthropologists can play in relation to international security analysis is that of a "culture broker." By interpreting the cultural and social world of societies with which the international security community must deal, the anthropologist can help keep international security discussions from becoming hopelessly mired in ethnocentric images of the other.—The Editors

In order to be judged a competent member of a group, an individual must not only be able to operate in a manner acceptable to its members but must also understand the cognitive principles by which its members construct the world.[1] A newcomer to a group must understand why members act as they do and accept their world view as "the way things are" if he is to be successful as a group member. Yet we know little about the actual process by which newcomers discover and acquire the rules of behavior and the underlying cognitive principles of group members.

This paper reveals the process by which I discovered the rules and principles guiding behavior of United States Navy wives during interaction in the Navy community. This action became necessary when I married a naval officer and found that both Navy personnel and their wives expected me to act without questioning this fully institutionalized role.

I felt my primary identity to be "social scientist" and was surprised that this identity was totally disregarded by other wives as well as the officers working with my husband. Unable to make sense of the expectations placed on me as well as the behavior I observed, I began a journal recording my observations and experiences in hopes of making sense of this foreign community.

Methodological Considerations and Procedure

As anthropologists in greater numbers begin to investigate American society, it is likely we will have opportunities to investigate groups of which we are members, or which we would like to join as members. Reporting on a setting in which one is a member is not a new approach. Hayano (1979:101) notes the advantages of such studies and comments, "Subjectivism and personal involvement need not necessarily be methodological 'problems,' but can be assets to deepen ethnographic understanding."

A number of social scientists have argued in favor of personal involvement of membership in the community one studies. In this way, the researcher has a unique opportunity to contribute both a highly personal knowledge of a community not available to the participant-observer, together with an explanation set within a theoretical frame-

work familiar to her colleagues. Thus the researcher becomes a link
between the world of the member and the world of social scientists.

Bittner (1983:151–153) argues against the assumption that a field-
worker can become just like another member since the circumstances
of members' lives are not the actual circumstances of her life. Emerson
(1983:105) agrees that even the experience of the member-researcher
is not exactly like that of the ordinary member. However, he points
out that it provides an experience much closer to that of the ordinary
member than other modes of research provide.

Whether or not the researcher-member can experience the community
in the same way as ordinary members also depends on whether he
can sustain a dual allegiance to the community of members and the
community of researchers. If the community is one whose principles
view intellectual analysis and independent thought as inconsequential
or even detrimental to the group, and the researcher is a member of
that group, she will have to determine if she can withstand the so-
ciocultural pressures to adopt that attitude. Full membership and the
conduct of research may create a conflict of interests. One may have
to concede that while approximating membership, one is not exactly
like other ordinary members.

The alternative is to relinquish one's role as researcher and become
the phenomenon (Mehan 1975:226–229). In this case, one will never
report back to the world of social scientists. For if one is not a
researcher, then he has no need to record, analyze, or report on the
community to non-members.

Nevertheless, one must calculate the risk and personal costs of doing
research as a researcher-member. A researcher-member does not wear
the emotional armor that a participant-observer does. He is open to
experiencing, and part of the human experience is feeling both positive
and negative emotions. Things happen to him, not just around him.
He must not only negotiate finding out about the group, but must
negotiate his place within the group.

The researcher-member struggles with a multi-layered approach to
knowing, including both rational and emotional elements. And even
in reporting back to fellow social scientists, he opens himself to "psy-
choanalysis" by his readers or audience through necessary self-disclo-
sure.

Because of my own personal background, I found it extremely difficult to perform competently as a Navy wife. That is why in doing
this study, I first focused on what it is one needs to know or do in
order to operate as a competent Navy member.

I reviewed the data—my journal entries and correspondence—for
evidence of rules that seemed to govern the setting. By searching for

major themes and recurring events, I constructed a list of rules which members recognized. I then looked for further confirmation of their existence in my future interactions with the Navy community. In addition, I informally questioned two other wives to see if they agreed that these were operative rules.

From these rules I abstracted general principles by noting similar features of the rules. Principles are broader than rules and give the member general guidelines to follow in diverse settings. For example, a rule might state: when the ship arrives in port, the Captain's wife (the CO's wife) is always the first to board and is escorted by a junior officer. The general principle under which this rule falls is: extreme deference is shown to the CO's wife. By knowing only the rule, the member will only be able to perform competently at ship arrivals. But by knowing the principle, she will be able to perform in whatever setting she again encounters the CO's wife.

It is critically important to the newcomer that she recognize the cognitive principles underlying the rules. This skill involves moving from concrete observable behavior to inferences about the relationships of certain rules and the abstract features common to them.

This paper presents the principles which govern interaction of officers' wives in the Navy community and the process through which these principles were discovered and which newcomers must go through in order to be considered competent members.

The Discovery of Rules and General Principles

Rules are instructions to behave in a particular way (Spradley 1972:14), which insure uniform behavior and thus, predictable behavior (Spiro 1973:106).

But rules do not instruct one how to think or believe; they only prescribe outward, observable behavior. Yet being socially competent in a culture requires more than just performing acceptable behaviors; one must also recognize the underlying cognitive principles of group members which generate appropriate behavior in new situations.

This is consistent with the classic definition of culture proposed by Goodenough (1957:167):

> A society's culture consists of whatever it is one has to know or believe in order to operate in a manner acceptable to its members . . . It is the forms of things that people have in their minds, their models for perceiving, relating, and otherwise interpreting them.

Members need to know not only how to perform competently but also how to conceptualize their world in a way acceptable to other members. Outward behavior and cognitive understanding are equally important.

Underlying the rules are cognitive principles; a way of seeing the world that provides both a rationale for the rules and criteria for rule construction. Rules may be thought of as prescriptions—they prescribe outward behavior—while principles are assumptions about how the world works.

These principles guide the enactment of appropriate behavior in new and diverse settings. Instead of trying to second-guess the inter-action from moment to moment, the new member can adopt a more relaxed attitude toward interaction once she knows that she shares the general assumptions of the group, or at least can act as if she does.

The following list of principles consists of those things which new-comers need to know or believe in order to operate successfully as Navy wives. This list is not all inclusive, nor could it ever be because one's prior experiences determine what it is one needs to know in a new environment. Nor is this list meant to imply that behavior always reflects these principles. But even the deviant member tacitly acknowl-edges the existence of these principles.

These principles are derived from those which govern officers' in-teraction. In many instances they are the same for officers and wives.

Principles Governing the Interaction of Officers' Wives Within the Navy Community

1. *A Navy wife's function is to serve as a support system for her husband in performing his military role.* Examples of support: meeting ships; maintaining uniforms; visiting the ship when husband is on duty (every third or fourth night); sending forgotten items overseas; maintaining the home well for visitors; attending social events; and for senior wives, hosting social events.

2. *A wife is an extension of her husband and his rank, and her behavior reflects on him, his command, and the Navy.* Wives are labeled according to function (staff wives, Airdale wives), according to ship (Buchanan wives, Vinson wives), or according to rank (CO's wife, XO's wife, Chap's wife, Chief's wife).

3. *Husbands are in command of their families, and therefore, "allow" and "permit" the activities of their wives and children.* Husbands may be criticized for their wives' inappropriate behavior since it is assumed that they permitted it to happen. Complaining about what one's husband

"lets" her do is acceptable since it demonstrates that their household operates in the acceptable chain of command.

4. *The needs of the Navy always come before personal needs. Loyalty to the group comes before loyalty to spouse.* Example: leaving the Navy to have more time with one's family is not looked upon kindly by other officers. However, divorcing because the wife objects to the amount of time spent apart is acceptable, and even laudable.

5. *Status within the group is solely dependent on one's husband's rank and function.* Such status is the primary consideration in all interaction. Persons are treated with the deference due their status and not on the basis of personal attributes such as age, occupation, talents, or social background.

A. Neither an officer nor his wife should fraternize (socialize) with enlisted personnel and their wives.

B. Junior officers (Ensign; Lt.j.g.; Lt.) and their wives do not socialize with senior officers (Commanders, Captains, Admirals) and their wives except at official command functions.

C. Deference is shown to wives whose husbands rank higher than your husband. Extreme deference is shown to the CO's wife. However, demanding deference because of your rank is poor form. Examples of deference: complying with all requests as far as possible; never expressing any disagreement; letting the senior wife make suggestions for activities and going along with them; making sure the senior wife is served and seated first at parties.

6. *Social events are obligatory for both the officer and his wife, and are conducted according to established protocol.*

A. Guests should arrive at the exact time stated on the invitation (which actually is more an announcement since R.S.V.P's never appear on them because one's presence is assumed).

B. Guests should not leave at their own discretion but wait until the most senior officer and his wife leave.

C. Social events are usually hosted by the CO and his wife. Other officers and their wives should not extend social invitations to the group unless they have the permission from the CO and his wife. However, if an occasion dictates that another officer should host a party, he cannot refuse, as in the case of celebrating promotions.

D. A married officer should not attend a social function alone unless his wife has a compelling reason for being absent (for example, is in the hospital; is at her mother's funeral). Nor does a wife not attend a wives' function without an equally justifiable excuse. (Separate wives' events are not held while the men are in port when the couples' presence is required at events.)

7. *All behavior should be appropriate for one's rank and in harmony with other group members.* Example: conservative clothing should be chosen in relation to what the other wives are wearing. For an evening party to which the CO's wife is wearing a blazer and pants, a long sleeved tailored shirt with dress pants would be appropriate for a junior wife. A red jumpsuit with big earrings, or a skirt would not be.

8. *Independent action which does not consider the other group members is frowned upon.* One must operate as a member of the group, not as an individual. Example: wives going to meet their husbands in foreign ports should make their plans together, coordinate their schedules, stay at the same hotel, fly on the same flight. The purpose of the trip is to reunite the group, not individual couples. Therefore, staying apart from the rest of the group is frowned upon.

9. *Group harmony is valued over individual expression.* Maintaining a group consciousness is one of the main tasks of social interaction. Disagreements are not openly expressed. Conversation is limited to neutral, non-controversial topics.

A. Common topics are:

1. *Shopping*—things purchased; where; your enthusiasm for shopping; upcoming purchases; past shopping trips.

2. *Children*—especially stories illustrating how you as a mother uphold values appropriate to a military family. Also child-related topics such as Cub Scouts, soccer team, schools, day care, labor and delivery of babies.

3. *Husbands*—especially stories which illustrate your husband's dedication to career at expense of family life. (Complaining about your husband's poor performance at home is tantamount to praising his dedication to work.)

4. *Household activities*—cooking, arts and crafts, cleaning, caring for children which show one's devotion to one's role as support system.

5. *Moving*—different Navy communities; moving sales; cost of housing; packing out; anticipation of the move; logistics of cross country drives.

B. Taboo topics include:

1. *Your interest in a career.* While many wives have jobs, especially part-time ones, they do not have careers. Moving every two years does not permit a wife to develop a career track. Also, expressing an interest in a career may be seen as detrimental to the joint career since it would impair the woman's ability to serve as support system. The needs of the Navy come first.

2. *Stories about your husband* which may make people suspect he puts your marriage before his work or the needs of the Navy.

3. *Sexual behavior* or "liberal" attitudes towards sex. Examples: how to cope with sexual frustration during deployments; a woman taking the initiative in sexual relations.

4. *Overt derogatory remarks* about other group members. (This includes nonverbal messages which contradict a benign verbal statement.)

5. *Complaints* about being left alone during deployments or having to move. Navy wives are supposed to be tough and stoic, and "do what they have to do," which includes everything from having babies alone to burying the dog. In case of moves, it may mean uprooting children from schools and friends, and giving up a job. But the good Navy wife does it all.

6. *Ship's business.* This is done not because women are incapable of understanding men's work, but because national security regulations stipulate that personnel do not discuss work matters with those who have no "need to know." Even if a wife did have some information, she would not jeopardize her husband's job by revealing it to others.

7. *Prostitutes.* Although the wives are aware of "foreign women," and even talk around the subject occasionally, they do not discuss the problem openly. The double standard is assumed and accepted by some wives. Others ignore the problem.

To make explicit the way in which I decided that each of these principles characterized the thinking of group members and guided their behavior, Table 1 outlines the steps in the process of achieving social competence in a new group as defined by my experience with the Navy. For conceptual purposes, I outlined the process in sequential steps, but in reality, steps may overlap or coincide.

Initially I had no sense of the rules or principles operating in the community I had just entered. I was aware that things were "not as usual," that this community was somehow different than other groups of people I had associated with, but I had only vague perceptions of what the differences were. I naively surmised that Navy people were perhaps unaware of how the rest of the world lived, and perhaps I could expose them to alternate ways of being and doing. (So much for recognizing my own ethnocentrism.)

I also was prone to attribute individual behavior to personality traits or psychological problems. If someone complained about being obligated to act in a certain way, I thought they were lacking in assertiveness. If someone seemed to fear the Military Police, it was because they had a personal problem in relating to authority.

In the beginning then, I was not aware of rules as such, but only knew I was in a community that was not operating in a manner I was used to. During this time I made many errors, but I did not yet realize they were errors. However, I soon began to recognize the regularities in some of the group's behavior. After seeing repeated instances of a behavior, I began to hypothesize some rules. Some of these rules were quite easy to infer.

Observing that officers' wives lined up according to rank to board the ship when it returns from deployment, and that they board before enlisted wives, makes it easy to assume there is a rule that wives board the ship according to their husbands' rank. When this same ritual is observed on other ships as well, one can safely assume this is a widely accepted rule.

In addition to hypothesizing from observation of others, I also discovered rules through breaching them and encountering negative reactions from other group members. For example, when making a trip to Hong Kong, a city I had visited previously, I planned to stop in Japan first and visit friends I had known when living there. Although the ship originally had planned on stopping there, it was uncertain whether it would still do so. I decided to go anyway since my plans were already made. From Japan, I would proceed to Hong Kong where I had reserved a room at a hotel on an island remote from where the rest of the group would be staying.

Initially I was asked if I planned on going on the same flight as the other wives. I told them I was going to Japan first, leaving a week before them. To this statement the XO's wife (second in command) reacted by saying: "I'm not the kind of woman who would go to a foreign country without my husband being there." ("Kind of woman" was said in the tone of voice used when referring to prostitutes.) I countered that I had no qualms about traveling alone, although I sensed the disapproval in her voice.

I was also questioned about where we were planning to stay in Hong Kong. Upon revealing we were not staying at the same hotel as everyone else, I was asked why we selected a different hotel. I said it was a sentimental place and spoke of how anxious I was to see my husband. The other women talked about where they were going shopping and what tours they were going to take together. No one mentioned being anxious to see her husband, assuming that he would go along with her plans. It was clear that the rest of the group would be seeing a lot of each other in Hong Kong.

I attributed all of this to insecurities about being alone. I was certain that my judgment was correct when I further observed that the wives were anxious about how they would get from the Hong Kong airport to their hotel, even though they would all be traveling together. In fact, wives from six ships would all be invading the city together and staying at the same hotel so I could not understand their anxiety.

Even though I explained the airport greeting system to the wives, they continued to express uncertainty about getting from the airport to their hotel. Therefore, I concluded that their behavior was due to a lack of confidence about operating independently.

When the CO's wife said that the wives would stay in the hotel and wait for the men to come there, I told her how easy it was to take the subway to the pier to greet the ship. I myself planned on doing that. However, the CO's wife said it would be better if the wives waited at the hotel. I again hypothesized that the wives were afraid to try taking the subway to the pier. This made sense to me in light of their anxiety in getting from the airport to the hotel.

When I returned from Hong Kong, I was called by both the CO's and XO's wives who both expressed dismay that they had not seen us in Hong Kong. I politely told them that I knew I could visit with them anytime in San Diego, but I could only see my husband for that one week out of seven and a half months, so wanted to spend that time alone with him. They talked about their meals with other officers and wives, their shopping trips, and the tours they had gone on together.

They said that they assumed we had "stayed to ourselves" because we were newlyweds but wondered why we hadn't joined them for at least part of the time. They continued to press me for details of what we had done "off by ourselves." I resented the questioning and felt it was an invasion of my personal life. However, I knew I couldn't be rude to these wives without it having repercussions for my husband.

It was a long time before I made sense of these events. Gradually from conversations with the wives and stories related by my husband, I came to understand that the worst social offense is not to function as a member of the group. People who did so were referred to as "loners," although by my definition I did not agree. I came to understand that our behavior in Hong Kong had been interpreted as antisocial behavior. I also realized that this goes against the needs of the Navy because in wartime sailors must be able to function as a cohesive group. Behavior in peacetime is practice for wartime.

However, I still do not know how to account for the wives' concern about getting to their Hong Kong hotel, even though they had been told that someone from the hotel would greet them and put them in a hotel limousine. It is possible that my original assumption was correct. The culture of the Navy lulls people into being dependent on it to take care of them. The occasions when independent action is required are few. Therefore, a need to take care of oneself, even with a group of other women, may seem threatening. I had observed similar reactions in Japan whenever certain officers or their wives planned to make trips off Base.

If I had been a different kind of wife, more anxious to show group belonging, I might have perceived the group's messages sooner. I might have jumped at the chance to be part of the group when asked if I was taking the same flight as the other wives. Or if I was not used to acting alone, perhaps I would have welcomed the company of other wives. But because of my independent nature, it took a longer time to discern the implicit rules for port visits. In not recognizing them, I breached the rules and experienced the negative reactions of the group.

After further reflection, I did not fault the wives for their prying. It is their duty to orient new wives and guide them in enacting appropriate behavior. They were only doing their job. In an occupation where a 24 hour per day commitment is required, there is little distinction between personal and professional life.

Learning the rules was made more difficult because of the amount of information I had to process simultaneously. Not being able to attend to multiple phenomena, I sometimes failed to recognize all the rules that were expressed in one interaction. For example, consider the following incident from my journal:

We had to go to a Hail and Farewell at the CO's house today. I wore . . . what I thought would be appropriate for a Sunday brunch. It was a cotton peasant blouse with a silk peasant skirt and flat sandals. I tied my hair back with a ribbon and wore gold hoop earrings. When we arrived, the CO's wife greeted me by saying: "You've got a skirt on!" She repeated this and then told me they are a very informal group and I didn't need to dress up. She was wearing walking shorts as were all the other women. Then the XO's wife came over and said to me in an indignant voice: "A skirt! Didn't your husband tell you what to wear?!" I assured everyone I was comfortable but that didn't seem to satisfy them.

My first reaction to this incident was that there was some kind of clothing rule which I had broken. But in attending to that rule, I at first missed the fact that there were a few other rules embedded in this incident. First, the fact that we "had to go" implies I had already learned that social events were obligatory. Second, the XO's wife's remark, "Didn't your husband tell you what to wear?!" inferred that my husband was in some way responsible for my behavior and that my dress reflected on him. Third, the information that *they* were an informal *group,* and the observation that all the women were dressed similarly should have been signals to me that group homogeneity was very important.

Since I was new to this group, I interpreted this incident as meaning that one would not wear skirts to Navy brunches and that the other women felt I was too dressed up for the event. Furthermore, I didn't understand why anyone should remark on my clothing. In my experience in the civilian world, if someone wears something different than the other guests, no one would call attention to it in the way that these women did. It was only after repeated incidents, and more breaching, that I was able to assimilate all the information that I had received and define the operative rule: one should dress conservatively and in relation to what the other wives are wearing. If in doubt, one should call the other women prior to each event to see what everyone will be wearing.

I came to discover rules then in two ways: either through observation of others' behavior, or though breaching them and experiencing the negative reactions of others. Gradually I became aware of similar themes or assumptions in several of the rules. In this way I was able to abstract a general principle from a set of specific rules. In so doing, I found that it was much easier to deal with new situations.

But does the existence of prevailing assumptions, the taken-for-granted way of perceiving the world, mean that everyone acts in accordance with them? Does everyone accept them as "the facts of life?"

From my observations this was clearly not so. Although everyone tacitly acknowledged the existence of the principles listed here, there were at least several types of responses to the principles. Some women completely accepted them as natural and normal, and the standard against which all other behavior was judged. Others resisted the principles and questioned their validity. In between these two extremes were inconsistent and ambiguous responses.

My next step, then, was to chart out the various responses I had observed during interaction with eighteen women. Some of these responses appear in Table 1 as direct quotes which I heard during conversation. Others are paraphrases of what I heard or synthesize statements of a few wives whose responses were similar.

In Table 1 I want to illustrate each response in the words of a member. I also name each type of response with a general term that characterizes a set of responses. While I occasionally noted a response that did not fall into any of these categories, they were too few to merit charting, hence this is not an all-inclusive list.

Although some members may not perform as ideal wives, they nevertheless give performances which are adequate to sustain membership in the group. They do this by at least appearing to share the cognitive principles of the group. However, a definite disregard for the principles, as demonstrated by unacceptable responses, is not tolerated by other members, and the deviant member eventually leaves the group through divorce or her husband's resignation. However, as long as one demonstrates a good faith effort to perform, she may still be regarded as a member even though her performance falls short of the ideal. Social competence might then be defined as the ability to maintain group membership rather than to give an ideal performance.

When the newcomer observes these various responses it is critical that she be able to identify which ones are acceptable to the rest of the group, lest she make the mistake of imitating a wife who responds unacceptably. If she aspires to be an ideal member, it is important that she be able to identify which of the acceptable responses is the ideal one.

The fifth and final step in the process of achieving social competence is demonstrating the acquisition of the "correct" cognitive principles and enacting acceptable behavior. It was this final step I was unable to take because of a conflict with my prior beliefs. This reflects the simple fact that the more congruent the group's principles are with those already held by a new member, the more likely it is that the newcomer will be successful in the group.

For me, actually accepting the group's world view as "the way things are" was impeded by my own strong beliefs in values which conflicted with those of the Navy community. Three fundamental conflicts which I defined were: 1) my belief in tolerance versus the moral absolutism I observed in the Navy; 2) my belief in autonomy: the right for each person to choose a course of action after considering all alternatives, versus the Navy's value of unquestioning obedience to authority; and 3) my belief that all persons are of equal value versus the Navy's way of relating to persons as statuses and treating them accordingly, assigning more value to some and little value to others.

Thus, moral absolutism, obedience to authority, and an emphasis on status as a criteria of personal worth are not only values held by military men at work, but also by their families, the auxiliary military members. Loyalty to these values results in a profound dislike for those American citizens who do not enact unquestioning obedience to authority. Members of peace groups are especially suspect since they not only question authority, but do not believe in the American Way as defined by the military community. Nor do they demonstrate the proper respect for high-ranking political officials whose status should automatically warrant it.

Conversely, the military value system is conducive to waging war in the name of "truth," "just causes" and "defending the American Way." It teaches a knee-jerk response to stripes and brass and subtle

TABLE 1: TYPICAL RESPONSES TO PRINCIPLES OF SOCIAL INTERACTION

PRINCIPLE	THE IDEAL RESPONSE	THE DUTIFUL RESPONSE	THE SOCIAL CLIMBER'S RESPONSE	THE ALTERNATIVE MOTIVE RESPONSE	THE MINIMAL RESPONSE	THE UNACCEPTABLE RESPONSE
I. Wife's function is to serve as a support system.	I love being my husband's partner in the Navy. I'm glad to help out.	I have to help my husband. That's my job.	I'll support my husband so we can move up in rank.	By helping my husband, I can maintain my marriage.	I'll offer just enough support to avoid criticism from others.	The Navy isn't paying ME - why should I perform support functions?
II. Wives are extensions of husbands' ranks.	I'm so proud and happy to be the wife of an officer. It impresses other people.	Having married an officer, I accept my place in life as a Navy wife.	My rank gives me social power. Lower ranking wives look up to me, and it helps me get what I want.	My husband's rank gives me privileges so I will accept being treated as his extension.	I won't object when I'm referred to by my husband's rank but I won't promote people thinking of me that way.	I'm a person in my own right with my own accomplishments and I want to be treated as such.
III. Husbands are in command of their families.	I like a strong man. I want my husband to be head of our household.	Men are heads of the house. That's the way it's supposed to be.	With my husband as head of the house, we can get ahead financially.	I can maintain peace at home if I let my man think he's the head of the house.	I'll support the image of my husband as head of the house but in reality we're equal partners.	This is an archaic notion and I don't mind saying so.
IV. Needs of the Navy come before personal needs.	Our career is serving our country and I'm proud to do it.	Duty comes first: that's a fact of life I can do nothing about.	That's what you have to do to make Admiral.	It's OK because it keeps us from focusing on our marriage too much.	I'll tolerate it to a degree but I don't agree that the Navy should always come first.	Sometimes my personal needs come first and the Navy can wait.

V. Status is primary consideration & people are treated accordingly.	It's important to know a person's rank so you know how to relate to them.	It's important to know people's rank because that's how the Navy works.	If you're going to get ahead you have to know who can help you and who's not worth your time.	It's nice to be able to assess which type of individuals are top performers.	I won't insult higher ranked people nor snub lower ranked but I'm also interested in others as people not statuses.	It doesn't matter to me what rank anyone is. I'm as worthwhile as others.
VI. Social events are obligatory and conducted according to established protocol.	It's fun to get together as often as possible. I enjoy all the traditions of the Navy.	You do what you have to do. Sometimes I like it & sometimes not. It's good to have set ways of doing things.	Socializing is necessary for moving up. It's good to be seen. You must also show you know the correct way of doing things.	I'm not doing this because of the Navy. I'm a real "people person" & love socializing. I like guidelines for what I'm supposed to do.	I'll attend most events but miss a few. I'll follow protocol when it's not too inconvenient.	I don't care to socialize with this group and often miss events. I think their little rules are silly.
VII, VIII, and IX. - The HARMONY PRINCIPLES One must behave in harmony with the group.	I wouldn't want to draw attention to myself. I want to be like the other wives. I find a lot of support & understanding in this group.	The Navy way is to fit in. I do what I'm supposed to do.	By showing how well I fit in the group, I will be seen as an ideal wife which will help our career.	I don't like doing things by myself or making decisions alone, so I'll try to fit in with the group.	I'll go along when it doesn't conflict with my own values or plans, but at times I act differently than the group.	I'm an individual with my own opinions & ways of doing things. I make my own decisions and follow my own star.

disregard for those occupying low statuses. Becoming a competent member of the military community entails adopting attitudes that are counter-productive in seeking peaceful solutions to conflicts.

Notes

1. An earlier version of this paper was presented at the annual meeting of the Southwestern Anthropological Association, Las Vegas, Nevada, March, 1986.

References Cited

Bittner, E. 1983. Realism in Field Research. In *Contemporary Field Research.* R. Emerson, ed., Boston: Little, Brown. Pp. 149–155.

Emerson, R. 1983. Introduction, Part III. In *Contemporary Field Research.* R. Emerson, ed., Boston: Little, Brown, Pp. 175–189.

Goodenough, W. 1957. Cultural Anthropology and Linguistics. In *Report of the Seventh Annual Round Table Meeting on Linguistics and Language Study.* P.L. Garvin, ed., Washington, DC: Georgetown University Monograph Series, No. 9, Pp. 167–173.

Hayano, D. 1979. Auto-ethnography: Paradigms, Problems, and Prospects. *Human Organization* 38:99–104.

Spiro, M.E. 1972. Cognition in Culture and Personality. In *Culture and Cognition: Rules, Maps, and Plans.* J. Spradley, ed., New York: Chandler, Pp. 100–110.

Spradley, J. 1972. Foundations of Cultural Knowledge. In *Culture and Cognition: Rules, Maps, and Plans.* J. Spradley, ed., New York: Chandler, Pp. 3–38.

7 / Loyal Citizens of the Republic: Morality, Violence, and Popular Support for the IRA and INLA in a Northern Irish Ghetto

Jeffrey A. Sluka

Jeffrey Sluka directly confronts the important role played by moral ideologies in the social dynamics of conflict. Like Pulliam, Sluka reports research based on participant observation, and calls into question the too easy distinction between facts and values in situations of conflict. He argues that the relationship between partisans and the communities that support them is a moral one, and that anthropologists have an obligation to present and interpret that relationship in the service of improving our understanding of situations of conflict. Sluka suggests that by scrutinizing these moral relationships anthropologists can help distinguish in a principled way between guerrilla and terrorist activities. In this way, he makes the important point that sustained commitment to a cause, including violent conflict, need not reflect the breakdown of social and economic systems, but may instead result from the affirmation of moral values. In common with other contributors to this book, he shows that it is important to distinguish between the moral and pragmatic contexts for conflict and violence and to treat both as important when seeking to improve our understanding of conflict and peace. Like Bateson, Sluka shows that it is dangerous to assume that there is homogeneity in the moral frames of the community. As in Iran, competing values coexist; yet, at a particular time one or the other set of values will be ascendant. His description of two contrasting moral frames in an Irish community (and of the shades of opinion between them) and of how these are used in the "discourse of legitimacy" provides important insights into the social dynamics of conflict. —The Editors

One of the most important contributions political anthropologists have made to our understanding of social conflict is that extreme and violent political behavior cannot be dismissed as exceptional, irrational, immoral, meaningless, a sign of social pathology, or the result of either the actions of "evil men" or the putative presence of "violent instincts."[1] Just as it was once believed that social conflict and violence were inherently dysfunctional or a sign of social pathology, today violence is still sometimes viewed as being inherently immoral and the result of either the failure of moral systems or a breakdown in social morality. However, anthropologists such as Gluckman (1955), Coser (1956), and Cohen (1969, 1974) have shown that conflict and violence are not always the result of a lack or breakdown of morality, and that in fact both the occurrence of conflict and violence and the forms they take are often closely related to the moral ideologies of the conflicting parties. Conflict and violence may be the result of rational and pragmatic appraisals of moral obligations, and they may represent an affirmation of the legitimacy of moral systems rather than a sign of their breakdown. While in some contexts moral values, obligations, and constraints may serve to bind individuals and groups together, in other contexts they may also serve to divide them into conflicting parties.

This paper addresses the general subject of the relationship between morality and political violence, with reference to the contemporary conflict in Northern Ireland. It is derived from a much larger study of the social dynamics of popular support for the Provisional Irish Republican Army (PIRA or IRA) and Irish National Liberation Army (INLA) in Divis Flats—a Catholic-Nationalist ghetto on the Falls Road in Belfast (Sluka 1986). The research from which the data derive was conducted over an eleven month period in 1981–82, and was based on participant-observation and interviews with 76 of the households in the community.

I argue that the relationship between guerrillas and the communities that support them is a moral one, and that the existence of this moral relationship provides criteria for differentiating between groups that should properly be defined as "guerrillas" and those that should be properly defined as "terrorists." I argue further that, by elucidating the moral basis of the relationship between guerrillas and their popular support among civilian populations, political anthropologists can make at least two important contributions. First, they can contribute to a better understanding of guerrilla wars in general. Second, they can make an important political contribution by engaging in what C. Wright Mills (1959) referred to as "the politics of truth."

Divis Flats

Divis Flats is a high-rise public housing project built between 1966–72 as part of slum clearance and urban redevelopment of the inner-city areas of Belfast. The complex is part of the Catholic enclave known as the lower Falls Road, an inner-city area of nineteenth century row houses in an advanced state of physical deterioration.[2] Immediately to the north of Divis Flats is the Shankill Road and to the south is Sandy Row, both staunchly Loyalist Protestant working-class districts. The Divis complex contained some 850 flats, of which 755 were occupied, with a total population of approximately 2,400 residents, at the time the research was conducted.

Politically, Divis Flats has been a flashpoint for the political troubles in Northern Ireland, and it is one of the districts in Belfast that has been hardest hit by the violence that began in August 1969 and has been going on now for over 18 years. Today, the complex is reputed to be a political hotbed, an IRA fortress, an INLA stronghold, and one of the most violent housing estates in the United Kingdom. Patrols of heavily armed, combat-ready British troops were a common sight, and the entire complex was under constant surveillance from an army observation post located on top of Divis Tower—at thirty stories, the highest building in the district. Because the residents did not accept the police (Royal Ulster Constabulary, RUC) and were antagonistic towards them because they viewed them as a politically biased (pro-Unionist/Loyalist) and sectarian (97% Protestant) force, and because the police themselves feared being ambushed in the complex and were not highly motivated to help a community they believed strongly supported guerrillas trying to kill them, there was no "normal" police presence in Divis Flats.

Over the past 18 years, Divis residents have been assassinated by Loyalist extremists and attacked by Protestant mobs; they have been killed and injured by plastic bullets fired during riots and periods of civil disorder; they have been harassed, intimidated, arrested, interned, interrogated, and brutalized by policemen and British soldiers; they have been caught in crossfire between the Republican guerrillas, the Security Forces, and Loyalist paramilitary groups; and some of them have been beaten up or kneecapped by the IRA or INLA for engaging in antisocial or criminal activities. It is in this context that the question of the relationship between morality and political violence in Divis Flats must be considered.

The Politics of Support

Sociologist Frank Burton, who analyzed the dynamics of the IRA's legitimacy in a Catholic community in Belfast during the first part of the 1970s, noted that "community support for the IRA is a complex variable which is in danger of being portrayed as static" (1978:85). Burton argued that support for the IRA is based on the Catholic community's assessment of its basic legitimacy, and that this assessment was "floating" or dynamic rather than static, increasing and decreasing over time in response to specific events. He found that in the community he studied, outside of the third or so of the population that was staunchly Republican, there was a see-saw relationship between the rest of the people and the IRA that was sometimes tilted in favor of the IRA and sometimes tilted against them as a result of their own actions and the actions of the Security Forces and Loyalist paramilitary groups. Burton (1978:68) referred to this as an ongoing "debate" within the community between those who held various views on the IRA, but it should be noted that, at least in Divis Flats, the British government, the Security Forces, and the Catholic clergy are also actively involved in this debate. They interject their own views on political violence and the IRA as well.

Essentially, Burton found that the IRA was constrained by what its supporters and potential supporters in the community defined as acceptable political action. He found that the legitimacy of the IRA's role as defender of the community against the perceived threat of attacks by Protestant mobs, Loyalist paramilitary groups, and the Security Forces was accepted and rarely questioned, but there was disagreement and debate over the legitimacy of the IRA's offensive role. While defensive actions swayed popular support in favor of the IRA, offensive actions sometimes alienated support—particularly those that brought down a harsh reaction or "backlash" on the community from the Security Forces or Loyalist extremists, or those in which innocent lives were lost.

The politics of legitimacy and support for the IRA and INLA is essentially a politics of morality (Burton 1978:90–91). The debate centers on the issue of the morality of political violence and the fine line that exists in the public mind between violence that is considered legitimate or moral (for example, defensive violence) and that which is considered illegitimate or immoral (for example, offensive violence). Burton argued that there are two moral frames of reference at work in this debate. Republicans and those who are involved in or strongly support the IRA and INLA appeal to the sanctity of conscience and the moral right to use violence in a just war, and they tend to view the suffering, injuries, and deaths that result from the guerrilla campaign as tragic but unavoidable in the cause of Irish Nationalism. But others in the community endorse a more absolute morality that is not vitiated by the morality of a just war. This is essentially the traditional moral stance of the Catholic church concerning violence—namely, that it is almost never justified in any cause other than self-defense. Between these two moral frames of reference are many shades of opinion, and Burton argued that the claims and counterclaims made by those in the community holding these various views "represent ideological struggles within a discourse of legitimacy. They are political arguments striving for moral authority in the community" (Burton 1978:104).

IRA Morality and the Politics of Support

The IRA and INLA believe in all conscience that they are morally right because they are fighting a just war. They base their legitimacy on the "natural" legitimacy of a "freedom struggle" for national liberation. They argue that because they lack peaceful means of ending partition, and because it is only maintained by force, it is entirely moral to employ force to end it and achieve a united Ireland. The IRA and INLA absolve themselves of moral responsibility for the violence by placing that responsibility entirely in the hands of the British government.

The IRA admits that in a guerrilla war it is inevitable that some innocent civilians will be killed by both sides, but they also realize that to retain popular support they must keep such casualties to an absolute minimum. Today, both the IRA and INLA on the one hand and the British government and Security Forces on the other strive to garner as much propaganda capital as they can from deaths and injuries caused to innocent civilians by the other side. These claims are part of the long-standing argument as to whether the IRA and INLA are "terrorists" or "freedom fighters." The distinction has become blurred because the British government has made it a matter of policy to try to discredit the IRA and INLA by labeling them terrorists and criminals (for example, their "criminalization" policy).[3]

The suggestion that the IRA and INLA make substantial efforts to avoid civilian casualties because they realize that these alienate popular support is a "pragmatic" explanation of this phenomenon, and it is only rarely suggested that there could be a moral explanation for this. The IRA and INLA believe that in a just war it is moral to kill people who are clearly defined as military or political targets, but immoral to kill innocent civilians. The government, Security Forces, and other critics of IRA and INLA "terrorists" scoff at any suggestion that there could be morality among them. Their view is that the IRA and INLA are made up of men and women who are entirely unscrupulous, pragmatic, and immoral, for whom any means is justified by the ends for which they strive.

This is neither the view presented by the IRA and INLA, nor that which is held by the residents of Divis Flats. The IRA and INLA deny that they will resort to "any means" to achieve their goals, and they have a well-elaborated code of what may be termed "operational ethics." They believe that murder is wrong but make a distinction between murder and killing in a just war, and IRA Volunteers can be court-martialed for murder. The IRA and INLA choose to make efforts to avoid death and injury to innocent civilians (Catholic and Protestant alike), not simply because of a pragmatic realization that this alienates their popular support, but because they consider it to be not only practically but also morally wrong.

It is the policy of both the IRA and INLA to kill only those they publicly and clearly define as political or military targets—such as members of the Security Forces (soldiers and policemen), politicians, and judges—and to avoid killing or injuring innocent civilians. This policy is now well-established, though it was not as well-developed or as strictly enforced in the first half of the 1970s as it is today.[4] One of the most important lessons the guerrillas have learned is that casualties among innocent civilians generate a moral backlash among their supporters, while those among representatives of the government and members of the Security Forces are generally much more acceptable to the public.

A secret British military report intercepted and published by the IRA in 1979 noted that "there has been a marked trend towards attacks against Security Forces targets and away from actions which, by alienating public opinion, both within the Catholic community and outside the province, is politically damaging."[5] The report also noted that there is an IRA "military code of ethics" which means, for example, that there have been "few attacks on the families of either soldiers or the RUC." The IRA claimed that the main lesson to be learned from this report is that the picture of the IRA that the British government and the Security Forces project through the media is very different from that which is held privately by British military intelligence. Since the government and Security Forces publicly try to discredit the IRA by portraying them as immoral "terrorists" who have a callous disregard for innocent lives, this represents an important moral element in the politics of support for the Republican guerrillas.

The IRA and INLA have a morality exemplified in their policies and codes of conduct. They clearly differentiate between legitimate and non-legitimate targets, and they do not kill indiscriminately or for sectarian motives. They condemn antisocial and criminal behavior, and help to enforce community values and morality. They take responsibility publicly for both their successes and failures. And they are prepared to discipline their volunteers for transgressions against these codes and policies. In 1973 the IRA produced a manual of good conduct for its volunteers, which included recommendations concerning relations with the civilian population, and both the IRA and INLA now have "disciplinary departments" (Faligot 1983:69, 154).

With regard to civilian casualties, the IRA and INLA say that while some innocent casualties are unavoidable, in all of their operations the volunteers are responsible for taking reasonable precautions to prevent these from occurring.[6] One major way in which this is done is by giving warnings for bombs planted in public places. The IRA has a "strictly enforced code of warning procedure" (*Republican News,* 1 July 1982). Warnings must be given with sufficient time for the authorities to clear the area of civilians. The IRA generally gives these warnings to more than one source, because it claims that in the past the Security Forces have resorted to the counter insurgency "dirty trick" of trying to discredit it by deliberately delaying or withholding warnings so that innocent casualties result.

While the IRA and INLA place ultimate responsibility for all of the violence and bloodshed on the British presence in Ireland, they have policies of taking responsibility for all of their operations—both the successful and unsuccessful ones. After any operation that results in injuries or deaths to civilians, an inquiry is held. If the volunteers involved are found to have been negligent in taking precautions to avoid mistakes or accidental casualties, they are disciplined and in some cases court-martialed. When mistakes are made, the IRA and INLA generally issue public apologies in which they acknowledge responsibility and explain the circumstances. They also publicly deny responsibility for incidents which are attributed to them, but for which they are not responsible.

Support for the IRA and INLA in Divis Flats

Support for the IRA and INLA in Divis Flats was a complex variable. Some residents were for them, some against them, and some were "neutral"—neither condemning nor condoning them. Some supported only the IRA or only the INLA, some supported both of them simultaneously, and some did not support either of them. Some were glad to know that they were there, while others did not want them there at all. Some were proud of the guerrillas, some feared them, and many simply ignored them. But it was clear that there was a great deal of popular support for the IRA and INLA in Divis Flats.

In the interviews I conducted, I asked people directly if they supported the IRA or INLA. Forty-seven percent of those interviewed said that they did not support either the IRA or INLA, and 47% said that they did support either one or both of these organizations (of the remaining 6%, 4.5% had mixed feelings, which I included under the heading "don't know," and 1.5% preferred not to answer). But the politics of support for the guerrillas focused primarily on the defensive and civil roles they played in the community. When asked specifically about these roles, 84% of those interviewed said that they believed that the community did need the IRA and INLA to defend them against the threat of attacks by Protestant mobs, Loyalist paramilitary groups, and the Security Forces, and 77% said that they believed that the community needed them to play a "police" role and control at least the worst forms of antisocial or criminal behavior.

Clearly, the fear of attack, which served as the primary basis of IRA support when the current troubles erupted in 1969 (Coogan 1980), remains today—over 18 years later—the single most important source of popular support for the IRA and INLA in Divis Flats. This is despite the fact that there have been no attacks by Protestant mobs on Divis Flats, and relatively few on other Catholic districts, since the early 1970s.[7] In June 1970 and August 1971 the IRA provided armed defenses against attacks by Protestant mobs and Loyalist gunmen on Catholic districts in Belfast. These ended the mass sectarian attacks that had occurred regularly throughout the nineteenth century and intermittently since partition in Northern Ireland (Boyd 1969), and both firmly established the legitimacy of the IRA and swelled their ranks and support (MacStiofan 1975). In fact, the Provisional IRA took the Phoenix as their symbol, claiming that they arose again from the ashes of the Catholic streets burned down by Protestant mobs in Belfast in August 1969.

The fear of attacks by Protestant mobs remains an entrenched and historically validated element of Catholic political culture in Northern Ireland, and the threat of such attacks remains very real in the minds of Divis residents. They attribute the lack of such attacks to the presence of the IRA and INLA, and not to either a change in the attitudes of their Protestant neighbors or the presence of British army "peace-keepers."[8]

The social control role played by the IRA, and to a lesser extent by the INLA, also served as an important basis of support among the people of Divis Flats. The guerrillas try to control at least the worst forms of antisocial or criminal behavior, such as rape, mugging, organized crime, and drug dealing. In a ghetto community where there is no "normal" police presence, it was not surprising to find that over three-quarters of the residents believed that they needed the IRA and INLA to play a "police" role.

Finally, in the interviews I also asked people if they believed in general that the community did or did not need the IRA and INLA, and if they would prefer to have the guerrillas in or out of the complex. Three-quarters (74%) of those interviewed believed that Divis Flats does need the IRA and INLA, and said that they would rather have them there than not have them there. Only 19% believed that the community did not need the guerrillas, and said that they would rather not have them in the complex. Thus, while less than half (47%) of those interviewed openly admitted supporting the IRA or INLA, three-quarters (74%) believed that these organizations were needed by the community and admitted a feeling of reassurance that they were present and active in the complex.[9]

Attitudes Towards Political Violence

Concerning the morality and legitimacy of political violence, there was a near-universal conviction among Divis residents that violence is probably inherently evil and should therefore be avoided if at all possible. However, 55% of those interviewed believed that it was right to resort to armed struggle to achieve a united Ireland, and only 32% said that they were opposed to political violence.

Those in Divis who approved of the armed struggle universally said that they preferred peaceful means, but believed that violence was necessary because they had become convinced that it was the only effective political means available to the Catholic minority in Northern Ireland. They argued that there is a moral compulsion to act to remedy injustice and end oppression, and justified their endorsement of armed struggle only because they believed that it was the last resort. They expressed their conviction that a united Ireland could only be achieved through armed struggle because history had proven that violence was the only thing the British and Unionists in Northern Ireland listened to, and the only way the Catholic minority could hope to get any concessions from them. They argued that the Northern Ireland Civil Rights Movement tried peaceful protest in 1968–69 but was beaten into the ground, that political reforms introduced in the 1970s have not worked, and that over a decade and a half of talking had achieved nothing. As one resident put it, for the Catholic minority in Northern Ireland it comes down to armed struggle "because our politicians have failed us, and their politicians have left us no other choice" (from interview).

Those in Divis Flats who did not approve of political violence generally gave one or more of four reasons for their disapproval. First, many of them believed that there were effective peaceful means for the Catholic minority to achieve their political goals, and they therefore argued that violence was unnecessary and immoral. Second, they were sometimes opposed to political violence on dogmatic religious grounds. They took a more absolute "Catholic" moral stance that violence was evil and sinful, regardless of how good the cause. Third, they often said that over a decade and a half of violence proved that it does not work. They believed that the only thing it has accomplished is to kill, maim, and embitter people. And finally, there were some residents who said that they were simply so fed up with death, bloodshed, and fear that they would even prefer to return to the pre-1969 situation of peace but second-class citizenship rather than go on with armed struggle indefinitely.

Public Criticisms of the IRA and INLA

Almost everyone I spoke with in Divis Flats, regardless of whether or not they supported the guerrillas, had some criticisms of them. These criticisms are significant, because they represent moral parameters within which the IRA and INLA must operate if they are to retain their popular support in the community. Public criticism of the IRA and INLA is often misinterpreted by the British government and the media as evidence that the guerrillas either lack or are losing their popular support. However, Catholics in Northern Ireland have always been critical of the IRA and INLA, and that they have criticisms of these organizations does not necessarily mean that they do not support or sympathize with them. There is nothing inconsistent about supporting the guerrillas' actions in some areas while at the same time criticizing them in others.

There was a great deal of criticism in Divis Flats of the IRA and INLAs' social control role. Some people complained that the guerrillas were doing too little to control antisocial or criminal behavior in the community, while others complained that they were doing too much. And, while some complained that the guerrillas' methods (primarily beatings and threatened and actual kneecapping) were too harsh, others complained that they were not harsh enough to be really effective. Some residents also criticized the IRA and INLA on the grounds that their presence and actions brought a violent backlash down on the community from both the Security Forces and Loyalist extremists. A few people thought that the higher ranks and command structures of the IRA and INLA were "lining their own pockets" and doing well out of the troubles.[10] They complained that these individuals made the decisions but took few operational risks, while the young volunteers at the bottom took the greatest risks and faced the greatest danger of being killed or of ending up in jail. And there was a great deal of what might be termed "tactical" criticism. For example, while some people approved of attacks on economic targets in Northern Ireland and bombing campaigns in Britain, others were critical of these tactics.

Divis residents were also quite vocal in their criticism of mistakes and accidents in which innocent people (Catholic or Protestant) were injured or killed. They almost universally condemned actions which seemed to display a casual or callous disregard for the safety of innocent bystanders. This was in fact so strong a popular sentiment that if the IRA or INLA were to engage in acts of indiscriminate bombing and killing they would very seriously undermine their support among the residents. People were very critical of actions which appeared to have been done for sectarian rather than political motives. And they were also critical of particularly inhumane or cruel actions, such as the assassination of off-duty or retired members of the Security Forces at their weddings or in front of their families. These actions were generally condemned and considered unacceptable, and their occurrence caused a moral backlash and alienated popular support among the residents for the guerrillas.

However, attacks on obvious military and political targets—such as soldiers, policemen, judges, British politicians, militant Unionist politicians, and members of Loyalist paramilitary groups—were viewed by Divis residents in a different light, and generally did not alienate popular support for the IRA and INLA. They generally considered such attacks to be justifiable and acceptable. Divis residents were prepared to accept as morally justified almost anything done in direct defense of the community, and attacks on members of the Security Forces were considered the most acceptable form of offensive guerrilla action. This was because there was little ambiguity concerning the army and police as the obvious and traditional enemy and as legitimate military (rather than "political") targets.

There was also a good deal of criticism of the contemporary guerrillas by comparing them unfavorably with the IRA men of the past. To hear some people, one would have thought that in the past all IRA men were saints. They told of how difficult it was to join the IRA "in the old days," and of how prospective IRA volunteers needed character references, could not have a criminal record, and were required to go through a probationary period before they were accepted into the organization. In contrast, they claimed that today it is easier to join the IRA or INLA, and complained that they thought that the character and moral fiber of the volunteers had declined in the current campaign.

However, Republicans dismissed this kind of criticism as little more than a case of looking at the past through rose-colored glasses. They pointed out that people have always been critical of the IRA, in the past as well as today, and they have always compared the guerrillas they knew unfavorably with those that preceded them. They said that in the 1950s the IRA was compared unfavorably with the IRA of the 1920s, and now the contemporary IRA and INLA are compared unfavorably with the IRA of the 1950s. Republicans appear to be correct in this perception. The Catholic population has never exhibited a blind or uncritical acceptance of the Republican guerrillas, and they have always been concerned with their moral character. This enduring public concern with the guerrillas' moral character is an important limiting factor on the forms of action the IRA and INLA can engage in without alienating popular support.

Counterinsurgency and Support

The role the British army and paramilitary Royal Ulster Constabulary play in generating popular support for the IRA and INLA cannot be overestimated. The British government and the Security Forces in Northern Ireland have made a very common counterinsurgency mistake. Because it is difficult for them to come to grips with the guerrillas themselves, they have applied military force in a highly indiscriminate manner against the civilian population they believe supports the guerrillas. This has served to alienate that population, and it has created and continuously reinforced popular support for the IRA and INLA. This appears to have become a vicious cycle, because as popular support for the guerrillas grows as a result of military and judicial repression, members of the Security Forces grow increasingly convinced that the civilian population "deserves" to be repressed because they are "all" guerrilla supporters or sympathizers anyway.

The people of Divis Flats believe that they have seen terror of every description carried out by the Security Forces in the name of "law and order." They do not view the RUC or British army as neutral peace-keepers, but rather as pro-Unionist forces employed in a counterinsurgency effort aimed at defeating the IRA and INLA and keeping the Catholic minority under control. They have been badly alienated from the British government and the Security Forces by the constant raids and searches in which thousands of Catholic homes have been ransacked; by the widespread and at times indiscriminate use of CS gas and plastic bullets; by the riot squads and baton charges; by the innocent people killed by the Security Forces; by the constant surveillance, identity checks, and intelligence gathering; by all of the petty and sometimes serious acts of verbal abuse, physical brutality, harassment, intimidation, and vandalism by policemen and British soldiers on their streets; and by the application of repressive "emergency" legislation that makes a mockery of civil rights in Northern Ireland— the constant stream of arrests, detentions, "screening" of suspects, harsh methods of interrogation, and juryless "Diplock" courts. Divis residents believe that they can be arrested at any time on suspicion alone, that they can be threatened and physically abused during interrogation, that they can be convicted and imprisoned on trumped- up charges on the word of any soldier or policeman, and that they can be killed, maimed, and brutalized by members of the Security Forces with impunity. They also believe that the army and police will get away with these abuses of power, and that nothing they can do will either prevent them from doing these things or bring those who engage in such actions to justice.

The constant presence of heavily armed troops and police patrolling the complex, stopping, searching, questioning, and sometimes abusing people creates tension in the community, and the residents view this as a daily experience of what they define as military repression. They also view these actions as a form of discrimination against Catholics. The problem is that the Security Forces engage in too many actions in which entirely innocent people suffer. Too many innocent people are hurt by CS gas along with the rioters. Too many innocent people are injured or killed by plastic bullets, have their homes ransacked in searches, are killed by Security Forces gunfire, are stopped, questioned, and searched on the streets, and too many innocent people are harassed and abused by policemen and British soldiers. The result is that many people have become convinced that violence against the state is morally justified, and much support for the IRA and INLA flows directly from this conviction.

These government policies and Security Forces' actions have fanned the flames of political violence in Northern Ireland, and they have done as much, if not more, to sway popular support in Divis Flats towards the IRA and INLA as anything done by the guerrillas themselves. Despite British government propaganda to the contrary, the IRA and INLA do not intimidate the civilian population. In fact, just the opposite is the case. The Security Forces intimidate the civilian population, and the guerrillas benefit greatly from this. As long as the British government and the Security Forces continue to employ military and judicial repression against the community, they alienate the people living in Catholic districts like Divis Flats. This ensures that they cannot win the battle for "hearts and minds," and it creates and continuously reinforces the popular support the IRA and INLA need to survive and go on with the armed struggle.

The point is that people in Divis Flats apply the same moral criteria to the British government and the Security Forces that they do to the IRA and INLA. The "bottom line" of this moral evaluation is suffering caused to the innocent. The residents of Divis Flats find suffering caused to innocent people by the IRA and INLA morally unacceptable, and they do not find it any more acceptable when caused by government policies and Security Forces' activities. From their perspective, it appears that a lot more innocent people suffer at the hands of the army and police than do at the hands of the guerrillas. Thus, it seems to them that there is a good deal of morality on the guerrillas' side and a good deal of immorality on the side of the British government and the Security Forces. Popular support for the IRA and INLA among the residents of Divis Flats is based on rational considerations and moral evaluations. To many, if not most, it is the guerrillas who hold the moral high-ground.

Support and the Catholic Church

The Catholic Church in Northern Ireland has consistently and steadfastly refused to support or condone violent resistance and has opposed all movements espousing a revolutionary ideology.[11] The hierarchy has described the current campaign as directly contrary to Catholic doctrine concerning the sanctity of human life, they have strongly condemned the IRA and INLA, and they have repeatedly called on them to declare an immediate cease-fire. The Bishops have declared that supporting the IRA or INLA is a sin, and that one cannot be a member of the Catholic Church and be involved in Republican violence at the same time. The Church's position is in line with that held by the British government, that all killing (except that done by the Security Forces) is murder, a crime, and a sin regardless of political motivations or circumstances. Each fatality resulting from IRA or INLA actions results in predictable, ritual-like public condemnations by the Catholic hierarchy.

The crux of the public debate has to do with the Catholic doctrines concerning the sanctity of human life and the conditions under which violence is considered to be moral and acceptable. The IRA and INLA argue that such conditions exist in Northern Ireland, while the Catholic hierarchy maintains that they do not. While the IRA and INLA argue that all Catholics of good moral conscience should support their armed struggle, the Catholic hierarchy sides with the British government in arguing that no Catholic of good moral conscience should support IRA and INLA "terrorism." The position taken by the Catholic hierarchy adds moral weight to the anti-Republican argument presented by the British government. The IRA and INLA are therefore compelled to present moral counter arguments against the position taken by the hierarchy, in order to convince or reassure their members, supporters, and potential supporters that, despite clerical condemnation, it is they who hold the moral high-ground. Nonetheless, the persistent condemnations of the IRA and INLA by the Catholic hierarchy have prevented many Divis residents from supporting the guerrillas.

The respective positions taken by the IRA and INLA on the one hand and the Catholic clergy on the other represent two moral frames of reference, and the conflict between them represents, as Burton (1978) has argued, a struggle over moral authority in the Catholic community. When a priest once said to me that the people of Divis Flats would like to see a united Ireland and have a "sneaking suspicion" that the only way they will ever get it is by the gun, but have a question of conscience concerning political violence, he was expressing succinctly how this debate between Republicans and the Catholic hierarchy comes to bear on them. Whatever position they choose to take, for the IRA and INLA or against them, people in Divis Flats must arrive at some personal reconciliation between their religious and political convictions. In this paper, I have argued that this personal reconciliation is arrived at on the basis of moral evaluations of the various positions represented by the IRA and INLA, the British government and the Security Forces, and the hierarchy of the Catholic Church.

Conclusion

Mao Tse-Tung, the Chinese leader and great guerrilla theorist, taught that without the sympathy, cooperation, and support of the people, guerrilla warfare must ultimately fail. The principle weapon of the guerrilla fighter is his relationships with the community in which and for which he fights (Taber 1965:21). That community becomes, in Mao's classic metaphor, like a sea in which the guerrilla swims like a fish. As Robert Taber (1965:23) points out:

> The . . . population is the key to the entire struggle. Indeed, although western analysts seem to dislike entertaining this idea, it is the population which is doing the struggling. The guerrilla, who is of the people in a way which the government soldier cannot be, fights with the support of

the noncombatant civilian population; it is his camouflage, his quarter-master, his recruiting office, his communications network, his efficient, all-seeing intelligence service. Without the consent and aid of the people, the guerrilla would be merely a bandit, and could not long survive. If, on the other hand, the counter-insurgent could claim this support, the guerrilla would not exist.

Public support is absolutely vital to the guerrilla, because while a guerrilla campaign may be possible even without the active support of the majority of one's own people, it cannot survive their active hostility. The IRA and INLA cannot hope to achieve their political objectives, or even survive for very long, without the active or passive support of the majority of people living in the communities from which the guerrillas originate and in which they exist and operate—communities like Divis Flats.

After 18 years of on-going violence, the current IRA and INLA campaign represents the longest period of sustained Republican violence in Irish history. Tim Pat Coogan, an authority on the IRA, has noted that this differentiates the current guerrilla campaign from all previous ones in Ireland by breaking the traditional pattern of cyclical Republican violence. It is no longer a matter "of generations coming to maturity and striking a blow to maintain the Fenian tradition of a Rising in every generation. This time the pattern is continuous—the IRA's 'fresh generation' is next year's school leaver, or his younger brother or sister" (Coogan 1980:577).

One important consequence of this is that the IRA and INLA have had to expend a greater amount of resources and engage in a much more intense and sustained effort to maintain their popular support than did the IRA men who preceded them. They are engaged in an ongoing moral relationship with the Catholic population, in which the moral values of the Catholic community represent important constraints within which the guerrillas must operate in order to retain their popular support. When the IRA and INLA transgress their supporters' moral values, they suffer a moral sanction in the form of loss of popular support. In a similar manner, the "immoral" policies of the British government and "immoral" repressive actions of the Security Forces grant moral power to the IRA and INLA in the form of increased popular support.

Today, observers often comment on the fact that the IRA and INLAs' level of military professionalism and proficiency has increased greatly since the beginning of the current troubles in 1969. But what is often not equally appreciated is that so too has their level of political professionalism. The increased proficiency of the IRA and INLAs' political wings (Sinn Fein and the Irish Republican Socialist Party) is a direct consequence of the "new" form of relationship that has developed between the guerrillas and the Catholic population over the past 18 years of the current conflict.

Political anthropologists have made an important contribution by elucidating the role played by moral relationships, moral values, moral obligations, and moral constraints in social conflict and political violence. They can also make an important and socially responsible political contribution by engaging in what C. Wright Mills referred to as "the politics of truth." Mills (1959:178) argued that:

> The very enterprise of social science, as it determines fact, takes on political meaning. In a world of widely communicated nonsense, any statement of fact is of political and moral significance. . . . In such a world as ours, to practice social science is, first of all, to practice the politics of truth.

The political role of the anthropologist should be to find out as much of the truth as possible, to tell it to the right people, at the right time, and in the right way, and to "deny publicly what he knows to be false, whenever it appears in the assertions of no matter whom" (Mills 1964:611).

In guerrilla wars, propaganda is one of the major arenas of combat between the insurgents and the forces of the state. Anthropologists should play a political role by presenting definitions of the reality of these conflicts that are more accurate than those presented by the parties involved—either the guerrillas or the governments combating them. By challenging such official definitions of reality, anthropologists risk trouble, but at the same time they justify their existence—both practically and morally.

Notes

1. This paper was originally presented in the session on "The Anthropology of Peace and War," held in honor of David G. Mandelbaum at the 1986 annual meetings of the Kroeber Anthropological Society, the University of California, Berkeley, 8 March 1986.

2. I use the term "Catholic" as an ethnic designation referring to those in Northern Ireland who define themselves as being of Irish descent, and the term "Protestant" as an ethnic designation referring to those in Northern Ireland who define themselves as being of British descent.

3. The criminalization policy was introduced by Prime Minister Margaret Thatcher in 1976. It included the withdrawal of political ("special category") status for Republican prisoners, which ultimately led to the hunger strike in

1981. While the hunger strikers failed to achieve their stated objectives, the prison campaign arguably generated more popular sympathy and support (both in Ireland and abroad) for the IRA and INLA, than any previous event in the history of the conflict. Roger Faligot (1983:188) identifies criminalization as a propaganda and counterinsurgency "psyops" campaign, and summarizes the tactics involved as an attempt to "'depoliticize' the conflict, to portray Republican leaders as Mafia-type 'Godfathers', and solely define IRA activities as 'hi-jacking', 'kneecapping', engaging in 'rackets', and in brief, 'terrorizing' their own supporters."

4. While the IRA rarely if ever claimed responsibility for the no-warning bombings of public places which occurred in the early 1970s, several of which have now been linked to Loyalist paramilitary groups, some of these attacks have been attributed—at least by the government and Security Forces—to the IRA. No-warning bombings of public places rarely occur in Northern Ireland today.

5. Titled *Northern Ireland—Future Terrorist Trends.* Prepared by Brigadier J.M. Glover of the Defense Intelligence Staff, and dated 2 November 1978.

6. The only time the IRA has deliberately caused civilian casualties is when they have engaged in intermittent bombing campaigns in Britain (Coogan 1980:476). However, a number of civilians have been killed by the IRA and INLA due to premature explosions, accidents, and faults in their warning procedures. Even IRA bombings in Britain are not entirely indiscriminate. For example, in June 1986 the IRA said that while attacks in Britain would continue, they had ruled out attacks on the British Royal Family. I would argue that bombings in Britain belong to a different moral universe than do those in Northern Ireland itself, and that the moral arguments differ between them.

7. The violence that accompanied the outbreak of the contemporary troubles in August 1969 was marked by massive intimidation. Between July and September 1969, 1,820 families fled from their homes in Belfast. Of these, 1,505 were Catholic. Thus, while Catholics represented approximately one-third of the population of Belfast, they accounted for over four-fifths of those intimidated from their homes. Farrell (1980:263) notes that this was the second and in some cases third time some of these families had been put out of their homes. Many of these displaced families fled to the Divis complex, which was still under construction at that time, where they squatted in vacant flats. Not surprisingly, these families have the most pronounced fear of attacks by Protestant mobs.

8. The most recent example of the IRA's defensive role occurred during the Orange "twelfth" celebrations in July 1987. The IRA fired on a Protestant mob attacking Catholic homes in the Ardoyne district of Belfast, killing one man and wounding another. Attacks like this reinforce Catholic fears, and IRA actions like this reinforce the IRA's legitimacy as a community defense force.

9. The IRA plays a social control role in all working-class Catholic districts, but this role is more pronounced in socially disrupted districts like Divis and Unity Flats than in the more well-integrated traditional "urban village" districts such as Ardoyne and Short Strand. This is because the IRA have to make

up for the breakdown of communal control mechanisms in areas that have undergone physical redevelopment and social disruption.

10. It is interesting to note that the previously mentioned secret British army report on the IRA—"Northern Ireland: Future Terrorist Trends"—specifically commented that there was no evidence to support this claim.

11. There is a long tradition of "rebel" priests in Ireland. There have always been a few who were prepared to defy the hierarchy and defend the moral position of the Republican Movement.

References Cited

Boyd, A. 1969. *Holy War in Belfast*. New York: Grove Press.

Burton, F. 1978. *The Politics of Legitimacy: Struggles in a Belfast Community*. London: Routledge and Kegan Paul.

Cohen, A. 1969. *Custom and Politics in Urban Africa*. Berkeley: University of California Press.

_____. 1974. *Two-Dimensional Man*. Berkeley: University of California Press.

Coogan, T.P. 1980. *The I.R.A.* Glasgow: Fontana Books.

Coser, L.A. 1956. *The Functions of Social Conflict*. Glencoe: The Free Press.

Faligot, R. 1983. *Britain's Military Strategy in Ireland: The Kitson Experiment*. London: Zed Press.

Farrell, M. 1980. *Northern Ireland: The Orange State, 2nd Revised Edition*. London: Pluto Press.

Gluckman, M. 1955. *Custom and Conflict in Africa*. London: Oxford University Press.

MacStiofain, S. 1975. *Revolutionary in Ireland*. Letchworth: Garden City Press.

Mills, C.W. 1959. *The Sociological Imagination*. London: Oxford University Press.

_____. 1964. On Knowledge and Power. In *Power, Politics, and People*. I. Horowitz, ed., New York: Ballantine Books, Pp. 599–613.

Sluka, J.A. 1986. *Hearts and Minds, Water and Fish: Popular Support for the IRA and INLA in a Northern Irish Ghetto*. Unpublished Ph.D. Dissertation. University of California, Berkeley.

Taber, R. 1965. *The War of the Flea: Guerrilla Warfare, Theory and Practice*. St. Albans: Paladin Press.

Part 3
Dynamics of Peace

8 / The Communist Ethic and the Spirit of China's Party Cadres

Jack M. Potter

In contrast to earlier chapters which analyze the role of symbols and values in the dynamics of conflict, Jack Potter's paper, and those that follow, show the importance of the symbolic and normative aspects of society for maintaining peace. Just as the symbols and moral ideologies that contribute to conflict in a society are not homogeneous, Potter shows that the ethical system of the Cadre contains within it important tensions, and that peace is maintained, in part, by their ability to adapt to shifts in which aspects of the system are ascendant. Drawing on his own ethnographic experience in post-revolutionary China, Potter describes the world-view of the Chinese Party Cadre, the principal decision-makers for China. He argues that it is impossible to gain a deep understanding of the dynamics of modern Chinese society without accurately discerning the important role of the ethical system which justifies Cadre activities. In order to interpret the social life of the Party Cadre for us, he draws an analogy between the Cadre and the early Calvinists. In the course of this comparison, he shows that the image of the "corrupt Cadre," widely held in the West, is dangerously mistaken. Like Brasset and Pulliam, Potter discusses the moral dimensions of power. In the Chinese case he describes, however, these normative dimensions serve to support peace, and to give meaning to symbols important for facilitating commitment and sacrifice on behalf of the internal development of the country. Potter, like Bateson, Brasset, and Worsley, argues that anthropologists have a responsibility to combat pernicious images of the other by interpreting and ex-

Reproduced with permission from *China's Peasants: The Anthropology of a Revolution,* by Sulamith Heins Potter and Jack M. Potter, Cambridge University Press, forthcoming.

plaining the people of one culture to another. By serving as culture brokers anthropologists will not only reduce the ethnocentrism of security discussions but provide critically important new information about the social dynamics of other societies with which we deal.—The Editors

Max Weber, taught us that in trying to understand a complex civilization it is useful to conceive of it as composed of various social strata, each with its own material interests, power, world-view, and concept of status honor.[1] Among these strata is usually a dominant group—the Brahmans of India, the aristocracy of Medieval Europe, the business class of the contemporary United States—whose influence is so great as to shape the entire character of its civilization. In contemporary China the cadres of the Chinese Communist Party are such a group; their values and their view of the world have shaped and molded post-revolutionary China. Since they make all decisions for China, if we wish to negotiate agreements with the Chinese to maintain world peace and security, it is essential that we understand the cadres of the Chinese Communist Party as fellow human beings, because it is with them that we and the rest of the world will have to deal.

It is my contention, and it is an old-fashioned one, that the major contribution that anthropologists can make to peace is to increase understanding between peoples by interpreting and explaining the people of one culture to those of another. This furthers the cause of peace because it is more difficult to engage in mass holocausts if you recognize the essential humanity of the people you are trying to kill. By its very nature, anthropology is the enemy of war.

In this essay I portray the way of life of the rural Chinese Communist Party cadres among whom I have lived and worked over the past five years while carrying out anthropological fieldwork in Zengbu, a brigade of 5,000 people and five villages, located in Guangdong province of southern China. (Cadre is a word used to translate the Chinese term, *ganbu.* It refers to any party member who fills a leadership role in Chinese society.) My purpose here is to combat the stereotype of the "corrupt Cadre," which clutters the pages of the Western press and social science literature on China and precludes understanding. As an aid to understanding people whose culture and lives are so different from our own, I shall employ an analogy between China's party cadres and the early Calvinists, as described by Max Weber, in his *Protestant Ethic and the Spirit of Capitalism.*

The Communist Party of China is the architect of modern Chinese society; it is the backbone of the society, a centralized and effective instrument for governing. Party members hold all important leadership and management positions, in all fields, from the pinnacles of bureaucratic power in Beijing, down to grass-roots level rural brigades, like Zengbu. They command overwhelming legitimate authority over the persons, the labor, the livelihood, and the thinking of the peasants.

Over the three decades following the Revolution, in 1949, the rural Party cadres gradually became the new elite of rural China. They became conscious of themselves as a special group with material interests of their own and with privileges they wanted to pass on to their children. The Party cadres developed a distinctive leadership "ethos"—a characteristic moral and ethical shape and tone to their lives. They came to share a distinctive 'status ethic,' a moral code that guides the behavior expected of a member of the cadre stratum. As a unitary group sharing a common set of values and a sense of honor, they have esprit de corps, which gives them solidarity as a group and sets them off from the general rural population.

Central to the understanding of the Chinese Communist Party and its cadres is the realization that it is the organizational expression of a quasi-religion—nonsupernaturalistic and nonanthropomorphic to be sure—but a religion nevertheless, if religion is defined, following Durkheim (1965:62), as "a unified system of beliefs and practices relative to sacred things . . . which unite into one single moral community called a Church, all those who adhere to them."

The sacred party things are the prophets—Marx, Engels, Lenin, and Chairman Mao—and the sacred canon of Marxist-Leninist-Maoist writings. The Party secretaries are priests of the faith and keepers of the ideology as well as administrators. Party meeting houses at all levels, from the brigade headquarters to the Great Hall of the People in Beijing, display the sacred symbols of the Party. Hung with Party icons and paraphernalia, the meeting halls in rural Party headquarters resemble a church as much as they do the meeting places of a bureaucratically organized political party. The periodic Party assemblies and small-group discussion meetings are inspirational in tone. In their use of witnessing and statements by individuals of the particular meaning to themselves of the values of the shared belief system, they often resemble the emotionally-charged revival meetings of some Christian denominations. Such assemblies serve to strengthen the cadres' belief in the central values and goals of the Party.

The apocalyptic and messianic prophecy of the Party—that history will culminate in an earthly communist utopia—is an article of faith to the Zengbu cadres, even though the less sophisticated of them have a limited understanding of the fine points of Party doctrine and define the aim of communism as simply "to make China rich." As the first Party member of the Zengbu Party branch told me, when describing his initiation into the Party in the early 1950s, "I had to demonstrate knowledge of the Party's constitution and program, to become the type of selfless person who serves the people and tries to realize communism—not only in China, but in the entire world."

The Party program that the old cadre refers to is contained in the central canon of China's Marxism, written by Chairman Mao and Liu Shaoqi. In *How to be a Good Communist,* a set of lectures which Liu Shaoqi gave in 1939, and later published as a pamphlet in 1964, he set out the basic ideology of the Party for its members in the form of a catechism, the substance of which all the local cadres know by heart:

> What is our most fundamental duty as Party members? It is to achieve communism. . . . [T]he whole world will be transformed step by step into a communist world. Will the communist world be good? We all know it will be. In that world there will be no exploiters and oppressors, no landlords and capitalists, no imperialists and fascists, nor will there be any oppressed and exploited people, or any of the darkness, ignorance and backwardness resulting from the system of exploitation. In such a society the production of both material and moral values will develop and flourish mightily and will meet the varied needs of all its members. By then all humanity will consist of unselfish, intelligent, highly cultured and skilled communist workers; mutual assistance and affection will prevail among men and there will be no such irrationalities as mutual suspicion and deception, mutual injury, mutual slaughter and war. It will of course be the best, the most beautiful and the most advanced society in human history (Liu 1964:35–36).

This message is of a kind with the Christian apocalyptic message in Revelations, describing life after the Second Coming of Christ. Like the Christian gospel, it seeks to guide people to salvation by reforming their disjointed and troubled society in accord with new, or reformulated, sacred values. Anthony F.C. Wallace (1956) called such movements, common in situations of social stress when the existence of a society is threatened, "revitalization movements." Chinese Communism is the ideological basis of a Chinese revitalization movement. Rural Chinese who become Party cadres enter a political party which is the organizational manifestation of the movement. The moral fervor generated in the cadres and, during the early years after Liberation, in the peasants as well, inspired the cadres to implement the great revolutionary changes of the 1950s. The charismatic power of this movement and of its prophet, Chairman Mao, weakened only after the cumulative disillusionments and failures of the Great Leap Forward and the Cultural Revolution.

Entry to this elite group of Party cadres is restricted to a chosen few. Candidates have to demonstrate through years of hard and self-sacrificing work and through exemplary personal conduct, that they are worthy of Party membership. Only those who work hard, take the lead in all things, and are willing to do the most difficult jobs, no matter what the personal sacrifice, are supposed to have a chance to become Party members.

The standing committee member in charge of the Zengbu Party organization told me that applicants for the Party had to be people "who took an active role in their work." "If the cadres tell people to plant seedlings on one plot of land, according to a certain standard, an activist will plant more than one plot, and do it at a level far above the accepted standard."

Most of the older persons recruited into the Party are invited by the brigade cadres to join because it is not culturally appropriate for them to openly ask to become a member. One is supposed to work very hard at one's task, not shirking self-sacrifice, until one's contribution is noticed and one is "called" to join.

Secretary Lu, the Party Secretary of Zengbu Brigade, compared the process of joining the Party with the process of courtship. He said with a twinkle in his eye:

> Most people are shy about saying that they want to join. They are afraid that they will be laughed at. In the countryside, most people wait to be asked, rather than applying on their own initiative. They would be embarrassed to put themselves forward in this way. So, when the Party recruits, we don't start off by saying, "Will you join?" We talk about work, the future of socialism, or the greatness of the Party. If the person being recruited says, "Oh, I am not up to the Party's high standard," it is like a young couple talking love and saying, "Oh, I am not good enough for you." So we take this response as an oral application for membership.

The dedication and sacrifice that the Party demands tends to weed out people who would like to advance themselves without having real political convictions. And it is necessary to have a real faith as well. The demands of the Party are not unlike the demands of a religious vocation, and the sacrifices are much more certain than the rewards.

Liu Gensheng, Party secretary in Zengbu after 1980, told me how he came to join the Party in 1959, while serving in the People's Liberation Army.

In the army I saw that the Party members were tougher in mind and body than ordinary people; they always volunteered for the most difficult and dangerous tasks. I wondered what gave them such strength and courage; and I wanted to become like them. I wanted to become better educated in the Party's policies; I did not simply wish to follow the policies blindly. I tried to modify my behavior so that I could come up to the Party's high standards. I performed the hardest work—I did things that ordinary soldiers were not willing to do; and I took the lead in everything, to set an example for other members of my unit.

Liu said that he was happy to finally become a Party member; but that with exhilaration came also a feeling that he now carried a heavy burden of responsibility to the Party on his shoulders: "I had to set an example for others and behave properly at all times."

Not everyone in Zengbu wishes to join the Party. Secretary Lu said that, in spite of the power and high status Party membership gave, some were afraid that Party membership would require them to work too hard, since Party members had to dedicate their lives to the organization, and had to take the lead in all things, no matter how difficult the task, to set an example for others. As one young candidate for Party membership put it, "You gain as a Party member, and especially as a cadre; you get a good salary, and you gain the respect of the villagers, who look up to the cadres; but you also lose because it is very hard work."

Secretary Lu pointed out that, in the past, the people who wanted to and did join the Party, did so from diverse motives. Although most applicants genuinely believed in the Party and wished to devote their lives to building a modern and prosperous socialist rural China, others had less idealistic motives. Some people who had been poor and who had no social standing before Liberation joined the Party to become officials and enjoy high social status and authority. "This kind of person," said Secretary Lu, "joined the Party so that he could scold the peasants and lord it over his fellow villagers." Still others, especially those who entered the Party during the Cultural Revolution, added Secretary Lu, reflecting the lasting bitterness of old Party cadres who had been attacked during the Cultural Revolution, were opportunists, who sought Party membership only to further their own careers: "These people thought that they could rise to the top of the Party's ranks like helicopters. Many of them have not been successful because they were incompetents who were not able to bear the sacrifices or do the work required by the Party." "Needless to say," Secretary Lu commented, "We try to weed out the insincere people and accept only genuinely dedicated and able people."

Not only must one be hard working, Secretary Lu pointed out when discussing Party recruitment, one must be intelligent, have the ability to lead the masses, be firm in the face of difficulties, and be ideologically flexible, able to change and learn as the Party develops new policies: the Party, he said, does not want rigid fanatics in its midst. One must also be able to take criticism and keep close watch on one's own thinking and behavior. Only this kind of extraordinary person, after tempering in practice, makes an ideal Party member. The people of Zengbu speak of "bringing themselves up to the required standard of being willing to give one's life to the Party," if they are seeking Party membership, and of "not being of a high enough level," if they have doubts about joining (or if they are being conventionally modest).

The Party expects its cadres to internalize its values, ethics, and goals when they join. As in religious conversion, Party members are supposed to remold their innermost beings and to subordinate themselves to the interests of the party—even to the point of self-immolation. Chairman Mao sketched the personality traits of a good Party cadre:

At no time and in no circumstances should a Communist place his personal interests first; he should subordinate them to the interests of the nation and of the masses of the people. Hence, selfishness, slacking, corruption, striving for the limelight, etc. are most contemptible (quoted in Liu 1964:46).

Not only must a Party member's thinking be remolded, his new personality has to be reflected in his everyday behavior. As chairman Mao said, "Working with all one's energy, whole-hearted devotion to public duty, and quiet hard work are the qualities that command respect" (Liu 1964:46).

Liu Shaoqi described the effect of the Communist Ethic in disciplining the personal behavior of Party members:

[W]e must modestly learn the Marxist-Leninist stand, viewpoint and method . . . and apply all this in our practice, in our words and deeds, our daily life and work.

A cadre has to be so committed to the Party that he is willing to give his life in its cause. These stringent standards are, again, summed up by Liu:

[A good Party member] is "the first to worry and the last to enjoy himself (a quote from a classical Chinese scholar!)." Whether in the Party or among the people he is the first to suffer hardship and the last to enjoy comfort; he compares himself with others not with respect to material enjoyment but to the amount of work done for the revolution and the spirit of hard endurance in struggle. He has such revolutionary firmness and integrity that "neither riches nor honor can corrupt him, neither poverty nor lowly condition can make him swerve from principle, neither threats nor force can bend him" (a quote from Mencius; Liu 1964:48).

If a Party member follows this strict inner worldly ascetic regimen, he gains a form of inner enlightenment and strength that enables him to withstand all trials and struggles: he achieves a state of grace. When that happens, Liu continued.

[H]e has nothing to fear. . . . Because he has the courage of righteous conviction, he never fears the truth, courageously upholds it, spreads it and fights for it. Even if . . . in upholding the truth, he suffers blows of all kinds, is opposed or censured by most other people and so finds himself in temporary (and honorable) isolation, even to the point where he may have to give up his life, he will still breast the waves to uphold the truth and will never drift with the tide (1964:48–49).

Strengthened by his faith, Liu (1964:49–50) said, the Party member "is the most sincere, most candid, and happiest of men. . . . [H]e has no problem of personal gain or loss. . . . Even when he is working on his own without supervision and is therefore in a position to do something bad, he is just as 'watchful over himself when he is alone' (a quote from Confucius) and does not do anything harmful."

The "state of grace" achieved by a Party member secure in his faith is similar to the internal peace and self-confidence of a born-again Christian. The Communist Ethic motivates Party cadres to work hard to create the Party's utopia on earth. It is intended to be a this-worldly ethic that molds everyday behavior and must be realized in actual practice. The psychological mechanism which encourages Party members to resolve doubts about their right to membership in the cadres' elite by demonstrating in their work and action their commitment to the faith, resembles the effects of the Protestant Ethic on the practical life activities of the Calvinist, described by Max Weber (1958).[2] The Protestant Ethic motivated people to work hard building God's Kingdom on Earth by sustained, ascetic, rationalized work in a specialized "calling," or profession. It came to be believed that worldly success was a sign that the person was saved, a member of the select few whom God had chosen for eternal life. One had to work hard and succeed in one's calling because there was no other way to demonstrate that one was a member of the elect.

The psychological tension generated in Party members, anxious to prove themselves worthy of membership in the Party is resolved in Zengbu by selfless and exemplary labor. Such a practice is precisely analogous to the Protestant's attempt to resolve his uncertainty about his own salvation through dedicated, systematic labor in his calling. Both ethics create in people a religious interest in working hard—in order to become a good Christian in one case, and a good Communist in the other. And just as the Calvinist ethic played a role in capitalist economic development in early modern Europe, the Communist Ethic has played a role in socialist economic development in China.

Since the doctrine of the Chinese Communist party has historically been susceptible to so many sudden and abrupt changes, China's party cadres are under even more psychological stress than early European Calvinists. Party cadres not only have to be steadfast, they also have to be flexible in adapting to policy changes that are often sudden, radical, and contradictory—witness the change from Chairman Mao's policies since his death. Over the three decades following Liberation, the frequent shifts in Party policy kept the cadres in a constant state of uncertainty, as they sought to adapt and bend with change while maintaining their unswerving commitment and loyalty to the Party. The orthodoxy of one period became swiftly, and often with little warning, the heterodoxy of another. Cadres were praised for following Liu Shaoqi's liberal rural economic policies in the early 1960s and then in charge during the Cultural Revolution. Then, with the fall of the Gang of Four, Liu's policies again were adopted, and the cadres had to shift back again. Many of them were blamed in the Chinese press for not shifting fast enough! The source of religious uncertainty and tension in Calvinist doctrine (the will of a transcendent and unknowable God) is paralleled by the will of a distant, secretive, and unknowable Central Committee in China. Both the will of God and the policies of the Party upper-levels are changeable and unfathomable; they must be obeyed on the basis of faith; and one can never be sure— either as Calvinist pilgrim or as Party cadre—that one is walking the correct road. Being a Communist Party cadre is a lonely business. Like the early Calvinists, who were taught to be suspicious and aloof— even from family and friends—because one never knew who might be members of the damned who might threaten one's own salvation. A prudent Party cadre has to maintain a distance from his colleagues who might, in the shifting arena of inner-party struggle, be denounced as anti-Party—or denounce him. Those cadres who have managed to survive such tempering in the furnace of the Revolution are extraordinary people.

In conclusion, I hope I have been successful in presenting the deep cultural background necessary for understanding and dealing with China's Party cadres. The doctrine they live by and the Party organization determines what it is to be a cadre, at the highest levels as well as the peasant level that I have described. China's cadres are people totally unlike the stereotyped "corrupt cadre" of the Western press and the academic circles. Most importantly, they are a group with whom we share certain important values and orientations that derive from similarities between the religious backgrounds of early modern Western culture and current Party doctrine. Without understanding the strength and intensity of their ethical motivation, we can not deal with them effectively. To stereotype the dedicated followers of an extremely demanding religious faith as "corrupt Communist cadres" is an unrealistic act that can only hinder rational negotiations. By understanding who these people are, we can successfully find common ground to negotiate and maintain peace with China and avoid world destruction.

Notes

1. An earlier version of this paper was presented in the symposium "Power, Change and Security Decisions" at the 1985 annual meeting of the American Association for the Advancement of Science, Los Angeles.

2. Since first writing this, I have discovered that others have noted the similarity between Christian and Chinese Communist ethics. Professor Franz Schurmann mentioned this idea briefly in lectures at the University of California, Berkeley many years ago (and may not now hold this view), Schwartz (1970) noted in a passing sentence that "Maoist virtue, one might say, was to play the role of a kind of Protestant Ethic," and Urban (1971:xii) remarks that "Maoism is a serious call to a socially responsible moral conduct which has a great deal in common with Christian rectitude, especially in its Protestant and Victorian embodiment." Mazlish (1976:157–158) uses Mao as one example of a "revolutionary ascetic," and quotes similar observations made by James Reston and Maurice Meisner. I hope that my detailed and full exposition of this idea, based upon unique data from the countryside, will add to the full development of this idea and add new insights.

References Cited

Durkheim, E. 1965. *The Elementary Forms of Religious Life.* New York: The Free Press.

Liu Shao-Chi (Liu Shaoqi). 1964. *How to be a Good Communist.* Peking: Foreign Languages Press.

Mazlish, B. 1976. *The Revolutionary Ascetic.* New York: McGraw Hill.

Schwartz, B.I. 1970. The Reign of Virtue: Some Broad Perspectives on Leader and Party and the Cultural Revolution. In *Party Leadership and Revolutionary Power in China.* J.W. Lewis, ed., Cambridge: Cambridge University Press, Pp. 149–169.

Urban, G. 1971. *The Miracles of Chairman Mao.* London: Tom Stacey Ltd.

Wallace, A.F.C. 1956. Revitalization Movements. *American Anthropologist* 58:264–281.

Weber, M. 1958. *The Protestant Ethic and the Spirit of Capitalism.* New York: Charles Scribner and Sons.

9 / Rivalry and the Rise of Swiss Neutrality: The Feud in the Peace

Jonathan Habarad

Jonathan Habarad's study of the origins of Swiss neutrality shows that the institutionalization of peaceful, rather than of military, social forms can be the end-product of conflict and rivalry. He argues that peace is a constant and dynamic struggle which depends upon the operation of counterbalancing social processes. Rivalry in some areas of social life may be checked by acknowledged interdependencies in other areas. These counterbalancing social processes support and must be supported by a system of symbols and sentiments. Thus, just as earlier papers showed that conflict emerged from the tension between conflicting elements in the normative aspects of a society, peace too can be the product of dynamic social tensions. Harbarad argues that this can be accomplished by establishing linkages between competing groups so that their interdependence is recognized and their rivalry is thus diminished. In those circumstances sentiments against conflict can be mobilized most effectively. The Swiss case presented by Habarad demonstrates the important point that peace does not result merely from the absence of social, political, and moral conflict. Rather, peace is the outcome of the effective and continuing management of competing aspirations. Establishing and maintaining peace clearly depends upon coming to terms with the social dynamics inherent in our relationships with others.—The Editors

Switzerland's enduring policies of non-aggression and non-intervention are said to date back to a formal announcement in 1674, as French and Austrian armies faced one another near Basel.[1] Historians trace the origins back somewhat further, to the mid-16th century, holding that Swiss neutrality results from: (1) a major defeat of Confederate forces by France at Marignano in 1515; (2) a political paralysis brought on by Swiss bi-confessionalism beginning thereafter; (3) Switzerland's geopolitical location on the strategic Alpine massif; (4) treaties of non-aggression established between individual cantons and surrounding nations; and (5) the rise of a balance of power in Europe (Bonjour 1946:12–21, Hofer 1957:7–8).

Understanding the origins of Swiss neutrality could illuminate much about the nature and dynamics of peaceful international relations, yet the processes leading to the overall policy of neutrality have remained unclear. All the above explanations point to Swiss neutrality as a fluke, owing to unique coincidence of location within a matrix of particular external forces, and not to any general processes operating within the Confederation. All assume Switzerland's neutrality to have arisen as an intelligent response to external pressures. Perhaps it is such. Nevertheless, the rise of neutrality in the Swiss case evinces some general processes that I shall attempt to demonstrate in this paper.

An Interactional Framework

Swiss history of the 15th, 16th, and 17th centuries gives evidence of interactive processes within the Confederation that throw into dramatic relief some of our current theories on the roles of conflict and unifying ideologies in peace and war. Indeed, while neutrality describes a stance assumed by one actor or state in relation to others, the assumption of that position does not necessarily result from external considerations. It may instead result from primarily internal dynamics. In contrast to the force of external pressures or any sense of unity and common interest, schism and local rivalries between cantons, from the mid-fifteenth century onward, increasingly prevented mobilization for external aggression and territorial expansion. Competitions for power within the Confederation increasingly led cantons to take positions that would limit expansion of neighboring cantons. The growing intensity of internal competitions actually led to the rise of an ideology of neutrality as individual cantons sought to undermine the legitimacy of expansive efforts by rivals. Rather than owing to a sense of unity therefore, I argue that processes of internal schism and division may, as in the Swiss case, divert the large-scale mobilization necessary for war.

For this reason I have sub-titled the paper "The Feud in the Peace," playing off of Colson's and Gluckman's understanding of how diversity and conflicts of (loyalties within) local groups lead to a "peace" in the "feud" (Colson 1953, Gluckman 1956). Where Colson and Gluckman focused on diversity, integration and interdependency as means of resolving rivalries and conflicts within acephalous societies, I am focusing on the rivalries themselves, as processes inhibiting unification necessary for expansive efforts. I show how (rivalries between) local societies bound together in an essentially "acephalous" but interdependent political confederation place constraints on a state's ability to wage war, and thus may contribute to peaceful external relations.

The Social Contexts of Neutrality

In the mid-fifteenth century the Swiss Confederation, with a three century history of dramatic military successes, consisted of a collectivity of eight small, but expanding states renowned as Europe's fiercest and most resolute warriors. The cantons were separated by a high degree of local diversity, as well as diverse linguistic and ethnic alignment among the surrounding great powers. These, and further disparities in economic class and rural or urban lifestyle, and their relative geographic isolation, had long inhibited the rise of a centralized government, and created the structural cleavages of identity that separated the Confederation into local units.

Each canton was formally regarded as equal to the others in rights and influence in terms of decision-making in the Diet of the Confederation, which served as the mediating body for matters of internal relations and mobilization. Each canton sent a spokesperson to the Diet to represent its positions in policy matters. Spokespersons had few decision-making powers, but carried out instructions issued in the canton seat, necessitating numerous trips between canton and Diet in the event of complex problems. Despite the constraints of participation in a defensive alliance governed by consensus, confederation made each canton a political-military entity sufficiently powerful to protect its individual autonomy from attempts at incorporation by outside powers and to act in relations *outside* the Confederation as if it were a major power. Indeed, the strength of the Confederation had provided members with the military support necessary for expansion.

By the mid-fifteenth century however, formal and informal patron-client relations between larger, wealthier or more aggressive cantons had led to the formation of "intra-confederational alliances." These enhanced existing schisms and created tensions that contributed to an intense rivalry between the cantons with respect to their power within the Confederation. The large and wealthy Bern and her neighbors Fribourg and Solothurn; the contiguous "Waldstetten" Uri, Schwyz and Unterwalden; and individually, the international linkages of the urban states Zurich and Basel, constituted alliances that allowed influence in the Diet disproportionate to the one canton-one vote rule.

Their varying successes in annexing neighboring territories and in recruiting related areas as client states affected the relative size, wealth and influence wielded by cantons, and created marked disparities in power. By the mid fifteenth century such disparities in power had begun to affect the real influence wielded within in the Confederation's Diet.

Local Interests and an Image of Limited Good

Cross linkages, described by Colson (1953) and Gluckman (1959) operated at the local level to create integration up to canton-scale (compare, Rappard 1948:79, Weinberg 1983). But the "loyalties" or interdependencies connecting cantons as an overall polity were single-stranded: cantons were bound together only by a need for mutual support *vis à vis* surrounding powers. This strand of interdependence for the most part prevented cantons from warring with one another. But their defensive cross-linkages cannot explain the trajectory of neutrality taken by the Confederation as a whole, for it hardly precluded the option of military expansion by independent cantons. Apart from this they were bound together only by their rivalries.

Cantonal governments constantly feared being overshadowed and dominated by the others in confederational policy and decision making. A shared "image of limited good" (Foster 1965) saw the Confederation as a more-or-less closed system where the enhancement of the power of any single canton threatened the status and power of the others. This tension not only heightened and underscored the existing differences between the cantons, but led to a sense of intense rivalry between them, more intense than any political attitude held with respect to the "outside."

Cantons were expected to contribute to the costs of defensive alliance in direct relation to population, territory and wealth. Thus if a rival canton should become embroiled in an international conflict because of efforts to expand its territory through annexation of an adjacent area, each canton in the Confederation would be formally bound to come to its rival's assistance, aiding in the expansion of a rival power at its own cost in blood and resources.

Thus during the 15th and 16th centuries, there arose a desire on the part of each canton to limit the territorial acquisitions and economic improvement of the others and to build informal alliances within the Confederation which would counter the voting power of rivals and their allies. Rivalry, in the context of the requirement for mutual assistance, led to efforts by individual cantons to limit the military actions of their confederates. They did this through three means: first, by refusing to assist in military ventures that were not clear-cut cases of self-defense; second, by discouraging individual states from making external treaties that might involve them in military ventures; and, third, to intervene by "behind the scenes" third party diplomacy to mediate in international difficulties between confederates and external powers. Through these means they sought to avoid involvement in wars which, if waged and won at their own costs, might result in the greater power of a rival. Fears and jealousies of intra-confederational domination led to the extreme reticence of cantons to support confederates attempting to expand their territorial control through annexation of areas outside the Confederation. In many cases this reticence resulted not only in a refusal to become involved, but often in active exertion in campaigning and negotiations against involvement.

The Politics of War and Peace

The development of neutrality as a principle of foreign relations was therefore neither an outcome of planning, of intelligent response to external pressures nor of political inertia, but came about as a result of active rivalries between opposed cantons seeking to limit the gains of their rivals, and to enhance their own positions within the arena of the Confederation. A few examples of such conflict, which abound in 15th and 16th century Swiss history, demonstrate these processes.

The Conquest of Mulhausen and Morat

In 1466 Bern was the largest and most powerful of the cantons. It had just succeeded in the annexation of neighboring Thurgau and hoped to expand further northward to the free city of Mulhausen. Austria too, however, sought to bring Mulhausen within its borders. Bern and its client cities Fribourg and Solothurn (not yet cantons), therefore offered to engage in Mulhausen's defense—against the consensus of the remainder of the Confederation. They sent a force but found themselves out-matched by the Austrian army. Bern invoked the oath of mutual defense and after considerable delay, was joined by a large confederate force that succeeded in repelling the Austrian forces. To consolidate its power in the area Bern, with confederate forces, further attempted to occupy several neighboring towns held by Austria, but failed. Assisted by Solothurn and Fribourg, Bern was, however, able to win from Austria a settlement of 10,000 guilders, with the right to re-occupy these areas should the sum not be paid.

As the Duke of Austria was hard-pressed to pay, Charles the Bold of Burgundy offered to pay the settlement on his behalf. Charles' offer both foiled and alarmed the Bernese. To provoke Charles, perhaps to pressure him to withdraw his offer to Austria, Bern, in 1476 moved forces into Burgundian territory near Lake Neuchatel. When Charles responded by sending troops, forces under Bernese command occupied a castle, met, and defeated Charles' army, winning spoils for which Bern took full credit. The Bernese then lorded their successes over even the cantons whose troops had provided support and claimed control of the spoils, further angering their confederates. Then, against the wishes of the Diet, Bern occupied Charles' garrison town of Morat.

By March 1476, Charles had reorganized his forces and advanced to expel the Bernese. Bern again called upon confederates to come to her aid. The Diet however, asked Bern to abandon Morat. The Bernese government refused. The Diet therefore agreed among themselves to raise a small contingency force of levies from Zurich, Lucerne, Schwyz, Uri, Unterwalden, Zug, Glarus, Appenzell, Thurgau and St. Gallen, not to assist, but to stand by in the event of trouble. At the same time the Diet continued its demands for Bern to withdraw. As Charles' forces neared Morat, Bern continued in its refusal to abandon the city, again urging the confederates to come to her aid. The Diet met in repeated conferences for several weeks before agreeing it would support Bern should the situation become desperate. When, on June 11, Bern reported Morat under siege, an army was rapidly assembled and sent, routing Charles' forces before Morat on June 22, 1476, capturing both his territories and nearly the whole of his treasury, for which Bern again attempted to take full credit and control.

Despite the extreme opposition of nearly all her confederates, the conquest of Charles the Bold's Burgundy in 1476 and 1477 at Bern's instigation resulted in Bern's annexation of much of the the French-speaking lands to the south, including much of what is today Canton Vaud. In addition, to reward its allies Solothurn and Fribourg for their assistance, Bern attempted to force an initiative for their acceptance as member states, introducing a further imbalance of power in the Confederation. Rappard writes of the conquest that: "the victorious cantons were very much divided on the desirability of territorial expansion to the west which could but enhance the already dangerously preponderant Republic of Berne." Indeed, the disputes over how to divide the spoils of this campaign nearly tore the eight-member Confederation apart, and led to the calling of the Covenant of Stans four years later in 1481, at which the first whispers of neutrality were heard.

By the 1470s the inner forest cantons of Uri, Schwyz, Unterwalden, Glarus, and Zug were nearly surrounded by their confederates, blocking possibilities for their own territorial expansion. In this context the rural and forest cantons felt profoundly threatened by Bern's acquisitions and by the growing power of Zurich. With Unterwalden threatening civil war, the Covenant of Stans was convened to prevent dissolution of the agreements that bound the cantons as a defensive Confederation. They met to decide whether or not the Confederation should continue, and to discuss questions of disposition of the newly acquired territories, the perceived marginalization of the forest cantons (Uri, Schwyz, Unterwalden, Glarus, and Zug), the admission of the Bernese allies and "city cantons" Solothurn and Fribourg, and the recent aggrandizement of Bern at the expense of the Confederation (Bonjour 1952:133). At Stans, representatives of the Cantons were barely able to carve out an agreement on means to divide the spoils of war so as to keep the precarious interests within the Confederation in a tenuous balance.

The following two decades saw the rise of Zurich under leadership of the entrepreneur Waldmann as a power within the Confederation, overwhelming Bern's influence. Seen to threaten the autonomy of the countryside, however, Waldmann was soon deposed. A subsequent shift of influence within the Confederation had returned the rural cantons to power by 1489. Subsequently, Swiss involvement in the Swabian War against the Austro-Hungarian empire had resulted, by 1501, in the inclusion of Basel and Schaffhaussen as full members of the Confederation, again shifting the balance of power to the northern "urban" states. These admissions were followed shortly by efforts from the "forest cantons" Uri, Schwyz and later, Unterwalden, to expand their territories into the Alpine valleys of the Duchy of Milan, beginning with the conquest of Bellinzona.

The Conquest of Bellinzona

In 1495 Louis VII, Duke of Orleans (shortly to take the French kingship as Francis I), had promised the territories of Bellinzona, Locarno and Lugano in exchange for the Confederation's help in a struggle against the Duke of Milan. The Confederation lent its support and Louis established his sovereignty over the Duchy of Milan, but then failed to fulfill his promise. In 1501, after five years of waiting, Uri and Schwyz occupied Bellinzona in the Duchy of Milan and invoked the support of the Confederation. Endless negotiations ensued in which the six more distant cantons insistently urged Uri and Schwyz to relinquish and "to leave to the King of France what belonged to him." Uri and Schwyz refused, determined to expand their territories, while the Confederation sought endlessly to negotiate a peaceful settlement forcing Uri and Schwyz to abandon the territory.

The arguments and refusals of support by cantonal representatives in the Diet were insufficient, however, to dissuade the Waldstetten from their own resolve to take the territories that had been promised to them. The dissenting cantons forestalled a rapid response from France through diplomatic efforts, acknowledging the legitimacy of the French position and promising they would press the forest cantons to withdraw. After three years of tense negotiation between the cantons, however, Uri and Schwyz now joined by Unterwalden, advanced further, provoking a French response that thus forced the northern and western cantons to commit their troops or destroy the union. Much against their wills, but with little choice, governments of the dissenting cantons sent military forces in support of the campaign. These won the concession of Bellinzona and brought the campaign to a close (Rappard 1948:89–93).

Subsequently in 1511, Schwyz initiated an excursion of its own, again within the Duchy of Milan, to further expand its southern reaches, again against the wishes of other members of the Confederation. Schwyz's demand for confederate support led to consternation in the Diet, and a resolution that "Whereas none of our cantons should in future start a war of its own accord against the advice of all others or a majority of others . . . an agreement should be reached so as to avoid the recurrence of such accidents and to maintain our commonwealth as it has been bequeathed to us by our ancestors."

This resolution was insufficient however, to quell Schwyz's determination to add to its territory. Schwyz's struggle became a polarizing issue within the Confederation, intensifying the sense of rivalry, wherein the Waldstetten saw the refusal to support Schwyz as a sign of the Confederation's desire to keep the inner cantons enclosed and without power. Three years later, when an agreement to assist Schwyz was finally reached, the Confederation's forces met with those of France on the field at Marignano. On the eve of the battle, the King of France promised payment of a million crowns to the Cantons not to engage, resulting in the withdrawal of troops of cantons Bern, Fribourg, Solothurn and Valais, leaving only the eastern cantons to face his armies. Swiss forces lost the battle, and some 8,000 men in a crushing defeat. In the concluding negotiations, the million crowns were paid, and the disputed territories ceded, Bellinzona, Lugano, Locarno, Mendrisio, Bormio, Chiavenna, and the Valtelline, for the Swiss Promise of Perpetual Peace of November, 1516, never again to fight against the armies of France.

The Rise of a Policy of Neutrality

The period preceding the Battle of Marignano was among the most warlike in all of Swiss history, with individual cantons seeking to capitalize on the strength of their allies to set up situations in which they could legitimately mobilize an offensive force on the claim of "self-defense" (Krebs 1902). Many more cases illuminating the role of discontinuity and rivalry can be gathered from the materials and writings in Swiss history.

At the time of Marignano the Confederation was more bitterly divided than it had ever been before. The intensity of internal jealousies and the awareness among the confederate states that their pledges were being manipulated for the aggrandizement of rivals effectively ended the period of Swiss expansion by conquest. The Swiss defeat at Marignano by French forces resulted from an astute exploitation of these divisions by the French, of which the cantons afterward became well aware.

Marignano demonstrated to the Swiss the interactive limitations of their Confederation, yet those limitations had operated to attenuate Swiss expansion for at least a half-century prior to the defeat. A major attempt at expansion was made only once more, again by the Waldstetten in 1531, resulting in an alignment of the Grisons with the Confederation. After this, in the face of the growing schisms of the reformation and the more rapid growth of urban powers, to prevent the disintegration of their defensive relationships, the cantons began informally but persistently upon a course of effective neutrality (Bonjour et al. 1952:144–145, Peyer 1978:42–43, Rappard 1948:96–97).

Though not formally declared as national policy until 1674, for all practical purposes the Swiss began the practice of neutrality in foreign relations—non-aggression, non-intervention and non-alliance—in 1516, following Marignano. Bonjour wrote of the consequences of Marignano that "many Swiss then realized that so loose a congeries of states, so half-baked a political organization as the Confederation was at that time, did not possess the necessary strength either for a uniform foreign policy or for clear-cut military aims . . . any advance in that direction [would have required] the centralization of the Confederation" and the sacrifice of cantonal autonomy. As discrete but interdependent sovereign states, this was something cantonal leaders were not about to allow. Their localized social and political interests, their profound concern for sovereignty, and jealousies over power within the framework of the Confederation set them at odds—except in terms of their common interest in mutual defense.

These same dynamics played a central role in the maintenance of neutrality, which has lasted with few exceptions, such as the breach by Napoleon's campaigns between 1798 and 1815, to the present. Institutionalized through formal international recognition of Swiss neutrality in the Congress of Vienna in 1815, neutrality was formally adopted as a constitutional principle with the formation of a more centralized national government in 1848. Indeed, the policy of neutrality had by that time become so pervasive and explicit a unifying principle that it became one of the primary justifications for the 1848 establishment of a federal government.

Neutrality in Switzerland, having achieved popular and formal institutionalization as an overarching cultural and political ideal, had become a central part of the complex of Swiss nationalism, synonymous with sovereignty and the national interest. Having become an institution in itself, the ideology of neutrality no longer rests upon the intercantonal rivalries out of which it was born. The connection between them is now so obscured that it is perhaps no longer recognizable, or of note, except in an historical view. It has perhaps only one importance today, and that may be what it can tell us of mobilization for war and the processes that inhibit it.

The Feud in the Peace

The marshaling of power requires a locus—a unified body to win, possess or wield it. A unifying framework for the mobilization of resources for an effective offensive force is a fundamental requirement for waging war. Shared interests or ideologies serve as bases of unification, creating a framework for mobilization in concerted action and a pooling of effort on the premise of a common good. In political unions, alliances or federations where no such fundamental bases of common identity exist, or where actual enmities exist, the unifying of force for the waging of war may be impossible. Groups may vie to limit their rival's gains in power by simply refusing to contribute to expansion, or more effectively, by mobilizing sentiment against it.

These findings are supported by comparison in contrast, for example, with the case of Nuer expansion throughout the southern Sudan (Kelley 1985:157–241). The Nuer, organized on the basis of more or less continuous segmentary lineage principles, did not experience the fundamental discontinuities and local divisions within the population created by Swiss diversity and rivalries. The Nuer ideology of lineage identity (compare Gluckman 1959, Kelley 1985) created a sense of homogeneity of interests *vis a vis* other groups. Lineage linkages attenuated processes of rivalry discussed here, connecting local groups within a highly flexible socio-political framework, and provided Nuer with an organization well-adapted for mobilization, conquest and expansion (Kelley 1985:160). In contrast, Dinka, whose territories were often raided by Nuer, were socially and politically organized in locally discrete units. Organized in competitive local groups, Dinka were less able to mount effective raids into Nuer territory (Kelley 1985:161, 170–182).

The Swiss data indicate then, that peace is not of an idyllic character, but instead involves a constant and dynamic struggle. It may be that peace results from the operation of social processes in contradiction, such as interdependence and rivalry, in a dynamic of social forces canceling out and inhibiting one another—as resting on division and structural oppositions that clash to make a dynamic balance, rather than as is usually assumed, deriving from principles of unity and homogeneity. If opposition and rivalry do not take place within a framework of interdependency they are apt to lead to polarization and war between competing groups. Within a context of interdependence, however, rivalry and contradiction may, indeed, contribute to the peace.

It is unlikely therefore, that national integration and unity, or unification across nations will provide any solution to the problems of war. The ideology unifying the Helvetic Confederation was direct and single stranded: mutual defense. Their differences, their emphasis on local autonomy and their resultant rivalries long precluded additional bases of unification—except finally, agreement on neutrality. It may be that homogenizing processes that override local level divisions such as nationalisms, religions and other ideologies, are the greatest of threats to peace: for they make possible the mobilization of both the sentiment and the resources necessary for war. In contrast to an increasing unification it may be that political decentralization into interdependent local groups would do more to promote the interests of peace.

At present and most frighteningly, this thesis is manifest in the existence of political ideologies that override local divisions within and between nations, and which preclude questions of local interests in the framing of foreign relations. The organization of modern states diffuses the rise of local divisions and encourages a narrow range of national or "bloc" interests formulated within fully integrated and centrally organized complexes of social, political and economic relationships. The unifying forces of nationalism and ideology have now made possible the marshaling of power to engage in total war instantaneously. Centralized control of these awesome powers for war shortcircuits processes of internal struggle that might otherwise prevent their use.

Notes

1. This paper was written while I worked as a research assistant for David Mandelbaum's study *Peoples Without War*. It was originally presented at a session of the 1986 Kroeber Society Meetings in his honor, entitled "The

Anthropology of Peace and War." I am grateful to Professor Mandelbaum for encouraging me in pursuit of the problem. I am also grateful to Professor Burton Benedict, whose reading and criticism of an earlier draft has improved the clarity of ideas presented here.

References Cited

Bonjour, E. 1946 *Swiss Neutrality: Its History and Meaning.* Translated by Mary Hottinger. London: George Allen and Unwin.

_____, H. S. Offler and G. R. Potter. 1952. *A Short History of Switzerland.* Oxford: Clarendon Press.

Colson, E. 1953. Social Control and Vengeance in Plateau Tonga Society. *Africa* 233:199–211.

Evans-Pritchard, E.E. 1940. *The Nuer.* Oxford: Oxford University Press.

_____. 1953. The Sacrificial Role of Cattle among the Nuer. *Africa* 223:181–197.

Foster, G. 1965. Peasant Society and the Image of Limited Good. *American Anthropologist* 67:293–315.

Gluckman, M. 1956. *Custom and Conflict in Africa.* London: Basil Blackwell.

Hofer, W. 1957. *Neutrality as the Principle of Swiss Foreign Policy.* Zurich: Schweizer Spiegel Verlag.

Kelly, R.C. 1985. *The Nuer Conquest: The Structure and Development of an Expansionist System.* Ann Arbor, MI: The University of Michigan Press.

Krebs, M. 1902. *Die Politik von Bern, Solothurn und Basel in den Jahren 1466–1468: Zeitgeschichtliches zum Muhlhauser Krieg.* Zurich: Buchdruckerei Berichthaus.

Peyer, H.C. 1978. *Verfassungsgeschichte der alten Schweiz.* Zurich: Schulthess Polygraphischer Verlag.

Rappard, W. 1948. *Collective Security in Swiss Experience.* London: Allen and Unwin.

Stein, N. 1979. *Burgund und die Eidgennossenschaft zur Zeit Karls des Kuhnen.* Frankfurt am Main: Peter Lang Verlag.

Weinberg, D. 1983. Conflicting Political Models in a Swiss Commune. *Ethnology* 221:17–26.

10 / Philippine Verticality and the Deflection of Class Conflict

James N. Anderson

Conflict may be avoided, as Habarad points out, by processes that link social groups in relationships of mutual interdependence. In the following paper, James Anderson shows that despite great socioeconomic disparities, the Philippines has traditionally avoided class conflict, and maintained an uneasy peace, as the result of social institutions which link people in personalistic inter-class relations. He argues that in a situation which might otherwise be expected to result in violent conflict, patron-client relations have served to permit effective vertical access for subordinates to resources controlled by others. He argues, further, that despite its appearance to outsiders as an exploitative system, the Philippine system of patron-client relations is perceived by participants as having (and often does effectively establish) complementary advantages. Because of this ideology inter-class communication is kept open, and members of Philippine society are often linked to persons in different social classes as much as they are to others of their own social class. Anderson points out that the system of indirect access to resources through personalistic vertical relations differs markedly from Western models of political activity, which emphasize social equality and class relationships. He argues, as does Kehoe, that imposing Western political constructs as a filter through which to interpret Philippine behavior is ethnocentric and misleading. To do so obscures rather than elucidates the social dynamics of peace and conflict in Philippine society. Like other contributors to this book, Anderson argues the critical importance of understanding the symbols and normative dimensions of other societies if we are to deal with them in a respectful and effective manner.—The Editors

Anyone familiar with the Philippines can testify to the shocking gap in socioeconomic status and living conditions between rich and poor in that country.[1] The gap is so great that it rivals that known anywhere in the world. Indeed, even the casual observer of the Philippines is led to wonder how, given the extent of poverty and excess, any degree of peace between such divergent classes can be maintained (see Worsley this volume). Basic structural contradictions are evident throughout the society. Class cleavages generate profound, apparently irreversible conflicts. The most apolitical person is led to ask, "How is it that a revolution has not yet occurred in this country?"

This paper seeks to provide one answer to this question and a fuller understanding of the way in which processes that generate social differentiation and create conflict may be deflected by the existence of vertically linking social institutions and networks of social interaction. The discussion is organized around a model of vertical relations which pertains only to the Philippines. However, certain implications appear to have more general relevance.

In brief, I suggest that definitive class relations and organized class conflict, remarkably, are only just consolidating in the Philippines. They have emerged periodically and locally, only to be minimized or co-opted in many historical circumstances during the past century through the responsive processes of what I call vertical intermediation. Elite power was exercised over (and accepted by) subordinates through vertical communication usually without excessive recourse to force and fraud (although these were often threatened or actually present). Vertical ties of complementary assistance created social bonds, communication and exchanges between members of higher and lower classes. In this paper I identify, analyze, and interpret the sociological and, more briefly, the historical circumstances that appear so long to have inhibited (and more recently encouraged) the consolidation of classes and the reinforcement of class conflict.

An important theoretical assumption for the conceptualization of order and disorder, and peace and war suggested by Vayda (1976) is that war is a *process* rather than something that either occurs or does not occur.

Viewing war as a process consisting of recurrent, distinguishable phases enables us to ask questions different from those usual in studies of war. We can ask not only about the conditions conducive to the outbreak of war but also about those conducive to escalation of one phase of war to another. We can ask not only about the inevitability of war but also about the inevitability of escalation. We can ask about the duration and frequency not simply of warfare but rather of particular phases of war processes. And we can ask about the relation of the temporal and other priorities of war processes to the problems or perturbations that the processes may be responding to (Vayda 1976:2).

If war can be viewed fruitfully as a process, as Vayda suggests, then so can its opposite: peace. My purpose here is to analyze organized conflict and violence (and their containment) between classes in Philippine society as a process that can be understood as managing social relations in ways that effectively contain inter-class conflict and reduce violence without massive state or private coercion. As class tensions have emerged, they have been countered by processes which have provided new access to the values of society. By contrast, the costs of using organized force alone to quell class conflict inevitably become enormous and must in the end fail. This paper tries to show that through a particular organization of vertical social relationships and the articulating process of complementary reciprocity open conflict and potential violence are diminished or averted. The analysis does not reflect a moral judgment about what is, in many respects, a pernicious social arrangement that has contributed to the perpetuation of a grossly unequal and unjust society. However, whether we find the arrangement morally reprehensible or not, it continues to operate broadly and demonstrate amazing persistence. The question is not whether but how and why.

I also draw on a concept that I find useful for portraying the character of those vertical relations which I suggest are crucial to the reinforcement or suppression of open class conflict and organized violence. This may be called the "interaction compass." It provides a classification of the processes of interactions between members of different classes along a continuum from relatively mutualistic complementary benefit to extreme competition and exploitation. The metaphorical needle of the interaction compass swings in response to socioeconomic changes which affect the character of the social interactions between superordinates and subordinates. My thesis is simply that those processes of interactions which permit an effective type of vertical access for subordinates (through patron-client relations and processes of vertical intermediation) reduce class conflict. Those that restrict or terminate vertical access or which become excessively exploitative tend to lead to horizontal organization, the hardening of class lines, and the escalation of class conflict. The rage of former subordinate dependents who are abandoned by their patrons and excluded from access to the wider social system often initiates violent responses.

This stark analysis obviously oversimplifies the situation. However, it cautions us against assuming that status subordinates are always totally without power or resources in negotiating the character of vertical interaction. It cautions us also against the assumption that exploitation necessarily is perceived as such by subordinates, in inter-class interactions. This is, indeed, an empirical question. Inter-class ties which convey positive benefits of cooperative interaction ranging from those characterized by mutualism (or commensalism) are not necessarily less common or important than those of competition. I suggest that it is precisely those inter-class relations based on the perception (and reality) of some complementary advantages, and that keep communication open, are the ones which effectively defuse the generation of class conflict. This complementary vertical relation struc-tures competition *among* competing lower class persons for patrons who can deliver the rewards of the wider society. The shift in the Philippines from a hierarchy based on vertical complementarity to a hierarchy based on exploitation and involving the breach of previous personalistic vertical access marks the beginning of processes which have reinforced class formation and the escalation of inter-class conflict.

The remainder of the paper deals with an elaboration of the critical issues which support the rather idealized model just described. First, I turn to questions concerning power, conflict, and violence in the Philippines. Next, I consider further the question of verticality diach-ronically as well as the question of the organization of Philippine political action. In particular, I discuss the subtle workings of inter-mediation in the de-escalation (and in its absence, escalation) of vio-lence and in conflict resolution. Finally, I relate some pertinent his-torical and recent events in the Philippines, to the thesis of the interrelationship of verticality, intermediation, and the reduction (or creation) of organized conflict.

Social Conflict and Violence in the Philippines

During the tumultuous last week of February 1986, a television news anchorman, commenting on a picture of young Filipinos leaning against tanks and presenting flowers to armed troops, said "Filipinos are not a violent people." Courageous and non-violent as their actions on that occasion were, his remark is patently false. Filipinos are, by any standard capable of surprising violence. Their violence is expressed in culturally specific, normally personalistic and rarely anonymous, ways.

Although social conflict and contradictions abound in Philippine society, the expression of violence tends to be highly interpersonal rather than inter-categorical. Historically, violence was embedded in the practices of inter-locality raiding and headhunting which were rampant in the pre-Hispanic Philippines. Interethnic violence against anonymous Chinese migrants to the Philippines *was* routine during the Spanish colonial period. They represented a convenient scapegoat for both Spaniards and Filipinos. Revolts against excessive Spanish tribute or labor exactions were organized on the model of local ruler-led raiding parties of the pre-Hispanic era. But mass collective violence against an anonymous person or group is actually quite uncommon. However, factionalism is endemic among Filipinos in any social situation which combines persons of different alliance groupings. Feuds between such alliance groupings constitute the major arena of social conflict. These feuds are just as typical of Christian Filipinos as they are of pagan (Barton 1919) and Muslim (Kiefer 1972) Filipinos. A killing or wounding requires vengeance by the allies of the aggrieved against the perpetrator or his allies. On the interpersonal level, a personal insult and sometimes just a slight, especially one given publicly is cause for retaliation, sometimes immediate, sometimes deferred. But an assault on one's ego is never forgotten. *Amok* (the syndrome involving frenzied homicidal violence) is the final resort to the frustration of having to accept personal insult and not being able to even the score.

Collective inter-class violence has been intermittent, brief and surprisingly moderate in the Philippines, despite its violent expression in the revolts and insurgencies especially in this century. Power holders are in a strong position to express their hostility against a subordinate at any time, but they rarely have to employ violence. The threat of force is usually sufficient to make actual violence unnecessary. Such is the social reproduction of obedience to hierarchy in the Philippines. Intimidation and force by the "private armies" of powerful members of provincial elites usually come prominently into play only when personalistic relations no longer exist.

The commonest expression of violence between Filipinos—interpersonal violence—is related to their fierce competition for social recognition, for influence, and for wealth. This is a ubiquitous, constantly waged competition which provides the structure within which patron-client politics operates. But it is a competition mainly waged between persons or between families, rather than between wider groups, ethnic divisions, or classes. (The exceptions are seen in the Christian-Muslim, Armed Forces of the Philippines, and New People's Army violence of the past two decades.)

Filipinos have little belief in an abstract conception of social equality. All of their experience argues that abilities, power, and wealth are unequally distributed. But while recognizing that this unequal distribution exists, Filipinos do not accept it unchallenged. Indeed, they constantly struggle to improve their relative positions and their influence over others wherever they stand in the hierarchy. Position and power were traditionally measured by the size of one's grouping of personal supporters. The contest for prestige and higher rank is fiercest between males and between persons and their groupings of allies who are near equals. This is where violence is most likely to occur. Slights given between competing near-equals are the most dangerous, especially if given in public. Because competitors vigorously assert themselves in their quest for power the possibility of violence is heightened. This active confrontation heightens the possibility of violence as the competitors strive to protect their self-esteem (*amor propio*) against assault and to maintain extreme sensitivity to possible criticism. Being a significant cause for the loss of relative status, influence, and perhaps even followers, positive self-image is worth fighting for.

In contradistinction to the foregoing, conflict with clearly superordinate power figures is normally avoided at all cost. Subordinates, especially personal dependents, do not wish to risk losing favor with their patrons or anyone else perceived of as possibly exercising power over them. And subordinates are very reluctant to risk certain punishment if they are presumptuous enough to challenge and thus offend a superordinate.

Vertical Mediation in Conflict Resolution and the De-escalation of Violence

The Philippines has long been a hierarchical society. Specific relations within the entrenched structure of inequality have changed over time yet the hierarchical structure has proven remarkably persistent and resilient overall (Carroll 1970). The gap between rich and poor has widened rapidly and become obvious during the past two decades. Such circumstances surely imply that a class struggle should be well advanced. Yet, because the Philippines is so dominantly vertically-oriented, at least to date, a significant part of the population remains linked in personalized solidarity with members of different classes rather than with members in the same class. Interclass ties historically have been articulated by sets of particularistic patron-client relations contracted between persons with very different statuses and with mutually complementary resources. These are pervasive throughout the society and they are dynamic. While best known in various parts of the agricultural sector, they dominate most political and economic relations, the conduct of bureaucracy, access to welfare, and even the sociology of religion. They persist because they are personally advantageous, permitting the construction of chains of personal linkage which constitute effective adaptive strategies for survival and for social, political and economic access in a wider system.

Western models of political experience which emphasize either class or primordial relationships, while capturing some aspects of modern conflict or traditional sentiments in the Philippines, are not sufficient to explain the character of political activity in the Philippines. As James Scott (1977:124) suggests:

> when we leave the realm of class conflict or communalism, we are likely to find ourselves in the realm of informal power groups, leadership centered cliques and factions, and a whole panoply of more or less instrumental ties that characterize much of the political process in Southeast Asia. The structure and dynamics of such seemingly ad hoc groupings can, I believe, be best understood from the perspective of patron-client relations.

The importance and generality of Philippine verticality, that is, the structural dominance and responsiveness of superordinate-subordinate relationships cannot be overemphasized. It is not just political. It lies at the heart of the entire social and cultural system. Verticality and ranking are key structural principle of Philippine society. Yet, while agreeing with Scott (1972), Lande (1965), and others concerning the importance of patron-client relations (clientelism) in understanding Philippine political activity, I would insist that the full scope of sociopolitical activity is appreciated only by going beyond the dyadic bonds of clientelism to encompass the critical longer chains of intermediary relations. It is these chains which permit the indirect access by many persons at the bottom of society to vital goods and services. They continue to provide effective, predictable relationships. And they continue to reassert themselves even in drastically changing circumstances.

Fegan (1982:119) in describing the social history of a village in the heart of the most radicalized region of Central Luzon describes how vertical linkages subverted the momentum of the tenant-peasant rebellion in the early post-World War II period:

> The process by which upper peasant families acted as political ward-healers for the two landlord dominated parties, in return for getting their children into civil service jobs may have prevented conversion of the militant class consciousness shown in the peasant movements of the 1917 to 1954 period into a peasant class party.

He adds, "the tension between millenarian hopes of radical social change and short-term pragmatic self-interest could be handled by peasant elders overtly playing the pork-barrel and patron-client game in electoral politics, while covertly supporting the rebels" (1982:129).

By the early 1970s the problem group in southern Nueva Ecija was no longer the tenants, whose position had improved perceptibly, but the landless laborers who were competing for scarce employment. "The villages no longer stand united against the landlord class in town. They are divided by internal class conflict" (Fegan 1982:121).

Beyond the widening gap in income and privilege, tensions in Philippine class relations reached a point in certain areas of the Philippines in the 1960s that initiated apparently irreversible changes (Kerkvliet 1977, Wolters 1984). The forces responsible for the quickening and sharpening class conflict are numerous. The most obvious of these are soaring population growth, high man-land relations, severe competition for resources, massive unemployment and lack of economic opportunities, and tendencies toward dramatic reorganization of production, narrow economizing, profit-making orientation, and sheer greed. Perhaps the clearest representation of this change is captured in the nature of inter-class relations which earlier were overwhelmingly multistranded and which performed a wide range of functions for superordinate and subordinate. These relations were rapidly rationalized by superordinates, who found it in their interests to deal in narrower economic terms with their dependents. Multistranded social bonds became strictly economic bonds. Inequality which was tolerable (because it was tempered by indirect access through intermediaries by a large proportion of the population) became intolerable as a closed class structure emerged regionally. In historical terms, relations between two principal classes came periodically under stress especially since the mid 18th century. By the end of the century the oligarchic structure of Philippine politics was in place. Only the faces of those actually in power at any moment have changed since. Thus, the basic structure and processes that have eventuated in the present circumstances have been building for decades (McCoy and de Jesus 1982). However, for most of this century members of the ruling class operated more like "big men" than absolute rulers. By the 1960s things had changed substantially (Doronila 1985). Structurally, Philippine class relations were part-vertical and part-horizontal.

Analytically, it might be said that earlier the nature of hierarchical relations was softened through the idiom of equivalence of social and economic opportunities. The maintenance of strong personal relations tended to guarantee economic security and access to the values of the social system. Class interdependencies between unequals dominated and forestalled strong class formation. The progressively more intense economic competition which has accelerated in the course of the 20th century continued to play itself out in the idiom of *social* competition

for higher status and for more powerful patrons and vertical intermediaries. The intensity of social jousting may be seen as a symptom
of increasing tensions within the older order. Increasingly these older
arrangements appear, at long last, incapable of reconciling the growing
contradictions generated therein. The social tensions reinforced by
deepening poverty, and made apparent by blatant inequalities (even
rampant exploitation, repression and terror) seem likely to destroy the
remnants of the existing structure, and to increase the level of socio-
political conflict. They must eventually result in a revolutionary change
in Philippine society. Or so our expectations would have it. What
surprises us is that this process does not necessarily follow either our
expectations or our timetable for change.

For me, the major change that has occurred in this century is that
personalistic inter-class relations in a number of regions have been
severed in a wholesale manner as those willing and able to serve as
patrons have declined the role. This occurred first and most completely
on the new agricultural frontiers (Kerkvliet 1977, McLennan 1982).
Provincial elites refused to serve or to continue to serve as intermediaries for rural Filipinos. With the rejection of the provision of security
offered under the system of social dependency and the denial of access
to the wider sociopolitical and economic system, peasants and agricultural laborers had no option but to organize themselves, as they
could, horizontally and seek alternative leadership. If we map the
distribution of agrarian unrest and of rapid politicization and radi-
calization of Philippine peasantry we find a close correspondence with
the areas where peasants and rural laborers were excluded from personal
patronage and vertical intermediation. Thus, the severing of vertical
intermediation has in my view strongly reinforced processes related to
the escalation of organized inter-class conflict. Government efforts to
make economic operations of small producers more efficient, and to
modernize the rural and industrial sectors rapidly, have only accelerated
the process. Today, while vertical intermediation has excluded significant numbers of the poorest and most vulnerable of Filipinos from
meaningful socioeconomic access and opportunities from any hope for
the future, it has continued to operate within the upper ranks of rural
producers, the growing middle class and the ruling elite.

Still, there are reasons to question whether the course of events will
follow as a "natural" consequence of the tragic inequalities and polarizing trends that are so apparent. At least events are unlikely to
follow as rapidly as has been predicted. One reason rests on the fact
of the continuity of vertical access through intermediation by millions
of Filipinos not yet cut off from access to the system. The other rests
on the persistence of the structure and ideology of verticality (even

within the New People's Army) and on the practical recognition by the individual that the macro-system cannot be changed. While pernicious to us and to those who wish to establish social movements based on ideology, verticality and its personal manipulability in accomplishing tasks is pragmatically highly effective. In its capacity for micromanipulation many Filipinos continue to see their best opportunities for improving their circumstances. The vertical structure of relationships has operated so long in the Philippines, and is so fundamentally entrenched in the institutional framework and in the conduct of interpersonal relations that it has become the major general process for the solution of problems—the master strategy of Filipinos on which they ultimately fall back. Remarkably, many Filipinos who objectively have lost all hope of vertical access through patrons, brokers, and chains of linking persons continue to think and to act in terms of the vertical intermediary model.

Notes

1. This is a revised version of a paper presented at the 1986 annual meeting of the Kroeber Society, session on the "Anthropology of Peace and War," in honor of David G. Mandelbaum.

References Cited

Anderson, J.N. 1968. Peasants as "Prey"? Rethinking Peasant Adaptations and Socioeconomic Change. Paper presented at the annual meetings of the Kroeber Anthropological Society, Berkeley.

Barton, R.F. 1919. *Ifugao Law.* Berkeley: University of California Publications in American Archaeology and Anthropology, Vol. 15, No. 1.

Carroll, J. 1970. *Philippine Institutions.* Manila: Solidaridad Publishing House.

Doronila, A. 1985. The Transformation of Patron-Client Relations and its Political Consequences in the Postwar Philippines. *Journal of Southeast Asian Studies* 161:99–116.

Kerkvliet, B. 1974. Agrarian Conditions Since the Huk Rebellion: A Barrio in Central Luzon. In *Political Change in the Philippines.* B.J. Kerkvliet ed., Honolulu: University Press of Hawaii, Pp. 1–76.

———. 1977. *The Huk Rebellion: A Study of Peasant Revolt in the Philippines.* Berkeley: University of California Press.

Kiefer, T.M. 1972. *The Tausug: Violence and Law in a Philippine Moslem Society.* New York: Holt, Reinhart and Winston.

Lande, C.H. 1965. *Leaders, Factions, and Parties: The Structure of Philippine Politics.* Yale University: Southeast Asia Studies.

McLennan, M.S. 1982. Changing Human Ecology on the Central Luzon Plain: Nueva Ecija, 1705–1939. In *Philippine Social History Global Trade and*

Local Transformations. A. McCoy and E. de Jesus, eds., Honolulu: University of Hawaii Press, Pp. 57–90.

McCoy, A.W. and E.C. de Jesus. 1982. *Philippine Social History Global Trade and Local Transformations.* Honolulu: University of Hawaii Press.

Scott, J.C. 1972. Patron-Client Politics and Political Change in Southeast Asia. *American Political Science Review* 661:91–113.

———. 1977. Patron-Client Politics and Political Change in Southeast Asia. In *Friends, Followers and Factions.* S.W. Schmidt, et al., eds., Berkeley: University of California Press, Pp. 123–146.

Vayda, A.P. 1976. *War in Ecological Perspective.* New York: Plenum Press.

Wolters, W.1984. *Politics, Patronage and Class Conflict in Central Luzon.* Quezon City: New Day Publishers.

11 / Fourth World Responses to External Threats: The Dené

Alice B. Kehoe

The importance of studying the interrelationships between symbolic and normative aspects of societies for better understanding the social dynamics of peace and conflict has surfaced in various ways as a common theme in the preceding articles. The following chapter by Alice Kehoe brings this theme into central focus. Emphasizing the place of normative commitments and of the effective manipulation of symbols in the service of self-determination and indigenous values, Kehoe describes how a small Canadian Indian group, the Dené, has thwarted the political and economic agenda of "more powerful" nation-states and multinational corporations. She argues that the Dené proceed on the basis of the indigenous view of peace as beginning and ending with a vision of a plurality of communities living out long-used modes of existence. This view contrasts with the Western view, which is tied to the concept that peace is the regulation of conflict. Based on their normative commitment to local communities living in harmony with their ecosystems, the Dené have been able to forge politically effective coalitions with other Fourth world peoples. In addition, they have been aided by Western peace and ecology activists. By their use of symbols in the world press, the Dené have achieved an ethical power far greater than the material power recognized by "political realists." In one way or another, each of the papers in this book has argued that in calculating the social dynamics of peace and conflict taking account of symbolic and conventional aspects of society is as important as counting the material and technological resources which a society controls. Indeed, as Kehoe shows, the normative

Copyright © 1988 Alice B. Kehoe

and symbolic dimensions of social life can trump brute force. Kehoe's study well illustrates the major thesis of this book: that the study of culture and symbolism can contribute to revitalizing international security. —The Editors

"The Dené are opposed emphatically to furthering the nuclear arms race," stated the Vice-President of the Dené Nation at a press conference in 1984 (*Akwesasne Notes* 16(6):4)

Who are the Dené? Where or what is the Dené Nation? Can their opposition affect the arms race? Denendeh, land of the Dené, occupies the Mackenzie River region of the western North West Territories of Canada. Approximately 9,000 Dené live in 26 communities in Denendeh. Denendeh also contains significant uranium deposits and the favored route for a major pipeline carrying oil and gas to industrial southern Canada and the United States. Georges Erasmus, former President of the Dené Nation, pointed out, "We're aware that the uranium for the atomic bomb that was dropped on Hiroshima and Nagasaki in 1945 came from Denendeh. We're also aware that over 85% of the uranium in the world is actually on aboriginal lands and so we see that we're definitely tied in with the anti-nuclear movement because we possess the resources" (*Akwesasne Notes* 16(6):4).

While most of the world focuses on the mythic confrontation of the titan superpowers, small communities of indigenous peoples, some like the Dené still subsisting by hunting and fishing, are asserting an inalienable right of sovereignty over their ancestral lands. These lands contain, as Erasmus noted, significant quantities of resources essential for modern weaponry and warfare. Shrewd leaders from the aboriginal communities are presenting their basic demand for self-rule within a framework of justice, human rights, and peaceful coexistence (see also Asch 1984, Krech 1984, Ørvik and Patterson 1976). This paper examines the developing coalitions between the Fourth World and peace activists.

Geologic formations rich in uranium stretch from Denendeh across the Athabasca region to Wollaston Lake in northeastern Saskatchewan. Since 1975, Eldorado Nuclear has been mining uranium there. It has operated one mine called the Rabbit Lake mine, and has been creating a second mine in Collins Bay of Wollaston Lake by damming and draining to dig in the former lake bed. Eldorado Nuclear is part of a uranium mining industry that began in the 1950s around Uranium City in the northwestern sector of Saskatchewan (in central Canada). These mines have been a boon to the province's economy and continue to look attractive to economic planners. To the Indians of northern

Saskatchewan, uranium mining has brought very little income and serious threat to their livelihood and to their lives. Eldorado Nuclear and other mining companies build what by northern standards are relatively luxurious accommodations for workers imported from southern Canada, rotated with leaves back home in the south. Local Indians and Métis are seldom hired, and then only for low-ranked and often temporary jobs. The company towns are enclaves wholly dependent on imports, lacking any integration into local economic or social structures. What northern Saskatchewan gets from its uranium mines is radioactive waste, an estimated 250,000,000 metric tonnes so far (CASNP 1985:17).

A Chipewyan community called the Lac La Hache Band occupies Wollaston Lake territory. Athabascan-speaking, these Chipewyans are among the easternmost Dené. They believe that radioactive tailings and the material remaining from the processing of the Rabbit Lake Mine uranium into yellowcake, its exported form, have affected the health and lifespans of the Wollaston Lake people both directly and through contaminating the fish, caribou, other animals and plants they harvest for subsistence. The Collins Bay project threatens greater contamination, during its period of operation and afterward when Wollaston Lake is to be allowed to flow back over the mine site. Seeing only negative consequences for themselves from the Rabbit Lake and Collins Bay mines, the Lac La Hache Band formally protested against Eldorado Nuclear. In the summer of 1985, the Indian band was joined by anti-nuclear and peace activists from southern Canada, forming the Collins Bay Action Group. A rolling blockade on the road leading to the mine site appeared in July, headquartered in the Blockade Camp down the road where civil disobedience tactics were taught and spiritual uplift was provided through Indian drum and dance.

The Collins Bay Action Group is an example of a growing phenomenon of the 1980s, the alliance of "Fourth World" self-determination strategists with peace/anti-nuclear/disarmament activists (see Brøsted et al. 1985). Canadian Indians and Scandinavian Sami (Lapps) are forging international links with the European Greens and New Zealand. In August 1985, an Inuit (Eskimo) representative flew with a Euro-Canadian protester over the United States nuclear submarine traversing the Northwest Passage. The leaflets dropped from the plane demanded world recognition of the unwillingness of the Inuit and the Euro-Canadian peace activists to allow a nuclear warship to invade what each identified as his group's territorial waters. Notwithstanding the opposition in Ottawa to Euro-Canadian granting of political status to Nunavut, the projected eastern, Inuit-controlled half of the North West Territories, inside the protest plane it didn't matter that Inuit and southerner were each claiming rights over the same waters. A common enemy, a common threat had been perceived.

To understand the dynamics of the coalition developing between "indigenous," or "Fourth World," peoples and a variety of peace and environmentalist groups, it is necessary to begin with the 1960s counterculture movement. The dialectics of protest in the 1960s against escalating nuclear armaments, unforeseen radiation hazards (for example, the discovery of strontium-90 in the milk of American and Canadian mothers), apparent rampant materialist values blazoned in the postwar onrush of consumer goods, and United States imperialist moves against smaller states (for example, Cuba and Vietnam), coalesced around the Nature pole of the familiar Western contrast between culture and nature.

Nuclear power development, whether for electricity generation or weapons, war, destruction of natural resources in industrial expansion, denial of political rights to quasi-colonial peoples including southern American Blacks, all were projected as aspects of an unholy crusade against Nature, a crusade destroying not only the natural environment around us but the good and beautiful facets of human nature. Rejecting Western "materialism" and its "murderous" tendencies, many Europeans and Americans sought to rejoin and protect Nature. Meadows were overrun by more-or-less naked celebrants of the beauty of Nature, ashrams in India received planeloads of devotees from overseas, and the residents of the more picturesque American Indian reservations bemusedly watched city-bred pilgrims fulfill their thirst for spiritual transcendence by earnestly dancing in powwows. Organized protests in the 1960s and early 1970s were as a rule disparate, focused on democratizing universities, obtaining civil rights for American Blacks, banning the bomb, ending the Vietnam war or at least the draft, or reducing the Bureau of Indian Affairs' control over Indians. Constituencies of protest groups might overlap, but organized protests preferred concrete distinct goals rather than diffuse expectations. The dominant theme of antithesis to "the Establishment" existed both in laid-back individualist hedonism and in organized group protest, but political alliance was not seen as a necessary principal means to the various desired ends.

During the 1970s, the clear and simple contrast between the good nature-lovers and the bad Establishment of the late 1960s began to muddy. Blacks gained rights but couldn't find jobs. Women became their own persons but were beset with agonizing decisions over the choices now thrust at them. Smoke from all the woodburning stoves brought palls over the bucolic retreats. Nudity appeared on movie screens and somehow didn't seem liberating. America pulled out of

Vietnam and the draft ended, soon to be replaced with registration for a draft for a war that wasn't being fought while American advisers congregated in Central America. A generation was growing up in the First World learning to curb their impulses, to assess situations assuming that every rainbow was associated with rain.

Demagogues' failures, in the late 1960s and early 1970s, to revolutionize First World societies allowed more circumspect politicians to advance to leadership and work toward developing and strengthening institutional bases for action. One such politician was George Manuel, a Shuswap Indian from British Columbia. Manuel worked from the 1950s organizing Indians to redress iniquities and injustices. Beginning with his own people in interior southern British Columbia, Manuel extended his contacts and issues until in 1970 he was installed as first president of the National Indian Brotherhood, a coalition of Canadian Indian leaders galvanized into a trans-regional body by the 1969 government White Paper proposing to abolish special status for Canadian Indians. Five years later, George Manuel had created the World Council of Indigenous Peoples to unite for political action representatives of what he had come to recognize as the Fourth World. Manuel notes that the term "Fourth World" was suggested to him by a Tanzanian diplomat in Ottawa, Mbutu Milando (Manuel and Poslun 1974:xvi).

Trips to New Zealand and Australia to see how Maoris and Australian Aborigines managed within their respective Commonwealth governments, and a visit to Tanzania to observe a former colony functioning as an independent nation, taught Manuel the common elements and goals of indigenous peoples subjugated within nations dominated by an alien cultural tradition, and also the differences between conventionally recognized Third World nations and the subjugated encapsulated Fourth World indigenous peoples. Poverty is the lot and the problem of the Third and Fourth Worlds, but the Fourth World peoples lack political recognition as well.

In Manuel's conception of the Fourth World, the still-subjugated indigenous peoples are pockets of poverty within wealthy First World nations. Even as he realized that the World Council of Indigenous Peoples ought to bring in representatives of Latin American Indians, Manuel preserved the contrast between the poverty of these subjugated peoples and the relative affluence of the dominant class in Third World nations. Manuel's use of the term "Fourth World" to emphasize indigenous subjugated peoples differs from such use as that of economists who merely refer to the poorest of the poor nations, or that of the Minority Rights Group (Whitaker 1973) which includes immigrant minorities, such as Jews in the Soviet Union or Blacks in Brazil, as well as groups formed by actions such as religious conversion, like Baptists in the Soviet Union.

Because of these varying uses, Manuel and his colleagues tend to use "Indigenous Peoples" or, more recently, "First Nations" to refer to the subjugated indigenous peoples, emphasizing both the political and the economic contrasts between the internal colonies and the nations of the First, Second, and Third Worlds. George Manuel worked hard through a lifetime to link anciently diverse Canadian Indian peoples into a potentially effective political movement; in the heyday of the Counterculture he received little attention, but today his model of action is followed by a younger generation of Indian and other "Fourth World" leaders who see the value of constructing a base integrating the broadest possible variety of interests sharing common principles.

What unites the Fourth World leaders and the First World peace and environmental activists is the shared conviction that contemporary economic practices include technology and modes of exploitation that are dangerously, and ultimately needlessly, destructive. The common goal of these diverse groups is a world in which the social and long-range economic costs of technology and political structures are regularly assessed and practices adjusted toward long-term equilibria encompassing health and a measure of economic security for all humans. Nuclear disarmament would be a necessary step toward this goal, since even accidental detonations of nuclear weapons could destroy our species. Heads of six second-rank nations expressed the unifying goal in the Delhi Declaration of the Five Continent Peace Initiative,

> [O]ur voices are joined in a universal demand in defense of our right to live. . . . [H]undreds of billions of dollars . . . are spent annually on weapons. This stands in dramatic contrast to the poverty, and in some cases misery, in which two-thirds of the world population lives (Alfonsín et al. 1985).

Underlying this "demand" is the Enlightenment principle of an inalienable right to life, liberty and the pursuit of happiness, to be carried out in societies honoring liberté, egalité, and fraternité. The United Nations Charter in 1945 put its purpose as follows:

> To develop friendly relations among nations based on respect for the principle of equal rights and self-determination of peoples, and to take other appropriate measures to strengthen universal peace (United Nations Charter, Article 1).

Self-determination—or, home rule—is thus regularly linked to the claimed inalienable human right to personal freedom for self-fulfillment and to conditions for peace.

Models of Peace

In the Western tradition, peace is simply, as the Oxford English Dictionary states in its first definition, "freedom from, cessation of, war." St. Augustine put it startlingly,

> Every man seeks peace by waging war. . . . They who make war desire nothing but victory . . . what else is victory than the conquest of those who resist us? and when this is done there is peace (*City of God* book XIX, 10–13, quoted in Marrin 1971:57).

Augustine articulates the *conflict resolution* model of peace, a model that dominates contemporary peace research, as can be seen in the title of the leading journal, *Journal of Conflict Resolution,* and of the Section for Conflict and Peace Research in the Oslo Institute for Social Research which became the International Peace Research Institute of Oslo. Oslo's leading scholar, Johan Galtung, sums up his professional studies as,

> a plea . . . for a view that sees conflict as entirely normal . . . a more positive attitude to conflict. . . . The basic idea is that if conflict is not to be acted out violently, an alternative has to be given, some other way of acting it out which somehow has to be isomorphic to violent conflict behavior (Galtung 1978:27).

He suggests (1978:480) developing "a world with a competitive kind of peaceful coexistence," competing in sports, productivity, Nobel prizes and similar "cultural contributions," "technical assistance contributions *per capita . . . happiness . . .* etc. . . . ." Conflict resolution as a model of peace stems from a metaphysics of oppositional dualism, which is fundamental to the Judaeo-Christian(-Muslim) religious tradition and well exemplified both explicitly and structurally in the Bible. Division, as in Genesis 1, "In the beginning God created the heaven and the earth. . . . God divided the light from the darkness. . . . And God . . . divided the waters," and so on, until in Chapter 2, God created the "knowledge of good and evil." Division and contrast are postulated as the most basic structure of the world created by the Deity.

The structure overrides religious commitment, finding tangible manifestations in innumerable artifacts from two-party governments and two houses of Parliament to on-off electric switches and binary computer languages. Division, contrast and competition are taught to Western children from their earliest years, when boy babies are dressed differently from girl babies, when children playing are divided into competing teams, when prizes are awarded for performances judged competitively. Competition and conflict are facts of social life in Western societies and are premised to be universal and natural. This "perspective" is said to be,

> consistent with scientific knowledge of human society, [it] sees peace as a state of social relations in which conflict is regulated so as to maximize its positive consequences for human beings (Baur 1983:81).

First God, now Science, legitimize and impose conflict upon the world.

If this essay were to conform to the common structure of Western discourse, it would now contrast the Western metaphysic of oppositional dualism with an Eastern metaphysic of harmony. The Chinese yin-yang complementarity, Indian (East or American) mystic oneness with Brahma or Nature, or even Zen riddling may be selected as the exemplar of unity opposed to Western dualism. Let me try to struggle free of this flypaper of tradition, to avoid the entrapment of structuring dualism which a moment's reflection reveals to be untrue—for example, the Bhagavad Gita is Indian and strongly structured in oppositional dualism, and so is much fifteenth-century poetry in Nahuatl, even of the philosopher-king Netzahualcóyotl of Texcoco. Imposing a contrast between Western conflict models and non-Western harmony models only perpetuates stereotypes.

If contemporary formal peace research were not so engrossed with conflict resolution, a generally overlooked but impressively viable model of peace might be better recognized: the Dumezilian "Indo-European" society in a dynamic tripartite equilibrium. According to Dumézil (1968), ancient Indo-European societies conceptualized three estates comprising the nation: the priest-judges (in English tradition, the Lords Spiritual), the secular lord charged with executing the laws (Lords Temporal), and the productive segment, peasants, artisans and merchants (Commons). No one of these was truly sovereign, for all three powers—knowledge, force, and productivity—are necessary to society. The three estates serve as checks and balances for one another, each citizen serving the greater good through the exercise of his or her proper capacity and all deserving respect. Dumézil saw traditional Hindu society with the three castes of Brahmin, Kshatriya, and Vaisya exemplifying this fundamental Indo-European structure; the three estates recognized traditionally in France and Britain would be additional examples, and the strongest example is surely the United States of America, formally structured into Supreme Court, President, and Congress by its classically-educated founders.

What might be termed the Fourth World model of peace premises neither inevitable conflict nor a highly structured equilibrium. Nor does it really invoke a mystical unity or harmony, though Western interpreters are prone to impute this. As R.B.J. Walker (1984) argued, the very concept of a universal moral order so easily assumed in the West is a product of the set of primitive postulates from which Judaeo-Christian(-Muslim) religious monotheism has been constructed. A Fourth World model of peace may be said to, in a sense, ignore peace; to ignore, to fail to construct, any universalistic order including a reification called peace.

The Fourth World position begins and ends with the plurality of communities living out modes of existence that have demonstrated their viability over generations. This conceptualization is much like that of the ecosystem, and the world as happening to exhibit a variety of ecosystems. The principles of evolutionary biology, that no ecosystem is inherently superior to another except in reference to the particulars of its habitat, that the instability of all habitats renders all adaptations ultimately imperfect, fit quite well the Fourth World attitude and allow its congruence with environmental activists' campaigns. What Fourth World leaders such as the Dené argue is that each local community should look to its environs to construct its subsistence, then from this position of primary independence work out mutually tolerable accommodations with its neighbors. Zero-sum (win-lose) games have no place in a world of living beings, from this perspective. Neither peace nor war, competition or hierarchy of power exist in this metaphysic of viability unbounded either in time or in space.

From the Western metaphysic, this is a model of peace because it does not posit conflict; peace activists can ally with Fourth World claimants for self-determination under the umbrella concept of a world of accommodation in place of competition in zero-sum terms.

Realpolitik

Peace advocacy is frequently contrasted with the alleged ubiquity of conflict, peace a utopian ideal at odds with "scientific knowledge of human society." Environmental melioration and efforts to obtain a greater measure of home rule are more "realistic" goals because they can be described in the rhetoric of strategies customarily used to discuss politics in Western societies. Both environmentalists' objectives and home rule could be gained by negotiation and compromise, like other political ends in *realpolitik,* so they may be within the "art of the possible."

The radical notion in Fourth World declarations is that small communities might exert influence over large nations. Fourth World leaders hold some trump cards nature dealt them, the presence of valuable raw materials within the territories of the Fourth World peoples. Denendeh includes uranium deposits, some hydroelectric potential, and several feasible routes for transcontinental pipelines. Can a few thousand Dené and Métis prevent Canada and the United States from exploiting these resources? Can they use these trump cards, or will the big bully nations grab the cards Nature dealt? How realistic is Dené insistence on their power to control the resources of their native land?

That a strong measure of home rule is quite possible is argued by the "First Nations" of Canada on the basis of Denmark's granting home rule to Greenland. Hans-Pavia Rosing, a Greenlander and president in 1982 of the Inuit Circumpolar Conference, addressed the first (1982) World Assembly of First Nations, in Saskatchewan, on "a practical example of how aboriginal peoples can recover control of their own destinies" (*Saskatchewan Indian* 12(6):18).

Greenland is of course remote from Denmark and has few valuable resources compared to Denendeh in the central Canadian landmass. Denendeh and Nunavut do nevertheless appear more possible since Greenland's achievement of home rule in 1979, Denmark's process and structuring of granting Greenland internal autonomy serving now as a model and proof of feasibility.

Dené and Inuit are not resting their hopes for home rule on Ottawa graciously following Copenhagen's example. Alliances with southern Canada and internationally are seen as essential in pursuing self-determination. Economic benefits are supposed to accrue to the Canadian government from northern self-determination because bureaucratic outlay and welfare payments are expected to lessen, but these promises are not so convincing that there is clear practical advantage to Ottawa in granting home rule to Denendeh and Nunavut. Northern peoples' strongest suit is the general acknowledgement of the inalienable human right to participation in a democratic representative government, a right enshrined in the United Nations Charter and many subsequent public pronouncements by world leaders. Dené and Inuit couch their demands in the rhetoric of human rights and gain favorable attention from writers, news producers, liberal activists, the United Nations Non-Governmental Organizations and the Russell Tribunal. Human rights rhetoric may be empty words but it traps politicians into appearing to bless demands for self-determination. The rhetoric is a means to capture international public attention and to build a claim on publicly unassailable principles. Once this virtue of the indigenous peoples' demands is established, the Indian and Inuit leaders can address the variety of interests of the outside groups now listening: nuclear control groups can see the uranium deposits in Denendeh and Nunavut, environmentalists observe the delicate ecology of the North, Greens note the strong overlap between their platforms and those of the Dené and Inuit—bioregionalism would produce a Denendeh and a Nunavut.

From the point of view of classical *realpolitik,* the Dené and Inuit are naive. They lack manpower and technology to repel invasion. A rolling blockade of a remote gravel road by a few dozen protesters is as easily crushed as a mouse by an elephant. That, of course, is the point: the elephant is afraid to step on the mouse. So long as the Lac La Hache band is assured of international publicity should its protesters be crushed, Eldorado Nuclear and its friends in southern Canada must respect the Indians. *Realpolitik* today includes the manipulation of international public opinion, and here the sophisticated Dené and Inuit leaders are not disadvantaged; if anything, they enjoy a privileged position before a public disposed to see them as the noble red men, as Karl May's Winnetou or Neihardt's Black Elk. The challenge to the Dené and the Inuit is to hold public support internationally, by the nitty gritty working out of links and joint activities with a diversity of groups, and by staging media events or issuing press statements that will be picked up.

Because Denendeh and Nunavut are in Canada, the Inuit and Dené have been given a unique opportunity to advance their demands through the patriation of the British North American Act, by which Canada was released from the ultimate sovereignty of the British Parliament. Canada wrote a Constitution at this time, which in its initial presentation in 1980 failed to mention Indians or Inuit. Leaders of the indigenous peoples quickly alerted officials and members of Parliament to the omission of the special status of Treaty Indians. This was rectified in 1981, but the Indians and Inuit were not satisfied. They realized that they could demand recognition of their sovereign rights as, in their own terms, First Nations of Canada. The Constitution was passed in 1982, but representatives of the indigenous peoples have been meeting annually in First Ministers' Conferences, negotiating with government officials over the meaning of "existing Aboriginal and treaty rights," the phrase in the Constitution.

In the larger context of renegotiated relationships between the federal and provincial governments catalyzed by the writing of the Constitution, the possibility of provincial status for Denendeh and Nunavut is conceivable. Debates over the clauses of the Constitution sensitized

Canadians to the conflicts and compromises smoothed over in the final document, so that the demands of the Dené and Inuit seem similar to those of other constituencies in Canada rather than going against a properly hallowed tradition.

Pragmatists must concede that the Dené were no simple-minded fools when they issued their declaration in 1975:

> The challenge to the Dené and the world is to find the way for the recognition of the Dené Nation.
> Our plea to the world is to help us in our struggle to find a place in the world community where we can exercise our right to self-determination as a distinct people and as a nation (*Native Perspective* 1975:19).

Appealing to the world community, the Dené served notice upon Canada that they were prepared to mobilize international opinion to counterbalance their apparent powerlessness within the structure of Canadian politics. Their decision to issue their Declaration in 1975 itself illustrates their savvy, for it followed a well-publicized government-sponsored inquiry into the rights and needs of the Dené, occasioned by their opposition to the building of a massive pipeline along the Mackenzie Valley.

Thomas Berger, a judge who had headed the New Democratic Party (Canada's socialist-leaning third party) in British Columbia, heard depositions from an unprecedented number of Dené, both in formal proceedings in the provincial capital of Yellowknife and in the Dené communities. Berger concluded that native rights were substantial and should carry weight in evaluations of Northern development projects. His sympathetic support of the Dené, vivified through televised broadcasts of the poor but dignified people pleading for non-interference so that they could continue their self-reliant hunting and fishing subsistence, convinced many southern Canadians that Dené ought to have the opportunity to make their livelihood and lives free from Government interference. Dené know very well that armies today can be hamstrung, if not totally controlled, by public opinion. The world-system is more than an economic system, and the Dené can play on the world stage.

Peace

What makes the Dené demand for home rule interesting for a volume on the social dynamics of peace and conflict is their insistence that self-determination will include a determination to withhold Denendeh's uranium from a world that already used it to destroy Hiroshima and

Nagasaki. The position fits very well into the 1980s major peace movements which, as Nigel Young (1983:5) notes, differ from earlier peace movements in being "a synthesis of antimilitarism, ecology, feminism, local and worker democracy, and political decentralism." Such an amalgam characterizes the Greens in Europe and their American version, the bioregionalists. A grassroots movement, it has been called, from its focus on municipalities declaring themselves nuclear-free zones and electing officials who will promote its goals, but the 1980s' peace movements are hardly populist movements. Ecology furnishes the model and the rationale, and a sophisticated fear of bureaucracy as a kind of pea-brained lumbering dinosaur ruling the swamps of the world-system inspires efforts to develop decentralized structures responsive to local needs, communities congruent with local and regional ecosystems with their potential for evolutionary adaptation.

The 1980s' peace movement is looking for a bloodless revolution. Informed by Gandhian non-violence principles (Young 1983:4), street-smart tactics of such as those developed by Saul Alinsky, bright ideas for media-eye-catching popular participation like the Pentagon Peace Ribbon, the movement as a whole seeks to break out of bourgeois institutions and move the world into new alignments. Arrayed against this radical decentralization are the interests of the world's major political parties and corporations, the inertia of bureaucracies and their staffs' job security, the universalistic hegemonic principle of the Judaeo-Christian-Muslim tradition, all the power of conservative forces. That the Davids of the peace movement should slay these Goliaths doesn't seem likely. What may happen are incremental shifts toward long-range environmental planning, toward reducing unemployment, strengthening Third World economies, and allowing a greater measure of home rule to indigenous peoples. These shifts are already in motion. Their cumulative effect may bring about a world in which as Aurelio Peccei, founder of the Club of Rome, observed, "the institution of war is no more relevant to the modern world than are the institutions of slavery and human sacrifice" (quoted in Becker 1985:11). In that world, Denendeh may very well be a province; one where uranium ore rests untapped within Mother earth.

References Cited

Alfonsín, R., M. de la Madrid, R. Gandhi, O. Palme, J. Nyerere, and A. Papandreou. 1985. *The Delhi Declaration of the Five Continent Peace Initiative.* Delhi, 28 January.

Asch, M. 1984. Dené Political Rights. *Cultural Survival Quarterly* 84:33–37.

Baur, E.J. 1983. College Curricula in Conflict Regulation, the Emergence of a Discipline. *Peace and Change* 91:81-92.
Becker, J.M. 1985. *Teaching About Nuclear Disarmament.* Bloomington, IN: Phi Delta Kappa Educational Foundation.
Brøsted, J., J. Dahl, A. Gray, H. Gulløv, G. Henriksen, J. Jørgensen, and I. Kleivan, editors. 1985. *Native Power: The Quest for Autonomy and Nationhood of Indigeneous Peoples.* Bergen: Universitetforslaget As and New York: Columbia University Press.
CASNP. 1985. Wollaston Lake Blockade; Wollaston: A Portrait, *The Phoenix* September: 10-12, 15-17. Toronto: Canadian Alliance in Solidarity with the Native Peoples.
Cuthand, B., editor. 1982. World Assembly of First Nations. *Saskatchewan Indian* 126:2-89.
Dumézil, G. 1968. *Mythe et épopée.* Paris: Editions Gallimard.
Galtung, J. 1978. *Peace and Social Structure.* Essays in Peace Research, vol 3. Copenhagen: Christian Ejlers.
Krech, S. III. 1984. Land Claims and Political Development—The Case of the Dené. *Cultural Survival Quarterly* 83:41-43.
Laraque, M. 1984. Dené Say "We Will Not Participate in the Arms Race." *Akwesasne Notes* 166:4, 25.
Manuel, G. and M. Posluns. 1974. *The Fourth World.* New York: Free Press.
Marrin, Albert, editor. 1971. *War and the Christian Conscience.* Chicago: Henry Regnery Co.
Native Perspective Staff. 1975. The Dené Nation. *The Native Perspective* 12:18-20, 45-46.
Ørvik, N. and K.R. Patterson, editors. 1976. *The North in Transition.* Kingston, Ont: Queen's University Centre for International Relations.
Walker, R.B.J. 1984. World Politics and Western Reason: Universalism, Pluralism, Hegemony. In *Culture, Ideology, and World Order.* R.B.J. Walker, ed., Boulder: Westview Press, Pp. 182-216.
Whitaker, B. 1973. *The Fourth World.* New York: Schocken Books.
Young, N. 1983. The Contemporary European Anti-Nuclear Movement: Experiments in the Mobilization of Public Power. *Peace and Change* 91:1-16.

CONCLUSION / Expanding the Anthropology of Peace and Conflict

Mary LeCron Foster

Although the study of peace and conflict in relation to international security is a relatively new focus within anthropology, we can begin to define theoretical hypotheses and to explore avenues for expanding our theoretical base.[1] The papers in this volume as well as in other anthropological publications and symposia provide a means to this end.

Some anthropologists stress the primacy of materialistic or biological factors in triggering conflicts that result in the outbreak of armed hostilities (for example, Ferguson 1984, Ardrey 1966), in contrast, the major emphasis of the authors in this and a growing number of other studies (for example, Foster and Rubinstein 1986, Simonis 1983, Turner and Pitt 1988) is on the determining role of dominant cultural structures. Such structures promote either peaceful or military solutions to conflicts—which, as all anthropologists would agree, are inevitable results of social living and differences in needs, priorities, and goals among and between social groups and their members. Cultural structures that favor peaceful solutions also serve to prevent conflict from developing, as papers in the section, Dynamics of Peace in this volume, illustrate.

More anthropological studies have, in the past, focused on structures of power and politics than on those of peace and war *per se*. To achieve our aim, theories of power need to be incorporated into the broader topic of peace and conflict. Also at issue is the task of uncovering both the varied cultural mechanisms that promote peace and cooperation and those which foster conflict and warfare. A non-materialist focus, centering on the interplay of underlying ideologies can make anthropology a useful—even perhaps essential—tool for those striving to create a secure world. Materialistic concerns are only relevant in the context of the cultural infrastructure of any given society (see Greenhouse 1987).

As well as making use of anthropological studies of power, it is essential to bring studies of social change to bear on the dynamics of peace and conflict. Cohen (1974) argues that a thoroughly entrenched view—usually implicit—shared by many anthropologists as well as other social analysts, is that social change leads only in one direction: "from 'primitive' society which is dominated by status to modern industrial society which is dominated by contract. From the non-rationality of custom to the rationality of bureaucracy" (Cohen 1974:49). Cohen argues effectively that it is only through abandoning this mistaken evolutionary premise and analyzing the composition of a variety of social dramas involving power and selfhood, guided by differing symbolic constructs—including those that seem to us most "primitive," or least "rational"—that we can begin to understand the equally unconscious forces that structure and determine our own social behavior and its changing nature.

Peace and War as Categories

War is not well defined as a category. It is not clear, for example, if the sporadic raiding of hunter-gatherer tribes, or the head-hunting of those of New Guinea, qualify as war or as some other form of organized violence. If war is poorly defined, peace is a still more nebulous category. In a recent paper, Tishkov (1986) suggested that if we are to hope to advance the cause of peace we should know what it is that we are advocating. Is it simply the absence of overt conflict, or is it something more dynamic, with characteristics of its own? If it is not simply the absence of war, what are the sources and what the manifestations of its dynamics?

To understand war and peace we must begin with conflict and cooperation. Self-interest is an inherited trait of sentient creatures, and each species has devised practices which protect against self-destruction. Territoriality is one such device, with respect for the territorial priority of others serving as a block to potentially lethal conflict. Another social device is domination by a powerful male, who protects a group against encroachment by outsiders. In both cases, fear of retaliation prevents external aggression while some degree of cooperation assures the survival of individuals within the group.

In human society, by providing shared belief systems to ensure cooperation, cultural norms serve as a means of self-preservation. These norms have the potential to extend altruistic sentiments beyond the intimate group by making it possible to think of the "other" as like, rather than dangerously different from, "us." The extent to which norms are generalized and adhered to broadens the security base. Norms are internalized during childhood by members of the group, perpetuating common psychological ground and resulting in the protection of group solidarity. For human beings, group solidarity in the form of shared belief systems and internalized cultural mapping of appropriate behavior is necessary for maintaining peace. Worsley (this volume) describes the dangers of loss of, or failure to develop, common values and practices. Peace is not just the absence of war but a social and cultural dynamic which reconstitutes common beliefs among potential adversaries before they come completely unraveled through the inevitable differentiation of goals over time and the striving for individual power. The potential for conflict is inevitable, but a secure cultural means for forestalling or resolving differences (thus gaining a stable peace) is a standard that can be worked toward if never totally attained. Anthropology can be most useful by throwing light on those cultural means of conflict avoidance and resolution that show a potential for assuring stable peace. Long term policy-making requires the kinds of insight that anthropology provides.

Peace and conflict (including various forms of inter-group violence) can perhaps be sorted into a typology of institutionalized violence, and another of institutionalized non-violence, or peace. Goldschmidt (1986, and this volume) presents cross-cultural data about types of, and motivations for, institutionalized fighting. Greenhouse (1986) also points out the extent to which shared value systems can foster a willingness to go to war. Worsley (this volume) indicates the extent to which images of a different group as less moral (or even less human?) than one's own can lead to a belief that their extermination is a moral imperative. A typology would be useful as a means to a cross-cultural determination of cultural structures and the underlying symbols that support each type. Such a typology might range from the activities and belief systems supporting such phenomena as urban street-gangs, as described by Lomnitz (1986), through, for example, those supporting police torture, ethnic extermination, guerrilla warfare and terrorism (usefully differentiated by Sluka, this volume; and see also Paul, in press) or such externally directed activities as raiding, headhunting, surprise attack, and, finally, declared war between nation-states, supported by permanent military establishments.

Many more categories can be isolated: internal wars also occur and can be revolutionary in the sense of battles between supporters of differing ideologies within the same polity, as Sluka has described for

Ireland; or in the sense of battles for territorial and administrative separation from a ruling polity, also true of Ireland. Wars that are fought internally can be induced and supported from outside, as is the case for Nicaragua. At the extreme end of a war typology we might place situations such as that described by Gamst (1986) of centuries of chronic warfare in the Horn of Africa, supported by many competing belief systems within an area of scarcity of economic resources and climatic instability. A materialistic view of warfare causation (Ferguson 1984) would typologize principally in accordance with resource competition, but other anthropologists, including those represented in this volume would include differences in ideology and cultural structuring as basic factors contributing to conflict and its resolution.

Much more information is available for construction of a conflict typology than for a typology of peace. Six anthropological volumes focused explicitly on cross-cultural analysis of war have been produced to date (Bohannon 1967, Fried et al. 1967, Otterbein 1970, Nettleship et al. 1975, Simonis 1983, Ferguson 1984) as against only four that also emphasize the need to analyze peaceful means of avoiding or averting bloodshed (Foster and Rubinstein 1986, Turner and Pitt 1988, Melko 1973, and this volume). Articles in anthropological journals are equally biased toward war. (See Ferguson 1984:1–81 for a survey of war research in anthropology.) Material on peaceful organization of culture and society can only be retrieved by careful reading of ethnographies to discover structures that promote peace. Despite this handicap, a peace typology might start with societies that anthropologists have described as having long lived amicably with neighbors, such as the Pueblo Indians of the American Southwest, or the geographically isolated Nilgiri tribes of India which live amicably in close proximity in a state of symbiotic stability because each has a different and mutually complementary economic base (Mandelbaum 1941). A probable cause of the lack of peace emphasis is that it is much more difficult to define peace than to define war. The tasks of defining and typologizing peace must be done if an adequate theory is to be developed. Along these lines, in this volume Potter describes the restructuring of Chinese society through creation of a shared ethic toward cooperation, Anderson describes a structure of vertical alliances that promotes social reciprocity, Habarad discusses creation of national solidarity through the necessity to unite against a common enemy, and Kehoe demonstrates the way in which self-determination can be advanced through collaboration with others who share some common ideological purpose, separately arrived at.

The Dynamics of Change

Recently there has been a worldwide upsurge of peace advocacy, show-ing a cross-cultural ideological shift. At the end of both World Wars there were similar movements. We need to study these movements in order to discover why, after initial enthusiasm, interest tends to lag, and in cases of anti-war movements of longer duration, under what conditions and over what time periods they persisted.

In the United States we have long had a Military Academy, and for many years a Department of War, which was later euphemistically renamed the Department of Defense, with no change in purpose. After much lobbying, legislation has recently established a United States Institute of Peace. The purpose is educational but its impact is un-certain. It is unlikely that this Institute will serve to institutionalize peace as the Military and Naval Academies (in conjunction with a standing military force) have institutionalized war, for these academies steadily reinforce a military world-view in their student-bodies. No Department of Peace, comparable to the Department of Defense, is contemplated, with comparable socialization for peace, nor is a standing force to maintain or foster peace. Of course, the purpose of standing armies is not envisioned as a promotion of war, but rather for purposes of defense. Yet, curiously, wars that have not been for revolutionary purposes have never been fought within our national boundaries and specifically for our defense, while we have fought or supported many within the territories of others. Under these circumstances it is difficult to accept a characterization of the United States as a peaceful nation, despite ideological expression of peace as a desired goal.

Some anthropological studies of the armed forces between wars have been undertaken (Randall 1986, Willems 1986, Brasset this volume, Pulliam this volume). It is more difficult for anthropologists to study the ongoing dynamics of war itself in their own or any other culture, although attempts have been made (Sluka this volume, Isbell 1987). First, it can be physically dangerous for an analyst on the scene, and second, aroused emotions of patriotism or fear that tend to distort the data are apt to be shared by him or her. However, studies of war dynamics are necessary if we are to work toward its elimination. It is easier to make studies when societies are at peace, but lack of war has rarely made the social dynamics that lead toward peace rather than toward war an obvious field of study.

Studies of symbolic or euphemistic usage that reflect war or peace proneness on the part of various societies could be extremely useful. Bateson (this volume), for example, shows a bipolar ideology that provides the potential for an extreme ideological shift. Another example of a symbolic shift is discussed by Kehoe (1986) as a factor in the history of Christianity, which designates Christ as "The Prince of Peace," but from the time of Constantine has invoked Christian symbols to justify war.

In an investigation of peace and war both vertical and historical anthropological approaches are of value. A vertical approach may be either historical or evolutionary. It can focus on change in cultures with recent and observable change, as both Bateson and Kehoe have done (this volume), or on historically documented change (Kehoe 1986, Gamst 1986), or it can rely on archaeological materials to investigate the prehistoric origins and evolution of war (Roper 1975).

Archaeological investigation suggests that war as an institution arose either in the Bronze Age or toward the end of the Neolithic. Detailed cross-cultural comparison of institutions supporting war or peace in ancient Mesopotamia and Egypt would be valuable. Both areas institutionalized war, but in Mesopotamia internal war was endemic because of the nature of the fragmented political structure, while in Egypt, after unification of the upper and lower empires, internal peace reigned for around 2,000 years.

A horizontal approach seeks out structures that seem to aggravate and sustain conflict, as against structures that seem to favor avoidance or resolution of conflict, isolating the variables and their relationships to one another and to the whole. Variables are of many kinds: symbols, institutions, belief systems, political structures, types of hierarchical organization, economic systems, availability of resources, ethnic composition, and many others. With analyses of data of this sort it should be possible to differentiate cultural structures that make warfare as a way of life: frequent, non-existent, practiced only as a result of attack from outside, practiced for territorial or economic gain, or practiced for ideological control of other peoples.

Cultural Themes

Ten cultural themes that recur in anthropological cross-cultural analysis suggest particularly fruitful avenues for the development of peace and war theory:

Cultural holism. The growth of symbolic anthropology in recent years is a direct result of the increase in anthropological awareness of the complex but covert ways in which cultural institutions and beliefs are interconnected, leading to redundancy in the expression of ideological meanings. Symbolic anthropology, like linguistics, seeks to uncover the unconscious patterns, meanings and interconnections between cultural phenomena. For example, our own culture is so war-oriented that war terminology permeates our vocabulary in myriad ways. In religion, we find songs like: "Onward Christian soldiers, marching as to war . . . ," in medicine, phrases such as, "the war (or battle) against disease," or, in business, "price wars." Sports and politics are particularly given to the adoption of battle metaphor. Cohn (1987) effectively demonstrates the role of euphemistic language in making nuclear weapons seem bland (or even endearing) rather than totally destructive.

Resistance to change. By means of the symbolic redundancies that it generates, the holism of culture always reinforces the status quo and sets up resistance to change and to the introduction of new points of view. In the United States, the Reagan administration has exploited this resistance by emphasizing its adherence to old-fashioned values in spite of the fact that it has at the same time made many drastic changes in economic practice. Thus, change has been made to seem conservative rather than radical. Points of resistance to change are particularly strong in the realm of the sacred, or the ideologically most powerful.

Lack of cultural unity. Careful study of social behavior reveals that culture is not monolithic, as it sometimes has seemed when anthropologists studied only the ideal and not the real. In every culture there are pockets or strands of behavior, with associated beliefs and institutions, that run counter to the generally accepted norm. Recently Gorbachev, speaking to a group of American scientists in Moscow, indicated that there are such strands in Soviet ideology that open avenues to social restructuring (Hal Harvey, personal communication). Sometimes both the dominant and deviant behavior or belief are practiced or held by a single individual, who remains unaware of any contradiction in his or her position (Bateson this volume). The understanding of change and factors that either motivate or block it is enhanced by awareness of variation in cultural patterning.

Bateson points out that it is the divergent patterns which exist in any cultural system that can provide a certain adaptability to changed circumstances and to the introduction of new modes of thought and behavior. While anthropologists can probably never predict changes, they can become sensitive to the range of possibilities for change in any given culture if they recognize the non-dominant as well as the dominant patterns.

Polarization of experience. Cultural polarization became apparent after an article by Robert Hertz (republished in Needham 1973), and was reinforced in the work of Lévi-Strauss. The search for examples of polarization inspired a collection of essays (Needham 1973) that explore the symbolism of good and evil within particular cultures.

Aside from the interconnection between categories following similar lines of polarization, we also find a universal tendency to assign the category of evil to social groups which differ from ourselves either in ideology of in practice, and to reserve the definition of good to ourselves and our own practices and beliefs.

Taboo and the sacred. Taboos adhere to sacred symbols and provoke strong emotion if broken. If the sacred is disrupted, emotional commitment must be recaptured through introduction of substitute symbols that can command similar devotion. Threat to sacred symbols, which often have military connotations, is apt to provoke war. Studies of sacred symbols and their ritual and military associations is essential for understanding problems of peace and war.

Power and social cohesion. Psychologists, like anthropologists, recognize that a motivating factor in human behavior is a need for control over the social and physical environment. This is the same as saying that we all need to have some sense of power if we are to function efficiently, or in a way that is not socially disruptive. Cultural ways of satisfying this need differ widely, but they must be provided if depression or the violent reactions born of frustration and a feeling of helplessness are to be avoided. Power over our environment means power over other people as well, but this need not mean, and in a smoothly functioning and well-unified society does not mean, dominion or tyranny. It simply allows us to sense that we are valued in some way within our own social group. We learn to acquire a position of respect by assimilating the values of that group and learning to manipulate these to our advantage. At best, our personal advantage is also the advantage of other members of the group. At worst, it is only self-seeking, hence socially destructive. Thus power-need, like other human drives, has both good and bad aspects. Anthropological studies can sort out destructive from constructive uses of power.

Cyclical ritual and rites of passage. Cyclical rituals can, through repetition, stress various aspects of the moral order. The patriotic festivities of nation-states tend to emphasize military heroism and commemorate past wars, with displays of military pomp and the playing and singing of military songs.

From Van Gennep (1960) onward, analysis of rites of passage has been a major focus of anthropological field studies. Male rites of initiation promote warlike behavior in some societies (Huyghe 1986). In societies without initiation rites, compulsory military service may serve a similar purpose. Other rites of passage may promote internal peace and cooperation. Fictive kinship rites in many Mexican villages operate in this way. Such highly ritualized linkages transcend normal experience and take on sacred connotations. Heightened emotional response is sought as part of normal activity, and gives it a transcendent quality. Thus, risk-taking and risk-seeking (Clark 1986) in war and elsewhere are readily linked with the sacred.

Reversal behavior. Theories about cultural reversal may also prove relevant for peace studies. This relates to a definition of the sacred as culturally determined periods and activities with heightened emotional group response, and of the profane as culturally determined periods with little or no group emotional stimulation.

Many studies show that behaviors that are taboo for normal purposes are, either at cyclically determined points in time, or under unusual circumstances, not only acceptable but required. These points are "sacred" because they provoke group emotion. Warfare sanctions killing which under normal circumstances is taboo. This is one of the important sacred reversals in our culture.

Vertical and horizontal struggles for power. Bateson's (1958:171–197) discussion of schismogenesis should be required reading for those interested in interactions leading to conflict. Schismogenesis can be conceived as one type of reversal behavior. (Perhaps all cultural reversals are schismogenic. This needs to be explored.) Bateson (1958:175) defines it as "a process of differentiation in the norms of individual behavior resulting from cumulative interaction between individuals." Schismogenesis can be either complementary or symmetrical (either vertical or horizontal). The former occurs between those with different social roles, which tend to be hierarchical, as parent and child, leader and follower, or husband and wife. Symmetrical schismogenesis involves interaction between those sharing a role or status.

Uninterrupted series of schismogenic interaction of either type, unless interrupted, will result in social fission. Ritual interruption of one series by symbolic displays representing the other type can effectively interrupt the progression toward social fission. Thus, schismogenic sequences of dominance and submission require interruption by displays suggesting role and status equivalence.

Warfare becomes an extreme example of the dynamism of the schismogenic model (Foster 1988). An outbreak of war serves to interrupt the peacetime dominance-submission interaction of the military hierarchy, substituting the horizontal interaction of warriors on the battlefield. Schismogenic interactions between dictators or other powerful leaders and their subordinates provide examples of "how the megalomaniac or paranoid (leader) forces others to respond to his condition, and so is automatically pushed to more and more extreme maladjustment" (Bateson 1958:186). Bateson discusses the symmetrical schismogenesis characteristic of international rivalries and the complementary schismogenesis of "class-war," and suggests (Bateson 1958:187) that whereas the complexity of such interactions in modern national and international situations makes them difficult to study, "It may be that when the processes of schismogenesis have been studied in other and simpler fields, the conclusions from this study may prove applicable in politics." Schismogenesis as a theoretical tool is a fruitful concept that has largely been ignored within anthropology (but see Foster, 1979 and 1988) and has the potential of providing insight into covert cultural operations that lead to war or peace.

Vertical and horizontal devices to reinforce mutuality. My impression is that peasant communities with rites of mutuality like fictive kinship may have sporadic violence but are rarely warlike. Wars are sometimes imposed from outside, and although villagers are sometimes required to fight in these, without governmental urban pressures it would seem that peace would be enduring. Current revolutions in Latin America have villagers as their major victims rather than as their perpetrators.

Anderson (this volume) points out that a vertical mutuality benefiting both superior and subordinate but in different ways can have the same kind of peace-promoting effect. Like the Philippines, as described by Anderson, Mexico has a strong tradition of patron-client mutuality. It may be that the stability of relations between the United States and Mexico are, at least to some extent attributable to this ideology. Habarad (this volume) points out that horizontal conflict (symmetrical schismogenesis) can be removed by transference of the competition to an outside party. Such interactions seem to be the opposite of schismogenesis, and might profitably be studied under some such rubric as "synthogenesis." Such studies would help us to appreciate the dynamism of peace.

Conclusions

Since weaponry has now become totally destructive, it is essential that warfare be eliminated from the human cultural repertoire. Warfare is not a natural phenomenon like earthquakes and floods; it is a human institution, institutionalized and sustained by means of symbolic structures which are both mutually reinforcing and semantically multivocal. Cultures change. Other humanly degrading institutions have been abolished; slavery is a notable example. Since warfare is itself the ultimate use of force, it is clear that warfare cannot be abolished by warfare, or by the threat of more force. The only recourse open to us would seem to be attempting consciously to reorganize human symbolism in such a way that warfare is no longer considered adaptive. Adaptation has, to date, not been a conscious process, but if we are not to have human culture destroyed by the technology that we have devised, adaptation must be induced through conscious effort.

If symbolism is to be reorganized so that warfare no longer has an appeal, one place to begin is with modern nation-states, which have the most destructive weapons. The task seems formidable, but if we have a grasp of both universal and particular symbolic processes it becomes less daunting. It will take a great deal of research and data analysis. More anthropologists will need to be drawn into the task. Scholarly publication will need to be followed by popular publication in order to begin to influence public thinking.

Cohen (1974) said that symbols begin not to work if they are made conscious. Anthropology is perhaps unique among sciences in its ability to use cross-cultural comparison as an avenue to this end. By revealing the symbolic mechanisms by which warfare is institutionalized and perpetuated and peace is induced and sustained it may be that anthropology provides the means to make warfare obsolete. It is worth a concentrated effort.

Notes

1. This chapter is expanded and reworked from Foster 1987. A preliminary version of the paper was first presented in August 1985 at the meeting of the International Union of Anthropological and Ethnological Sciences, Commission on the Study of Peace held at the Academy of Sciences of the Union of Soviet Socialist Republics.

References Cited

Ardrey, R. 1966. *The Territorial Imperative: A Personal Inquiry into the Animal Origins of Property and Nations.* New York: Athenaeum.

Bateson, G. 1958. *Naven.* Stanford, CA: Stanford University Press.

Bohannan, P., editor. 1967. *Law and Warfare: Studies in the Anthropology of Conflict.* Garden City, NY: The Natural History Press.

Clark, M.M. 1986. The Cultural Patterning of Risk-Seeking Behavior: Implications for Armed Conflict. In *Peace and War: Cross-Cultural Perspectives.* M.L. Foster and R.A. Rubinstein, eds., New Brunswick, NJ: Transaction Books, Pp. 79–90.

Cohen, A. 1974. *Two-Dimensional Man: An Essay on The Anthropology of Power and Symbolism in Complex Society.* Berkeley: University of California Press.

Cohn, C. 1987. Slick'ems, Glick'ems, Christmas Trees, and Cookie Cutters: Nuclear Language and How We Learned to Pat the Bomb. *Bulletin of the Atomic Scientists* 43(5):17–24.

Ferguson, Brian, editor. 1984. *Warfare, Culture and Environment*. New York: Academic Press.

Foster, M.L. 1986. Is War Necessary? In *Peace and War: Cross-Cultural Perspectives*. M.L. Foster and R.A. Rubinstein, eds., New Brunswick, NJ: Transaction Books, Pp. 71–78.

———. 1979. Synthesis and Antithesis in Balinese Ritual. In *The Imagination of Reality: Essays in Southeast Asian Coherence Systems*. A.L. Becker and A.A. Yengoyan, eds., Norwood, NJ: Ablex, Pp. 175–196

———. 1987. Cross-Cultural Approaches to Problems of Peace and War: The Generation of Theory. *Newsletter of the Commission on the Study of Peace, International Union of Anthropological and Ethnological Sciences* 5(1): 2–8.

———. 1988. Cultural Triggering of Psychological Reversals. In *Progress in Reversal Theory*. M. J. Apter, J. H. Kerr, and M. Cowles, eds., Amsterdam: North Holland.

———. and R.A. Rubinstein, editors. 1986. *Peace and War: Cross-Cultural Perspectives*. New Brunswick, NJ: Transaction Books.

Fried, M., M. Harris, and R. Murphy, editors. 1967. *War: The Anthropology of Armed Conflict and Aggression*. Garden City, NY: The Natural History Press.

Gamst, F.C. 1986. Conflict in the Horn of Africa. In *Peace and War: Cross-Cultural Perspectives*. M.L. Foster and R.A. Rubinstein, eds., New Brunswick, NJ: Transaction Books, Pp. 133–151.

Goldschmidt, W. 1986. Personal Motivation and Institutionalized Conflict. In *Peace and War: Cross-Cultural Perspectives*. M.L. Foster and R.A. Rubinstein, eds., New Brunswick, NJ: Transaction Books, Pp. 3–14.

Greenhouse, C. 1986. Fighting for Peace. In *Peace and War: Cross-Cultural Perspectives*. M.L. Foster and R.A. Rubinstein, eds., New Brunswick, NJ: Transaction Books, Pp. 49–69.

———. 1987. Cultural Perspectives on War. In *The Quest for Peace*. R. Vayrynen, ed., London: Sage Publications, Pp. 32–47.

Huyghe, B. 1986. Toward a Structural Model of Violence: Male Initiation Rituals and Tribal Warfare. In *Peace and War: Cross-Cultural Perspectives*. M.L. Foster and R.A. Rubinstein, eds., New Brunswick, NJ: Transaction Books, Pp. 25–48.

Isbell, B.J. 1987. An Anthropological Dialogue with Violence. *Newsletter of the Commission on the Study of Peace of the International Union of Anthropological and Ethnological Sciences* 5(4):2–8.

Kehoe, A.B. 1986. Christianity and War. In *Peace and War: Cross-Cultural Perspectives*. M.L. Foster and R.A. Rubinstein, eds., New Brunswick, NJ: Transaction Books, Pp. 153–173.

Lomnitz, Larissa 1986. The Uses of Fear: 'Porro' Gangs in Mexico. In *Peace and War: Cross-Cultural Perspectives*. M.L. Foster and R.A. Rubinstein, eds., New Brunswick, NJ: Transaction Books, Pp. 15–24.

Mandelbaum, D.G. 1941. Culture Change Among the Nilgiri Tribes. *American Anthropologist* 43:19–26.

Melko, M. 1973. *52 Peaceful Societies.* Oaksville, Ont: Canadian Peace Research Institute.

Needham, R. 1973. *Right and Left: Essays on Dual Symbolic Classification.* Chicago: The University of Chicago Press.

Nettleship, M.A., R.D. Givens and A. Nettleship, editors. 1975. *War: Its Causes and Correlates.* The Hague: Mouton.

Otterbein, K. 1970. *The Evolution of War.* New Haven, Conn.: HRAF Press.

Paul, B.D. in press. The Operation of a Death Squad in a Lake Atitlan Community. In *Harvest of Violence: Guatemala's Indians in the Counter-Insurgency War.* R.M. Carmack, eds., Norman, OK: University of Oklahoma Press.

Randall, A. 5th. 1986. The Culture of United States Military Enclaves. In *Peace and War: Cross-Cultural Perspectives.* M.L. Foster and R.A. Rubinstein, eds., New Brunswick, NJ: Transaction Books, Pp. 61–69.

Roper, M.K. 1975. Evidence of Warfare in the Near East from 10,000–4,300 BC. In *War: Its Causes and Correlates.* M.A. Nettleship, R.D. Givens and A. Nettleship, eds., The Hague: Mouton, Pp. 299–343.

Simonis, Yvan, editor. 1983. *Guerres et Stratégies.* Special Issue of *Anthropologie et Sociétés.* Vol. 7, No. 1.

Tishkov, V.A. 1986. War and Peace: The View of a Soviet Scholar. In *Peace and War: Cross-Cultural Perspectives.* M.L. Foster and R.A. Rubinstein, eds., New Brunswick, NJ: Transaction Books, Pp. 223–244.

Turner, P. and D. Pitt, editors. 1988. *Cold War and Nuclear Madness: An Anthropological Analysis.* S. Hadley, MA: Bergin and Garvey.

Van Gennep, A. 1960. *The Rites of Passage.* Chicago: University of Chicago Press.

Willems, E. 1986. *A Way of Life and Death: Three Centuries of Prussian-German Militarism, an Anthropological Approach.* Nashville, TN: Vanderbilt University Press.

Name Index

Subject Index